The Orig
of
WARWICK PARK
and the Nevill Ground

The Home Farm as seen from Warwick Park road, 2nd January 1899

John Cunningham

**Royal Tunbridge Wells Civic Society
Local History Monograph No.6
June 2007**

Published in Great Britain in June 2007 by
The Local History Group of
The Royal Tunbridge Wells Civic Society.

All rights reserved.

No part of this publication may be reproduced,
stored in a retrieval system, or transmitted,
in any form or by any means,
without the prior permission
of the copyright holder.

Within the UK, exceptions are allowed
in respect of any 'fair dealing' for the purpose of
research or private study, or criticism or review,
as permitted under
The Copyright, Design and Patents Act, 1988.

©Royal Tunbridge Wells Civic Society, 2007

The author has asserted his right to be identified
as the author of this work in accordance
with the Copyright, Design and Patents Act, 1988

The Publishers have made every effort to establish the copyright
of all illustrations in this monograph
and apologise for any unwitting oversight or omission.

ISBN 978-0-9545343-7-0

The text is set in Bookman Old Style 10 pt
and the cover in Bookman Old Style 9–34pt.

Front cover and title page:
The Home Farm of the Marquess of Abergavenny,
as taken by Henry Vaux Wild on 2nd January 1899.

Printed and bound by
The Inkpot Lithographic Printers
Southborough, Tunbridge Wells, Kent

CONTENTS

	Page
Ordnance Survey Map of Home Farm Estate, 1897	iv
Ordnance Survey Map of Warwick Park Estate, 1909	v

Introduction   1

CHAPTER

1.	TUNBRIDGE WELLS BEFORE WARWICK PARK	5
2.	THE ABERGAVENNY FAMILY AND ITS INCOME	14
3.	DRAMATIS PERSONAE	27
4.	THE ORIGINS OF WARWICK PARK	49
5.	THE RATIONALE FOR, AND SEQUENCE OF DEVELOPMENT OF THE HOME FARM ESTATE	57
6.	THE NEVILL GROUND	74
7.	ISSUES AND PROBLEMS	93
8.	ROADS, BRIDGES AND LANDSCAPING	100
9.	THE COST AND PROGRESS OF DEVELOPING THE HOME FARM ESTATE	108
10.	THE DEVELOPERS AND BUILDERS OF WARWICK PARK	111
11.	THE ARCHITECTS OF WARWICK PARK	127
12.	THE NAMES OF THE ESTATE AND THE ROADS	137
13.	ASSESSMENT OF THE WARWICK PARK DEVELOPMENT UP TO 1914	141
14.	SUBSEQUENT DEVELOPMENT AFTER THE FIRST WORLD WAR	145

APPENDIX

1.	Parliamentary Acts and Settled Land Acts affecting the Abergavenny family	154
2.	Abergavenny Rent Account 1895-1909	155
3.	Abergavenny Household Running Costs 1890 -1903	156
4.	Abergavenny Ground Rents in Tunbridge Wells 1899	157
5.	Warwick Park Estate: Plot Details: pre-1914	158
6.	Warwick Park Estate: House records from TWBC Archives	161

Sources, Bibliography, Maps and Plans   166

Acknowledgements   169

INDEX   170

iv

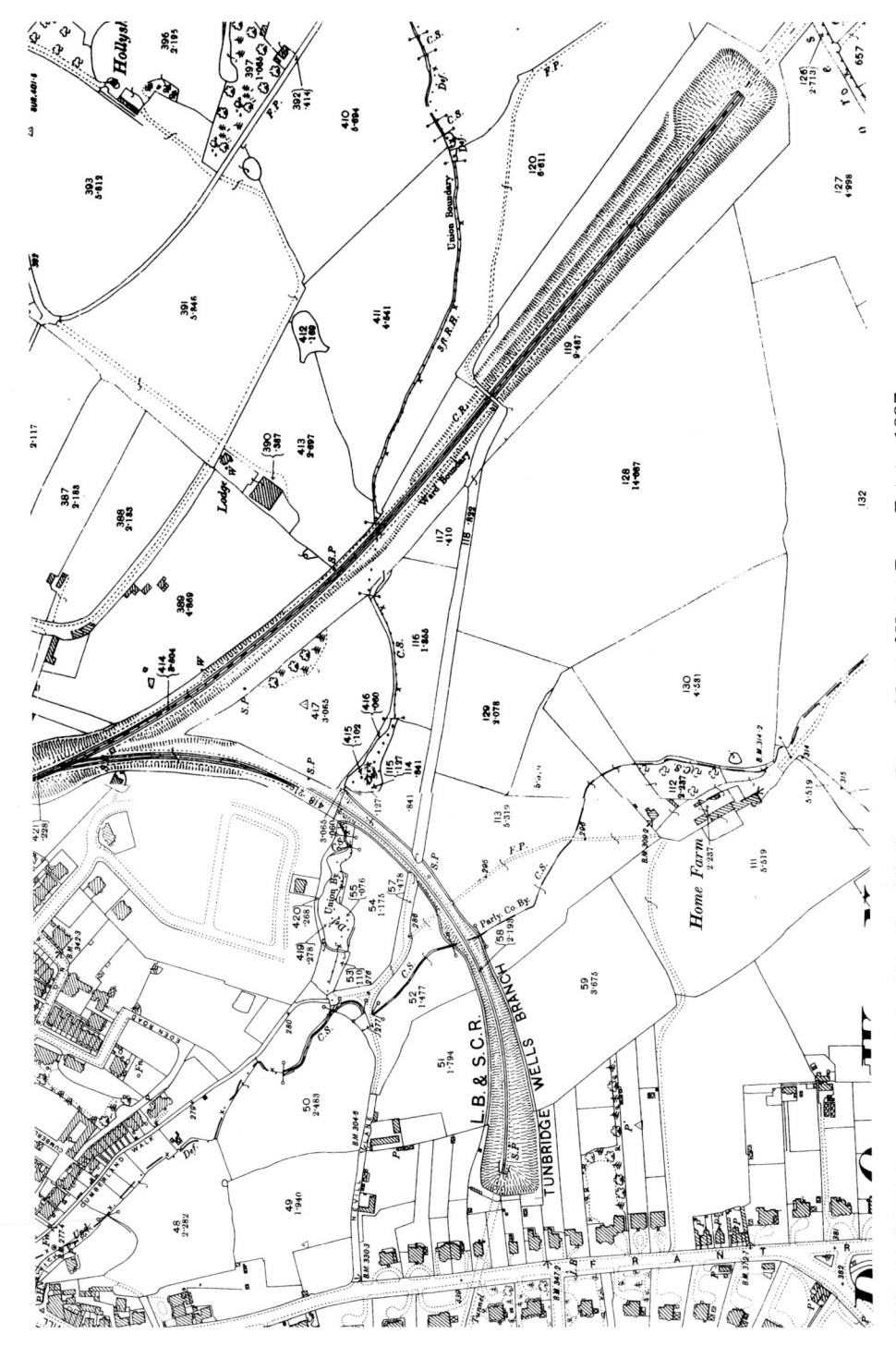

Section of Ordnance Survey Map of Warwick Park Estate, 1909

Enlargement of part of Jan Kip's print of Tunbridge Wells in 1719.
It is interesting to note that although Warwick Park was not to be built until the 1890s, the entrance to it already seems to have existed in 1719. The cart track just above the four horsemen on the right, is where Warwick Park joins Nevill Street today.

INTRODUCTION

Warwick Park is a middle-class road in Tunbridge Wells, built mainly around the end of the 19th/beginning of 20th century. As such, it might not seem to deserve its own history, except that its origins are unusually well-documented in the archives. They reveal a background of interesting and very different people, alternative plans, conflicting circumstances and differing motivations, which should make it a subject of interest to the social historian as well as to local residents.

Even residents may not realise that Warwick Park and its ancillary roads were intended to be an Estate, following in a somewhat less grandiose fashion the evolving 'Park' style created by Decimus Burton in Tunbridge Wells with Calverley Park (1828-1838), and by others in the Italianate Nevill Park (1845-1870), Camden Park (1853-1863), Hungershall Park (1853-1880) and the Neo-Gothic Broadwater Down (1860-1880).

Few will also be aware that another inspiration for Warwick Park was the town of Eastbourne, which had been developed in just thirty-two years, from a 'village' of just over 3,000 in 1851, to an Incorporated Borough with a population of 40,000 in 1883. In many respects, it was a role-model of how it was thought the development of Warwick Park might be. Eastbourne had been a considerable social success for upper-middle class England, as well as a financial success for its developers; and it was hoped that Warwick Park would inject some of that success into Tunbridge Wells. That Warwick Park never quite succeeded in its aims – it was certainly not a failure, but it was not the success hoped for – is due to a number of factors which this book, it is hoped, will make clear.

The book, it is worth stating, had however a more modest origin – in the search for information about the architect of the Lutyensesque No. 69 Warwick Park, where I live. This led to the wider study of Warwick Park as it is; then as it was; and finally as to why it was, and is; and to the 5th Marquess of Abergavenny on whose land the Warwick Park Estate was built. When I approached him to ask whether I could study his archives, he guided me towards where the archives had been deposited since 1963 – in the East Sussex County Records Office in Lewes. Without his very friendly and interested direction, this study would not exist and I am deeply indebted to him.

I was extremely fortunate to find a very full Archive which, although it had been 'weeded', nonetheless provided a great deal of information about the Abergavenny family and the development of the Home Farm Estate into the Warwick Park Estate. Few archives contain records of conversations and discussion – most are records of what was done – but the Abergavenny archive did contain a number of letters as well as the official legal documents and accounts. These gave a considerable insight into the discussion between all the parties, but even with such information, there are gaps and so I have often had to use intelligent speculation as to *why* something was done, or not done.

The same consideration applies to all the Minutes which, of their nature, remove any hint of controversy or disagreement at a meeting; and the very concise Minutes of the Tunbridge Wells Borough Council Committees are no exception to this. They record what was decided, but do not list the pro's and con's, or what other alternatives were available or possible. So here again, the reader must rely on what I hope is objective analysis and judgement, in the absence of clear documentary evidence.

I should emphasise that this study is essentially concerned with the *origins* of the Warwick Park Estate and therefore in many respects it does not go beyond the First World War. Nonetheless, it does include later data in order not to leave the reader 'hanging in the air', but it is **not** intended as a comprehensive history of *all* houses in the Estate up to the present day.

I have sought to put the origins of the Warwick Park Estate into a wider context by providing background about the development of Tunbridge Wells; about the coming of the railway; about the Abergavenny family and the other principal people involved. The first chapters of the book cover this general background.

A problem for all authors where research is involved, is to decide when and where to stop (the research, that is.) Each new piece of information opens new avenues, some very minor but some potentially quite important. If one pursued every avenue, one would never publish. I have therefore decided to call a halt to my research in order to publish, in the certain knowledge that as a result, I will have missed vital information and that some readers may well be able to correct me, or provide additional information. I would stress that readers' comments and corrections are truly very welcome.

Any errors of fact or interpretation are mine, and mine alone. However, I would like to acknowledge the kind assistance of:

- ❖ the late 5th Marquess of Abergavenny and the generous help of the late John Hillyer, OBE, the nephew of Harold Hillyer, the architect of 69 Warwick Park and therefore the inspiration for this book;
- ❖ Dr. Ian Beavis, the Museum Officer of the Tunbridge Wells Museum and Art Gallery;
- ❖ Roger Farthing, the late and distinguished local historian of Tunbridge Wells;
- ❖ Mrs. Josephine Butler, the daughter of Richard Millard and great-niece of Vincent Millard, the former owners of No.69 Warwick Park;
- ❖ John, Peter and Ivor Beale, respectively grandsons and great-grandson of Louis Beale;
- ❖ Ann Bates, granddaughter of Thomas Bates;
- ❖ and Hugh Bredin, Duncan Rawson-Mackenzie, Eileen Hellicar, Christopher Masters, Erica Royston and particularly Chris and Charmian Clissold-Jones and Sue Brown, who have read the draft with expert eyes and made many constructive comments.

Warm thanks must also be given to the staff of

- the East Sussex County Records Office at Lewes;
- the Centre for Kentish Studies at Maidstone;
- the Tunbridge Wells Museum and Art Gallery;
- the Tunbridge Wells Reference Library, and particularly Sue Brown, the Local History Librarian;
- the Tunbridge Wells Borough Planning Department (and particularly Mrs. Lynda England, without whose help Appendix 6 in particular would not have been possible);
- the Probate Office in London;
- and the Public Records Office in Kew.

It could be said that they were only doing their job, but *didn't they do it well* – with knowledge, understanding, efficiency, speed *and with a friendly smile.*

I can only hope that readers' reaction to my book will not be the same as the small girl who, when asked to review a new book about penguins, wrote 'This book told me more about penguins than I wanted to know.'

Finally, I would dedicate this book to my dear wife, Sheila, with my thanks for her help, patience and forbearance.

John Cunningham

Easter Sunday,
8th April, 2007

CHAPTER 1

TUNBRIDGE WELLS BEFORE WARWICK PARK

Warwick Park is a small (although in the eyes of the cognoscenti, a significant) part of both Tunbridge Wells and its history. Before beginning the history of Warwick Park, it is apposite to provide the reader with a brief summary of the history of the development of Tunbridge Wells, first as a fashionable spa village, and subsequently as a *town*, as both a background and a context for the development of Warwick Park.

Most readers will be familiar with the story of the origin of Tunbridge Wells in the early 17th century – how Dudley, the 3rd Lord North (1581-1666)[1], while recuperating from a malaise – described as 'a lingering consumptive disorder' – stayed with his friends, the Bergavenny family at Eridge, and chanced upon a spring, the taste of whose water seemed familiar, since while travelling through the Ardennes (then in the Spanish Netherlands, but now in Belgium), he had visited the town of Spa, the original health resort which has given its name to so many others. He drank of the waters of this new Well and felt much improved.

According to the legend, he recognised a similarity with Spa water, and he was right, since Tunbridge Wells and Spa are both chalybeate springs (i.e. impregnated with iron). He attributed his own recovery of health to his consumption of the Wells water and had the water analysed (insofar as fairly crude analysis existed in those days). As a result, he (and probably others, including the Bergavennys) must have started to

* The use of *Tunbridge* and *Epſam* waters, for health and cure, I firſt made known to *London*, and the Kings people; the *Spaw* is a chargeable and inconvenient journey to ſick bodies, beſides the mony it carries out of the Kingdome, and inconvenience to Religion. Much more I could ſay, but I rather hint than handle, rather open a door to a large proſpect than give it.

Margin note in Lord North's 'A Forest of Varieties' (1645).

---
[1] This Lord North was incidentally the great-grandfather of the Lord North who was George III's Prime Minister and who played a major part in the loss of the American colonies. His great-grandson, when forced from office in 1783, retired very appropriately to Tunbridge Wells.

recommend the spring, since people started to flock to it, but there is absolutely no evidence that North benefited or even sought to benefit commercially from it. (Indeed, it is clear that Lord North was largely unaware of the significance of his discovery since it merited only a marginal note in his *Forest of Varieties*, published 30-40 years later in 1645.)

The spring was in the middle of the countryside away from any habitation and on land which was generally described as a barren area, but its situation was to cause complications since it was very close to no less than *three* parish, *two* manor and two county boundaries – the *parishes* of Speldhurst, Tonbridge and Frant; the manors of Rusthall and South Frith; and the counties of Sussex and Kent. The closeness was a matter of between 20-50 yards, which as to be a material factor in the way first the village, and then the town, was to develop.

'Word of mouth' recommendation (the only form of 'advertising' which then existed) led to the six-week visit in 1629 of Queen Henrietta Maria, the French wife of King Charles I. She had just had a miscarriage and came to recuperate and take the waters. In those days, there was little or no local accommodation and Queen Henrietta Maria camped on what is now Tunbridge Wells Common. The result of her visit was that she was delivered of the future Charles II, just nine months after returning from the Wells. This understandably had a considerable influence on attendance at the Wells, which was interrupted however between 1641 and 1660, first by the Civil War and then by Cromwell's Protectorate.

Royal patronage was confirmed in 1663, with the arrival of Charles II and his Queen, Catherine of Braganza. From that point, Tunbridge Wells was to take off as a fashionable venue and the number of visitors justified the building of permanent and specific lodging accommodation. But visitors were still essentially seasonal, with virtually all coming between April and September.

Queen Henrietta Maria.

The first chapel – now the Church of King Charles the Martyr – was built in 1678.[2]

The Pantiles were the centre of social activity during the late 17th and the 18th centuries. With an Upper and a Lower Walk, visitors promenaded up and down the 400 yard length. At one end (the northern) was the Spring, at which visitors were encouraged to drink as many as 15 pints of the water every day; in the middle were the Assembly Rooms over which Beau Nash presided as Master of Ceremonies for 26 years from 1735 to his death in 1761 (although he spent most of his time in a similar role at Bath).

Chapel of King Charles the Martyr in the 18th century.

Jan Kip's engraving of Tunbridge Wells in 1719.

---

[2] Originally and somewhat unliturgically, it faced north. But an expansion due to demand some twelve years later, turned the direction of the church west for almost 200 years until a further expansion in the 1880's, turned the axis of the church towards an orthodox east.

But one should be realistic about Tunbridge Wells in the 18th century. It was still very much a village, although a fashionable one. While Tunbridge Wells in the 17th century had been a prime influence in creating the fashion among the rich for 'healing waters' and can truly claim to be the first spa resort in England, it had been overtaken by Bath, which had started later but which had become much bigger, much grander, more stylish and much less seasonal. Bath and its waters had been known of course since Roman times and in medieval times it had been a prosperous town – witness the Wife of Bath in The Canterbury Tales – but it had no reputation as a fashionable resort for society until the beginning of the 18th century.

Tunbridge Wells did not lose its fashionableness and it prospered throughout the 18th century, although overshadowed by Bath. Its attraction was that besides its 'healing' waters, it was much closer to London – only about 35 miles – compared with the 85-95 miles distance for Bath. It could be reached in one day and therefore visited for only a few days – allowing the 18th century equivalent of the 'long weekend', when the 'rigours' of the journey to and from Bath demanded a stay of at least a fortnight, if not a month.

Richard 'Beau' Nash.

The part of the 'village' which developed first was slightly to the north and east of the Pantiles on and around Mount Sion and this was part of the parish of Tonbridge. It is possible that it took its name from the principal parish to which it belonged, namely Tunbridge, but what is more probable is that it took its name from the nearest town, Tonbridge[3], some 5-6 miles away, which would have made it much easier for visitors, particularly coming from London, to find.

In 1801, the estimated population of Tonbridge was 3,400 and of Tunbridge Wells only 1,000.

---

[3] Tonbridge was originally spelt with a 'u' and not an 'o'. Hence the spelling for Tunbridge Wells. The change in spelling for Tonbridge from 'u' to 'o' occurred in the latter half of the 19th century for no reason except perhaps to differentiate itself from its now larger sibling and as a quite separate railway station, while the spelling of Tunbridge Wells remained unchanged.

But by the 1841 Census, Tonbridge had been outstripped in population by its offspring. Tonbridge's population at 3,000 was static, if not in slight decline; while the population of Tunbridge Wells had increased to 8,302, due to the increase in permanent residents, (of whom returning [i.e. retiring] East India Company 'nabobs' and refugees from the French Revolution are identifiable segments), rather than seasonal visitors.

It is therefore not surprising that from the early 19th century, Tunbridge Wells should seek to govern itself and not be governed by a smaller parent. After several years of agitation, Tunbridge Wells became a town in its own right through the Tunbridge Wells Improvement Act in July 1835. This Act gave relatively limited self-government. It was for 'lighting, watching (i.e. policing), cleansing, regulating, and otherwise improving the town of Tunbridge Wells... and for regulating the supply of water and establishing a market within the said town.'

The town's new government was by Improvement Commissioners who were not elected but were *all* men of property, who owned or occupied land worth not less than £50 a year.

The visitors to Tunbridge Wells continued to be 'of the highest quality' and probably the most-prized was the Princess Victoria who, as heir-apparent, visited the town five times between 1822 and 1835 before she became Queen Victoria in 1837.

It was however the coming of the railways to Tunbridge Wells from the late 1840's which gave the town its biggest boost in population, as the following Census figures show:

Population of Tunbridge Wells

Year	No.	Increase
1801	1,000 (est)	–
1831	5,929	4,929
1841	8,302	2,373
1851	10,587	2,285
1861	13,807	3,220
1871	19,410	5,603
1881	24,309	4,899
1891	29,296	4,987

(It was these growth figures which were to mislead the Marquess of

Abergavenny and his agents into developing Warwick Park – but more of that in later chapters.)

Before the arrival of the railway, the only way of going to London had been by stagecoach – a distance of some 36 miles via Sevenoaks, taking eight hours to get to London. Nonetheless, some 31,000 passengers took the stagecoach in 1838 – an average of about 600 a week, or just under 100 a day, which with an average of 12 passengers per coach meant about 8 coaches a day, in *each* direction.

The railway to Tunbridge Wells was developed by two companies which initially had separate franchises but became increasingly competitive:
- the South Eastern Railway (SER) incorporated in 1836 to build a railway line through Kent to Dover;
- and the London, Brighton & South Coast Railway (LB&SCR) incorporated in 1837 to build a line to the South Coast.

Initially both shared a line from London to Redhill and then it divided in different directions:
- SER to Tonbridge and Dover, which was reached in 1844;
- and LB&SCR to Brighton and the South Coast, reaching St. Leonard's and Hastings in 1846.

SER then developed a branch line from Tonbridge to Tunbridge Wells (reaching Tunbridge Wells Central Station in 1846) which was extended to reach Wadhurst in 1851 and Hastings in 1852.

Tunbridge Wells Central Station c.1850.

In 1866, LB&SCR opens the second Tunbridge Wells railway station – Tunbridge Wells West (or Brighton) Station – with a direct route via Redhill to London.

At the same time in 1866, there was a degree of cooperation between SER and LB&SCR when a spur (or loop-line) was opened between the Central and the new West Station. This[4] ran directly across the Marquess of Abergavenny's Home Farm Estate which was to become 30 years later, the Warwick Park Estate, and its existence was certainly a factor in the break-up of the Home Farm Estate and the development of the Warwick Park Estate.

In 1868, SER became more competitive by opening a new shorter route to London via Sevenoaks, which reduced the journey from $49\frac{1}{2}$ miles to $34\frac{1}{2}$ miles.

While the development of the railway obviously played an important part in the growth of Tunbridge Wells, there are other indicators of the development of Tunbridge Wells as a *town*, which can be summarised:

1843	Gas Company formed
1845	Fire Brigade formed
1869	General Hospital **re**built
1872	Tunbridge Wells Courier first published
1878	Eye and Ear Hospital established
1887	Telephone Exchange opened

The 1835 Tunbridge Wells Improvement Act by putting local government in the hands of £50 freeholders and lessees, had set up a self-perpetuating oligarchy which was increasingly unsuited to an expanding town. Minor changes were achieved by the Town Improvement Act of 1846, which tightened procedures, redefined some boundaries and abolished turnpike trusts, but management was in the hands of a select and somewhat reactionary few. By 1860, when the population had grown to almost 14,000, the number of people eligible to be Commissioners had grown to 200-300. Despite this, it was difficult to get a quorum of seven for meetings of the Commissioners.

---

[4] Traffic on the spur was initially very low. In 1867, there was just one daily freight train and it was not until 1876 that the spur carried passenger trains. In 1888, there were only four round trips a day, which had increased to seven by 1925 and to twenty by 1933. By 1956, the spur carried 58 passenger and two freight trains daily, making it the busiest stretch of single track in the country for most of the year, except for summer Saturdays in the Isle of Wight. One can only wonder why it was subsequently closed, when it was apparently so busy.

Reformers, including the Rector of Frant who was Abergavenny's brother-in-law, and William Delves who was his Steward, forced through at public meetings in 1860 the elective clauses of the Local Government Act of 1858.

This 'improvement' was to last nearly thirty years, but from 1881 when the population had increased to over 24,000, there was growing pressure for reform, particularly from the Tradesmen's Association. Eight stormy years later, with the Incorporation of Tunbridge Wells as a Borough, democracy came to at least the male, and also a few female, ratepayers of the new Borough.

On 22nd. January 1889, occurred the most important development since 1835: Tunbridge Wells was granted its Charter and was incorporated as a Borough with four Wards, 24 *elected* Councillors and eight Aldermen.

Whether Incorporation stimulated the inhabitants into becoming far-sighted, progressive and innovative; or whether they were already so, which is why they achieved Incorporation, is difficult to say. But certainly the 15 years which followed Incorporation were probably the most stimulating in the town's history. The Council somewhat

22nd January 1889. The new Town Clerk, W. C. Cripps, reads the new Borough Charter outside the Town Hall.

unconventionally appointed far-sighted and pro-active Mayors, such as Sir David Salomons, Bt (in 1894-5)[5], and Major J.R. Fletcher Lutwidge (three times in 1895-6, 1896-7 and 1902-3), who were **not** members of the Council; opened their own Borough Electricity Works (in 1895); set up an Omnibus Company in 1896, set up the first municipal telephone system in England in 1901 (long before Kingston-upon-Hull); and approved the building of an Opera House for Tunbridge Wells which opened in 1902.

These were very stimulating times for everyone in Tunbridge Wells and it is in this very positive and optimistic atmosphere that the original idea of developing the Home Farm Estate into what would become the Warwick Park Estate was first considered; and against which the reader should view all that is about to be related.

Before however we consider this in detail, there is another subject – the Abergavenny family and in particular the 1st. Marquess – which needs to be considered first.

---

[5] Sir David Lionel Salomons, 2nd. Baronet (1851-1925) was a wealthy engineer, scientist and inventor who lived at Broomhill near Southborough and was the heir of his uncle, a former Lord Mayor of London. He was a pioneer of electricity and motorised transport and was the second Englishman to own a motor-car. During his term of office, he inaugurated Tunbridge Wells' first electricity supply and organised Britain's first 'Horseless Carriage Exhibition' which was held at the Agricultural Showground off the Eridge Road (now part of the Showfields Estate). He campaigned successfully against legal restrictions on the use of cars on public roads and drafted the technical clauses of the Road Locomotive Act of 1896, which replaced the 1865 Act, abolished the man with the red flag, and raised the speed limit for vehicles from 4mph to 20mph. His mayoralty was also famous for his Inaugural Mayoral Dinner held at the Great Hall and attended by 300 guests, including the Lord Mayor and Sheriffs of London, the Marquess of Abergavenny and the Astronomer Royal. According to 'The Times', The Duke of Cambridge, Lord Salisbury, the Archbishop of Canterbury, the Lord Chancellor and the American Ambassador 'were prevented from being present'.

CHAPTER 2

THE ABERGAVENNY FAMILY AND ITS INCOME

The importance of the Abergavenny family to Tunbridge Wells cannot be exaggerated, since it is true to say that:

- if they had not been one of the principal local landowners,
- if they had not been friends to Lord North,
- and if Lord North had not been staying with them at Eridge in 1606,
- then the Wells might never have been discovered
- and Tunbridge Wells might never have been developed.

And over the next 300 years:

- much of the land which was developed in Tunbridge Wells was Abergavenny land, despite relative lack of interest or enthusiasm on the part of the family,
- and was developed somewhat belatedly, with the help of local developers and builders.

The Marquess of Abergavenny was, and still is, a major landowner in Sussex and, to a lesser extent, in Kent. In 1899, his estates in Sussex and Kent totalled 22,182 acres, of which the Eridge Estate (which comprised Frant, Rotherfield, Mayfield, Buxted, Broadwater Down, Speldhurst and Tonbridge) totalled 13,690 acres. He also had further estates along the diagonal line of Monmouthshire, Herefordshire, Worcestershire and Warwickshire, totalling 7,305 acres, as well as a somewhat isolated 11 acres in Norfolk. The Abergavenny total acreage in England and Wales was just under 30,000 (to be precise, some 29,487) worth in 1899 some £40,008 in rent a year, which was less than it had been in 1890.

Originally the family title was Lord (of) Bergavenny. This was changed by the 14th Baron in 1734 to Abergavenny and

Arms of the Marquess of Abergavenny.
Note the punning motto.

his heir (the 15th Baron) became the first Earl of Abergavenny in 1784. A later descendant, the 5th Earl, became the 1st Marquess just under a century later in 1876.

But more important than the family title is the family name – Nevill. The Nevill family with its many branches has played a major part in English history since at least the 12th century. They were the most powerful family in England during the 15th century with Warwick the Kingmaker, the head of the family, making and unmaking kings during the Wars of the Roses.

Before 1500, branches of the family held the Dukedom of Bedford, the Marquessate of Montagu, the Earldoms of Westmoreland, Salisbury, Warwick, Kent and Northumberland, and the Baronies of Nevill, Furnivall, Latymer, Fauconberg and Bergavenny.

Our Nevill branch did not settle in Sussex until the 15th century when Sir Edward Nevill KG married Lady Elisabeth Beauchamp, the only daughter and heiress of Richard Beauchamp, Lord of Bergavenny, who owned much land in the Weald. As a result, the Nevill family were to benefit from the rise of the iron industry in the Weald during the 15th, 16th, 17th and the first half of the 18th centuries when the Weald became one of the industrial centres of its time[6].

The Nevill family had been visited at Eridge for six days in August 1573 by Queen Elizabeth, but it was not their principal residence, reputedly because of the noise and smoke of iron-making at Eridge. However in 1787, the 2nd. Earl built a Gothic Revival castle at Eridge and lived there until his death in 1843, aged 88.

The neo-Gothic Eridge Castle, built in 1787 and demolished in 1935.

---

[6] The size of this industry should not be under-estimated. There are 527 known sites in the Weald for bloomery (i.e. direct reduction) iron-making - 76 were Roman bloomeries and 180 water-powered sites, of which 86 were furnaces, 71 forges and 23 combined furnaces and forges. Between 1490 and 1540, the industry changed from bloomery to blast furnace and finery forge as Continental technology, and particularly French workers, were introduced.

The two eldest sons of the 2nd. Earl pre-deceased him, so it was the third son, John, who became the 3rd Earl. John had taken a Cambridge MA, served in the Army during the Peninsular War and then taken Holy Orders, becoming Chaplain to the Prince Regent in 1818 and subsequently being the Rector of several Norfolk livings. He died at Eridge Castle, unmarried and 'of delicate health', in 1845 at the age of 55, only two years after succeeding to the title. He was succeeded as the 4th Earl by his younger brother, William (the 1st. Marquess's father), who was also in Holy Orders and was Rector of Frant, on the border of Eridge Park, and also of Birling in Kent. He lived at Birling Manor where he died in 1868, aged 76, leaving an Estate valued at probate at just under £300,000.

Since the discovery in 1606 of the chalybeate spring which gave Tunbridge Wells its name, the Abergavenny family had shown surprisingly little inclination to build on their land except in the immediate vicinity of the spring. This may have been because the well was not actually on their land. They owned in effect the Lower Walk, but not the Upper Walk of the Pantiles, and as they did not control the well, they may have seen little point in developing the area. The source of the Wells water is still a matter of debate, but some of the water must come from the (still-existing) streams which flow down the hill on which the Home Farm Estate lies, and of which the principal is the Grom Brook. But the Wells were a crucial twenty yards beyond the Grom Brook, which flowed on to Groombridge and the Medway, and which was both the Abergavenny boundary and, until 1894, the Kent-Sussex county boundary as well.

While the Abergavenny family did not own the Wells, they did however own some land in Kent, that is across the Grom Brook – in particular, the land between the brook and Cumberland Walk (originally known as Patty Moon's Walk or Lane[7]), which was part of the Home Farm Estate; and also the land further west in Kent, which would subsequently become Nevill Park and Hungershall Park.

It was the coming of the railways to Tunbridge Wells from 1845 which particularly helped the town to develop and the fact that the Abergavennys were slow or reluctant to be involved[8], must have been

---

[7] Patty Moon, or some say Paddy Moon, is thought to have been a dipper at the Wells, or possibly a lodging-house keeper.

[8] The first lot of land for the railway was a thin strip a few yards wide, which ran to Frant and beyond, but which nonetheless amounted to over 27 acres in total. It was in effect compulsorily purchased through the South Eastern Railway Company Act of 1846 from the Earl in 1848 for £2,600 - just over £96 an acre. A dispute arose about compensation for tenants, which was still continuing in 1855.

a significant factor in the direction, mainly north and west, which the town's development took in the latter half of the 19th century.

Certainly they were not averse to all development, but what they did, was peripheral rather than central to the town and its development. From the 1840s, they developed Nevill Park and then Hungershall Park in the south-west, and then allowed development up the Frant Road and along Broadwater Down in the south-east in the 1860s, but the Home Farm Estate (on which Warwick Park was to be built) remained untouched. Perhaps it was a question of other priorities; perhaps the Home Farm Estate was thought to be too hilly for development (but that had not deterred other developers nearby); perhaps the Estate was still viable as an agricultural unit.

The Abergavennys or their estate managers must have been aware of losing out on the development opportunities in Tunbridge Wells, from which others were undoubtedly benefiting. But the then current Earl – the Rev. William Nevill, 4th Earl of Abergavenny and 18th Baron Nevill – was old and probably did not have the energy to set major developments under way. The 4th Earl was to die on 18th August 1868 at the age of 76 and he was succeeded by his son William, the 5th Earl, who was 42.

The 5th Earl was a remarkable man who was highly regarded and respected in his day, but is now largely unknown. A short biography of him outside of the context of Tunbridge Wells and Warwick Park will be found in Chapter 5, while this chapter continues with its theme of the Abergavenny family, Tunbridge Wells and Warwick Park. It was the 5th Earl (created 1st.Marquess in 1876) who was the head of the family during the key period of the development of Warwick Park.

1st Marquess of Abergavenny

It is clear that from an early date the new Earl wanted an up-to-date assessment of what he owned, with no doubt a view as to how he could improve both value and income.

A survey was carried out in 1870 by the surveyors, T.S.Cundy and R.L.Cobb, on a large non-urban part – some 12,472 acres – of the Eridge and South Down Estates. They estimated the annual value as

£11,864-11s-6d or (in decimal currency) £0.95 an acre. By comparison in 1899, the average agricultural acre on the Eridge Estate was producing an average annual income of £1.29.[9] So there had been a real increase in income, but the Marquess would have been open to any scheme which promised a better return for his investment. As we shall see, urban development was just such a development.

It is relevant to look at the financial situation of the Marquess at this time since it was to have a considerable bearing on the development of the Home Farm Estate into Warwick Park.

The Marquess was obviously a rich man, as far as capital was concerned, with so much land. But his income was mostly from rents and these (in the now familiar phrase) could go down as well as up, if too much property was unlet or there was an agricultural recession. And in the 1890s, there was an agricultural recession and his rent income did fall. This created what in modern parlance would be called a cash-flow crisis.

Abergavenny's Income
Abergavenny's Rent Account for all his Estates shows a total of £45,339 in 1895. This fell to £40,008 in 1899 – a fall of some 12% in four years. The fall was even greater – some 15% – in his Southern England Estates, which accounted for over 60% of his rents. His Eridge Estate, which also included Tunbridge Wells and Rotherfield, was over 70% of his Southern England Estates. (See Appendix 2 for a detailed Table of the Rent Accounts from 1895-1909.)

He would have been well aware that urban rents per acre were considerably higher (in fact ten times higher) than agricultural rents. As an example of this, the average rent per acre in 1899 on the Eridge Estate was £1.29 for agricultural land and £12.61 for commercial or residential land in Tunbridge Wells. The pity was that he had 13,690 agricultural acres on the Eridge Estate producing a total rent of £17,595, while the 391 urban acres he had in Tunbridge Wells produced a rent of £4,930 (in other words, the urban part of the Eridge Estate which was less than 3%, produced just under 22% of the Estate income). So he would have been more than aware that urban development pays, but it also required an investment up front before income could be generated; and this need to invest could create

---
[9] They incidentally charged £467-14s-0d for their services - not a huge sum by today's prices but nonetheless just under 4% of the then annual value.

difficulties when one's other sources of income were in decline. (See Appendix 4 for a more detailed listing of Tunbridge Wells rents.)

Two other factors were relevant to his financial situation.

The first was that with such a large estate, it was important to protect and preserve the estate intact for future generations. The Abergavennys had started to do this as early as the 16th century when their estates were entailed. (See Appendix 1, which lists the Parliamentary Acts which cover the Abergavenny estates.) It was common practice by the second half of the 19th century for large estates to be put into Trust in order to avoid or minimise Death Duties (as Inheritance Tax was then known), which were considered then as now, to be punitive. The Marquess would have been advised to put all his property into a trust of which he and his successors would have been the beneficiaries and which would have made him the tenant-for-life. The status of 'tenant-for-life' still left him with considerable power and autonomy. The trust situation was covered by a number of Settled Land Acts, the most recent being 1890 (See Appendix 1). When the Trust was set up is as yet uncertain, but it was certainly in existence on 9th August 1885 when an Order was made in the Chancery Division appointing the Earl of Cranbrook (then only Lord Cranbrook) and the Hon. Ralph Pelham Nevill, the 1st Marquess's brother, as Trustees under the Settled Land Acts. While the trustees were relatives and friends, they could not afford, if they were to carry out their duties responsibly, to 'rubber-stamp' the Marquess's wishes. Indeed their independence was declared by them using a separate firm of solicitors, who would advise and represent impartially.

There was an additional family issue which required Trustees to be appointed. The eldest son (Reginald, Earl of Lewes, born in 1853) of the first Marquess was to grow up and be officially certified as 'a lunatic – non compos mentis'. His condition, although kept as far as possible from public knowledge, must have affected decisions by both the Marquess and the Trustees of the estate. He lived quietly for much of his life in a country house in Cheshire, attended by his domestic staff. Although still a 'lunatic', he was to succeed as the 2nd. Marquess in 1915 at the age of 62 and was not to die, unmarried, until the age of 74. His condition and the legal need for Trustees (particularly from 1915) may have had some influence on the development of Warwick Park. His death was recorded in the Courier of 14th October,1927, in just three lines which referred to him as having been 'an invalid for many years'.

The second factor which has been touched on earlier, was that in the early 1890's there was developing what would be called today a 'cash-flow' problem. In simple Micawber terms, expenditure was exceeding income and this had been disguised by a number of eccentric accounting practices.

The Eridge Estate, representing at it did some 45% of the Abergavenny Estates, bore the brunt of all the costs. All the Estates were audited as if from Eridge and the auditors presented consolidated audited accounts.

The Eridge Estate paid the household running costs for the Castle, the Gardens, the Park, the Stables and the Game Account amounting in 1890 to £7,726, as well as the cost of running the London House in Dover Street[10] (a mere £445 in 1890) and Nevill Court[11] in Tunbridge Wells.

But the Eridge Estate also paid a large part of the costs of running the Monmouthshire, Herefordshire and Worcestershire estates, and the income from those estates amounting to close on £20,000 a year, was not paid into the Eridge account but into the private account of the Marquess at Child's Bank. It was therefore not surprising that the Eridge Estate was in the red from 1893 with an overdraft, at first with 'Messrs. Molyneux & Co.' (of which William Henry Delves, the son of William Delves the Marquess's Steward, was the manager) and then subsequently with Barclay & Co. Ltd., of some £10-15,000. (See Appendix 2 for a detailed breakdown of Abergavenny rents.)

The Monmouthshire, Herefordshire and Worcestershire income was definitely considered to be the personal income of the Marquess and did not have to go to meet household or estate running costs.

The Marquess was not doing anything wrong in the way his income was handled, although by today's practices it might be seen as irregular. He did, after all, own all the property and how he chose to distribute its income was his own business. He did make good in due course any deficiency or overdraft on a specific account. He also instituted economies in expenditure when it became clear in the early

---

[10] The Marquess had two London houses - 54 Portland Place, purchased in 1845 for £4,725 and sold to Lord Skelmersdale for £8,700; and 34 Dover Street, purchased in 1872 from the Duke of Leeds for £25,000 and sold subsequently to the Bath Club for £34,000.

[11] Nevill Court, an Italianate mansion standing in 50 acres, lay between Nevill Park and Tea Garden Lane, and was demolished in 1930 to make way for The Midway and The Crossway.

1890's that there had been a fall in income. So there can be no question about his probity.

The household running costs were reduced from a peak of £9,361 in 1891 to a trough of £3,339 in 1898. This was due principally to the running costs of the Castle itself being reduced from £6,892 to £1,529, from which one can infer that the Marquess changed from living mainly at the Castle and moved to Nevill Court which was less expensive to run.

Nevill Court.

But the 1901 Census shows him living once again at the Castle, with one son and daughter-in-law and grand-daughter, three young visitors, and twelve female staff, ranging from a Housekeeper, Cook, two Lady's Maids, and eight Housemaids and Kitchen and Scullery Maids; and twenty male staff, with a Butler, a Valet, three Footmen, eight Domestic Grooms, four Domestic Gardeners, a Coachman, a Domestic Porter and 'a Steward's Room Boy'.

His use of his London House in Eaton Square seems to have remained fairly constant, if its running costs are any guide. The costs of running the Eridge Gardens and Park were not large and would have remained largely the same, whether the Marquess was there or not. However the cost of the Stables did fall through the 1890's from a high of £1,178 in 1891 to a low of £92 in 1898, although this was to some extent counter-balanced by an increase in the cost (loss) of the Game Account from under £200 up to 1894, rising to £704 in 1902. The cost of the Game Account was essentially game given away, or at least not paid for. The comment of the Auditors in 1902 probably explains it all: "Your late Head Keeper was extremely irregular in keeping his accounts." We do not know whether he was the late Head Keeper because he had died, or had been dismissed. (See Appendix 3 for a detailed breakdown of Abergavenny Household expenditure.)

The Auditors commented each year in suitably subservient terms on the irregularity of the direct payment of the Western Estates' income (Monmouthshire, Herefordshire, and Worcestershire). They urged that the expenses of these estates should be met out of their income and only the net balance should be paid to the Marquess's private account. Each year the Marquess chose to ignore them.

The Eridge overdraft rose from £1,998-10s-0d on 1st January 1894 to £6,050-10s-10d at 1st January 1895 and £10,685-16s-11d at 31st December 1895. In their report on 1896, the auditors comment on the reduction in overdraft of £604-12s-11d over the year, but say that the overdraft "still stands at £10,081-4-0 and occasionally we note that it is as high as £15,000. We urge Your Lordship to release a portion of the Monmouthshire, Herefordshire and Worcestershire income." This income in 1897 was £19,662-11s-8$1/_2$d. The Marquess once again chose to ignore their request about how the income was paid, but he did make a payment of £4,000 which helped to reduce the overdraft by £2,600, to £7,379-3s-1d on 1st January 1898. This was despite what was listed as 'extra-ordinary expenditure' in 1897 of £74-17s-1d on Queen Victoria's Jubilee Celebrations.

It is clear that while overall income was not increasing, expenditure was being reduced and by 1st January 1899, the overdraft was down to £2,699-9s-6d, with the help of *only* £1,000 contribution from the Marquess. The Auditors' Report for 1899 was able to state proudly that "The Estate has been able to clear off the overdraft of £2,699, pay its way during the year and have a balance in hand at the finish." So prudent housekeeping had won the day.

But while the Auditors had been subserviently pushy about the distribution of income, there were two material considerations of which they were unaware, or kept unaware, and they were not to learn of them until 1899 and 1901.

They were also the Auditors for the Trustees and they were completely unaware until 1899 that the Trustees had a second and separate bank account, which was dormant except to receive income from certain sources. Its existence only surfaced when the Trustees' current account went into overdraft. The Auditors reported for 1899 that "despite realisation of £7,649 London & NW Railway Debentures for £7,820, and a temporary advance from Messrs. Drake & Lee (their solicitors in Lewes) of £3,000, income amounted to £15,485-16s-0d while expenditure was £16,383-14s-11d, with the result that the overdraft at Messrs. Child has increased by £897-11s-11d to £3,213-17s-7d." When Messrs. Child charged no interest on the overdraft, it emerged that there was a second account with £3,983-6s-8d in it. This had never been drawn upon, but was treated as a set-off against the current account. "We were not aware of its existence until this year."

The second consideration of which they seem to have been unaware until 1901 was that the Marquess and/or his Agent had been letting many farms for quite a number of years at below their valuation. What happened was that the tenant did not pay the full rent and what he did not pay was put in a separate account for future payment, but often future payment never occurred. In 1896, these rent 'arrears' were some £5,992 on a rent account of £44,214 – nearly 15% of the total. This situation could be interpreted as either a philanthropic Marquess being sympathetic with his tenants; or a realistic Agent knowing the limit which a tenant could take, particularly at times of agricultural recession. The pip squeaked only when the Marquess's expenditure was exceeding his income.

It is reasonable to express surprise that the auditors took so long to realise this situation. They had been the auditors since at least 1895. It is possible that, as City auditors, they did not understand country ways, or that they were overawed by dealing with a Marquess. Or it could just be that they were not very good auditors.

As will be shown in the next chapter on the origins of Warwick Park, the 1890s and early 1900s were to be fairly traumatic times for the Marquess. At one stage he wrote that he feared that the Home Farm/Warwick Park development would prove 'ruinous' and he bitterly regretted starting it. But by 1906, the sun was beginning to shine because from that date he had a new and major source of income which out-performed any building development.

That source was mineral rights in Wales – the rent and royalties received from the Blaenavon Iron & Steel Co. and the Nantyglo & Blaina Ironworks Co., which were about five miles from the town of Abergavenny (See box at the end of this chapter). The Abergavenny Trustees had made a loan to the companies and the loan was repaid by instalment and with interest and some element of royalty payment, no doubt related to the original lease of 1787. Typical annual payments to the Trustees had been of the order of just under £3,000 but with the end of the loan in 1906, new terms called 'Minimum Rent and Royalty' were introduced which created a quantum leap in the Mineral Rights payment and at the same time and for the first time, the increased income was to be divided, with only a quarter going to the Trustees and three-quarters going to the Marquess. The scale of increase was roughly ten-fold, from £2,773 in 1906 to £29,513 in 1907, £22,057 in 1908 and £22,128 in 1909, so the Marquess's income leapt about 50% in just one year and he was richer than he had ever been.

There can be no doubt that this new income must have removed any financial worries and reduced the pressure on or need for other investments, such as the Warwick Park Estate, to perform. It must therefore be considered a major factor (if not possibly the major factor) in the slowing down of the Warwick Park development, which would be compounded by the start of the First World War a few years later.

The subsequent history of the Nevill family is outside the scope of this study which is about the origins of the Warwick Park Estate.

But readers might like to know that when the 1st. Marquess died in1915, at the age of 89[12], having held the title for nearly 50 years, he was succeeded as the 2nd.Marquess by his 'lunatic' eldest son, Reginald William Bransley Nevill, who died, unmarried, in 1927 at the age of 74. He was succeeded as the 3rd. Marquess by his younger brother, Henry Gilbert Ralph Nevill (who features in this study as Lord Henry Nevill). Ralph, as he was known, was a great fox-hunting enthusiast who was killed in the hunting field at the age of 84. The 3rd. Marquess, although a widower twice and married three times, had no surviving male issue and consequently, when he was killed in 1938, he was succeeded as 4th Marquess, by his nephew, Guy Temple Montague Larnach-Nevill (the son of Lord George Montague Nevill, the youngest brother of the 2nd. and 3rd. Marquesses, and third son of the 1st. Marquess).

The 4th Marquess died in 1954 at the age of 71 and was succeeded as 5th Marquess by his eldest son, John Henry Guy Nevill, who was born in 1914, was educated at Eton and Trinity, served (ultimately as a Lt.-Colonel) in the Life Guards in the Second World War; as a member of the East Sussex County Council from 1947-54 and as Alderman from 1954-62; as a Vice-Lieutenant of East Sussex from 1970-4 and Lord-Lieutenant from 1974; was appointed a Knight of the Garter (KG) in 1974 and was appointed Chancellor of the Order in 1977; and held a number of directorships, including that of Lloyds Bank plc.

---

[12] When he died on 12th December 1915, he left 'effects' (excluding the value of the settled lands) valued at £173,680-14s-9d - about £8 million at today's value.

The 5th Marquess died in The Nuffield Hospital, Tunbridge Wells, on 23rd February 2000 at the age of 85, and since his only son died tragically of cancer in 1965 at the age of 17, he was succeeded in the title by his nephew, Christopher Nevill, the second son of his younger brother, the late Lord Rupert Nevill, a former private secretary to the Duke of Edinburgh. The 5th Marquess left a personal estate probated at £4,143,000, in addition to the Settled Lands which pass down with the title.

The 6th Marquess is now the only peer belonging to the great historic House of Nevill. In their time, the Nevill family have given to their country a Marshal of England, more than one Lord Chancellor and Lord High Admiral, two Archbishops of York, ten Knights of the Garter and a Queen of England, besides many other statesmen and soldiers.

It will be noticed from the previous history of the family, that the descent of the title for some 200 years has not been direct descent, but a diagonal line through younger brothers.

The Blaenavon Iron & Steel Co. and the Nantyglo and Blaina Ironworks Co.

The Blaenavon Ironworks had started in 1787, when the developers leased 12,000 acres from the Earl of Abergavenny. This land was perfect for iron-making. Seams of coal and iron ore were close to the surface; limestone needed as a flux to remove impurities during smelting was also there; as was clay and sandstone for building furnaces.

Blaenavon and some four other sites were to make South Wales and Merthyr Tydfil in particular, the iron-producing capital of the world in the mid-19th century. But this was not without its problems. As with all early industrialisation, there was a 'feast-or-famine'/'boom-or-bust' economy, which depended on the still-uncoordinated balance between demand and supply.

Industrialisation not surprisingly produced great social unrest and physical strife – following the impact of the French Revolution on public opinion and attitudes, 'Reform' was in the air in the 1820s and 1830s and from it there followed 'The Hungry Forties', the Chartist Movement and the development of trades-unionism.

It is worth noting that at least 16 workers were killed and the Red Flag was flown for the first time anywhere in the world, in the Merthyr Rising of 1831, just a few miles from Blaenavon.

Blaenavon was to concentrate between 1840-1870 on producing rails for the rapidly expanding international railway market, with orders from Britain, Brazil, India, Russia and many other countries.

Blaenavon Ironworks.

South Wales however faced growing and severe international competition – none more so than from a new manufacturing process – the Bessemer process invented in 1856 – which offered significant economies in production of iron and particularly wrought-iron rails. In the ten years to 1880, British production of wrought-iron rails slumped by 90%. So Blaenavon had to modernise, or die.

In doing so, it would seem that the companies overreached themselves financially, and in 1877 for reasons and terms not yet researched, the two companies received a 30 year loan of £6,000 from the Abergavenny Trustees (and probably further money from other sources as well.)

Blaenavon's role as one of the key places where the Industrial Revolution began, was recognised in 2000 by being designated by UNESCO as a World Heritage Site.

CHAPTER 3

DRAMATIS PERSONAE

Before describing Home Farm and the sequence of events which led to it becoming Warwick Park, it is pertinent to introduce the reader to the principal 'players' who were to perform on the Warwick Park stage and to give some indication of their characters.

They divide into three groups:

* **The Marquess** and his advisers:

  - George Macbean, his Agent
  - William Brackett, a surveyor, valuer and estate agent
  - William Roper, a surveyor
  - Augustus Drake, one of his solicitors
  - Henry Currey, an architect
  - Henry Michell Whitley, a surveyor

* **The Tunbridge Wells Borough Council**, and specifically:

  - W.C. Cripps, a Solicitor and first Town Clerk of the Borough of Tunbridge Wells
  - T. E. W. Mellor, Borough Surveyor

* **The developers and builders** of Warwick Park, and particularly:

  - Louis Beale
  - Henry Vaux Wild
  - Thomas Bates
  - Samuel Edwin Haward

✿ ✿ ✿ ✿ ✿ ✿

The Most Hon. William Nevill KG, 1st Marquess of Abergavenny, 5th Earl of Abergavenny, 5th Viscount Nevill and 19th Baron Bergavenny (1826-1915)

The Marquess appears rarely in the Archives and only when he disagrees with what is being proposed. In 1893, he was aged 67; was a Knight of the Garter and the 1st. Marquess (as well as being the 5th Earl and 19th Baron); owned 30,000 acres; and was Lord Lieutenant of the County of Sussex. He was clearly a very important and influential person locally and also nationally; and he also took a very active interest in his estates and their development.

The first Marquess was a benevolent patrician, a man of great charm and persuasion, much admired and loved by both his equals and his tenants; a political organiser or party manager rather than a politician, responsible in large part for the reorganisation of the Conservative

The 1st Marquess of Abergavenny by Sydney Hodge, 1887.

party between 1858 and 1874; a great friend of two Prime Ministers, Disraeli and the Marquess of Salisbury, to whom he owed respectively his Marquessate (granted in 1876) and his KG (appointed in 1885); and yet he is hardly known today, when lesser contemporaries are still household names. He has a very brief entry in 'Who was Who' and did not appear in the Dictionary of National Biography until the 2004 edition. He rarely features, and then only fleetingly, in the standard histories of the political parties and their organisation, by Blake, Feuchtwanger, Hanham, McKenzie, Ramsden, Roberts, Seldon & Ball, and Shannon. Yet during his lifetime, he was very influential and very well known, liked and respected.

The simplest explanation of his subsequent anonymity is that he rarely took the front of stage, except on his estates. He was an *eminence grise*. He rarely made speeches in the House of Lords, he never held political office as such, although he was instrumental in creating the National Union of Conservative Associations and was for many years its Chairman, and he worked untiringly for the organisation of the party. He rarely went on public platforms and he never wrote any books, let alone memoirs. His identity may also have been obscured subsequent to his death by having had two names in his political career, since until he succeeded his father in 1868, he would have been known as Viscount Nevill, the eldest son's courtesy title, and not as Abergavenny. He certainly saw no need to court publicity, since his position in Society put him well above that. He would have had the natural arrogance and confidence of the completely self-assured man or, should we say, aristocrat. His lineage was impeccable – the Nevills in one branch or the other had served England, certainly since the 12th century and probably since the Conqueror.

It is a slight surprise therefore to find that he was brought up in the ecclesiastical branch of the family, to which 3rd and 4th sons of aristocratic families were conventionally condemned in the 18th and 19th centuries.

William, the 1st. Marquess, was born on 16th September 1826 without any title, or certainly any immediate prospect of succession, since his grandfather (who was the 2nd Earl), his uncle (who was the third son of the 2nd Earl, and became the 3rd Earl) and his father (who was the younger brother of the 3rd Earl, and became the 4th Earl) were still alive. Probably because he was in the line of succession from birth (unlike his uncle and father who had come to it much later), he did not follow his father or his uncle into the Church, but he was always a strong Churchman, although a relatively Low one. In due course, he was to become the Patron of some 24 livings and it is said that he would accept no candidate for a living unless he was 'an Evangelical, a Conservative and a gentleman'.

He followed the more mainstream traditions of the family and went into the Army. After Eton, he took a commission at the age of 18 in the 2nd. Life Guards and in due course became a Lieutenant.

In 1848, at the age of 22, he married Miss Caroline Johnson, the daughter of Sir John Johnson, 2nd Bt., of Hackness Hall, Scarborough, Yorkshire. Miss Johnson was the sister of one of his friends at Eton. By her, he was to have eleven children, of whom nine reached adulthood and two were twins – the Ladies Rose and Violet Nevill, who, according to the Kent & Sussex Courier, created a sensation at their coming-out ball, and 'had more than the ordinary share of Nevill good looks, and were the cynosure of all eyes, whether in the ballroom or in the hunting field'. For the next 20 years until he succeeded to his father's title, and when military duties permitted (which can be assumed to be often), he lived principally in Yorkshire at Hope Hall near Tadcaster in the centre of the Bramham Moor country. Why he removed himself from the traditional Abergavenny areas of South-East England and Mid-West England/South-East Wales to Yorkshire is not known, but a number of reasons can be speculated: the influence of his dearly-beloved wife; his personal liking for the county; or the better sporting (and particularly hunting) opportunities in Yorkshire.

He was a great sportsman throughout his life and there can be no doubt that his love of sport and his skill at it, played an important part in all aspects of his social and political life. He preferred hunting with the hounds to shooting, but was said to be a crack shot till extreme old age. To quote his obituary in the Kent & Sussex Courier (which ran to two whole broadsheet pages), 'There was no more popular member of the Bramham Moor Hunt than the cheery Viscount (Nevill), who kept open house at Hope Hall...'.

When he became the 5th Earl in 1868, he moved to Eridge where his younger brother Ralph had lived for many years. Ralph had hunted with the West Kent Hunt[13] for nearly twenty years and was the MFH,

---

[13] After nearly 200 years of separate existence, the West Kent Hunt held its last meet near Penshurst on Saturday 20th March 1999. Its end was attributed to urban sprawl reducing the amount of countryside suitable for fox-hunting. From 1st May 1999, the West Kent Hunt merged with the further western Old Surrey and Burstow Hunt. Since then, fox-hunting with hounds was made illegal in 2004.

but when the Hunt was moved towards Sevenoaks in the 1870's, the Marquess whose sons *and daughters* were also keen huntsmen/women, decided to create a new pack, the Eridge Hunt, which was established in 1878. The Eridge country was consequently separated from that of the West Kent. But good relations were kept with the West Kent, and one son, Lord George Nevill, was Deputy Master under his uncle. The Eridge Hunt primarily hunted fox, but within the 2,000 acres of Eridge Park also hunted red deer.

What has been written above suggests that the Marquess was a typical 18th century English Squire – sporting, down-to-earth, popular, unintellectual – in a phrase, a High Tory with all its reactionary associations. The first three adjectives certainly seem to fit him, but the last one and its summing-up could not be further from the truth. It will take much more research and a separate study to get to the heart of the matter, but for the purposes of this study it suffices to say that the Marquess (who was probably the first party *manager* for the Conservatives), was a key influence in turning the 19th century Tory *faction* into the 20th century Conservative *party*. As the Conservative party has held office for 70 of the 100 years since 1895 and their success has often been attributed more to their better organisation than their policies, some credit for this should be given to the Marquess who built the right foundations for it, in the 1860's when he was still Viscount Nevill with his home in Yorkshire; and in the 1870's and 1880's when he was the Earl and then Marquess of Abergavenny, living at Eridge Castle.

At the time of the Reform Act of 1832, there was nothing which could seriously be called a party system, either inside or outside Parliament. The Conservative and Liberal parties were created from the 1850's onwards out of (respectively) the Tory and Whig *factions* and they were the first true political *parties* in the United Kingdom, with structure, organisation, policies, paid membership and a growing and democratic electorate.

The Tories were descended from the Court Party which supported the Stuarts, Charles II and James II, and who were opposed by the Country Party, known subsequently as Whigs, who in due course became the mainstay of the Hanoverian kings. In many respects, there was little difference between Tories and Whigs except emotional attachments, since both sides were drawn from the same very small and privileged groups with the same self-interests; and were elected by a very small electorate who were totally unrepresentative of the population.

The impact of the Industrial Revolution in the second half of the 18th and the first half of the 19th centuries and its accompanying social upheaval was enormous. Social 'Revolution' particularly after the French model was a constant fear, if not a threat. New industrial towns, particularly in the North and Midlands, were being created without any representation in Parliament and the first Reform Act (of 1832) was introduced to remove anomalies of *Parliamentary*, rather than *electoral* representation. The Act was considered 'revolutionary' in its day, although all that it did was to abolish some 56 'rotten boroughs', such as Old Sarum with two members and two electors, and Bossiney in Cornwall which had two members elected by only one voter; and to give parliamentary representation for the first time to 'new' towns such as Manchester (with a population of 180,000) and Birmingham, Leeds, Sheffield, Wolverhampton, Huddersfield and Gateshead. But the net effect of the Act was only to increase the electorate from 220,000 to about 400,000, out of a population of some 14 million, that is from a mere 1.6% to a hardly significant 2.9% of the population.

The widening of the electorate was to come later with the second Reform Act of 1867 which gave the vote to a further million – all *male* householders in *towns* – and in doing so, tripled the electorate; and also with the third Reform Act of 1884 which extended the vote to all male householders. Also of significance was the introduction of the secret ballot in 1872, after three previous unsuccessful attempts to do so, which did much to reduce or even remove undue influence on the voting behaviour of a growing electorate.

What should be of interest to us was that the 1st. Marquess was at the centre of all these events and the changes they created; and that he played a significant, if now unsung, part in all of them. He was among the first to appreciate not only the importance of the new growing and increasingly educated electorate, but also the power of the Press among an increasingly literate population, and the importance of having that Press on one's side politically. He took this belief as far as actually helping to found newspapers which would be guaranteed (by ownership) to be Conservative; and among these were both The Yorkshire Times in 1866 and the Kent & Sussex Courier (The Tunbridge Wells Courier) in 1872.

According to his obituary in 'The Times', "he wielded great power in the innermost councils of the Conservative Party... His peculiar gift of heartiness and geniality won over many a wavering constituency.

His enthusiasm and keenness for the Conservative cause earned for him the sobriquet of 'The Tory Bloodhound' [first given him by Lady Dorothy Nevill, who was his cousin by marriage]. Endowed with a considerable gift for organisation, he did much valuable work as one of the founders of the Junior Carlton and Constitutional Clubs and continued to act as the Chairman of the former up to comparatively recent years. For a considerable period he was the Chairman of the National Union of Conservative Associations. [*In fact as Nevill, he was one of the principal founders of the National Union.*] His influence with the old 'county members' was extraordinary, besides which he possessed the faculty both of forming strong and lasting friendships and of obtaining devoted service from those who had to work with him. In the distribution of rewards for services to the party, he had for many years a predominant voice. His power in this respect, indeed, was so great that it was once said of him that, if he could not lay claim to be called 'The King-maker' like his ancestor, the Earl of Warwick, his title to the name of 'The Peer-maker' could not be disputed.

Besides his political interests, the Marquess also played a (Sussex) County role to the full. He had been a Sussex JP since 1866 (two years before his father's death and before he lived permanently in Sussex) and regularly attended the Quarter Sessions at Lewes. (He also regularly attended Lewes Races 'although not an active patron of the turf' according to the Courier obituary, possibly because he owned Lewes Downs and Racecourse and had his own private stand there.) He became Lord Lieutenant of Sussex in 1892, a post which he relinquished in 1905 'owing to failing eyesight'. While Lord Lieutenant at the time of the South African War, he was instrumental in raising the Imperial Sussex Yeomanry, of which a platoon was stationed at Eridge. He was also President, Patron, Governor or Trustee of innumerable County or local Hospitals, Associations, Societies, or Clubs.

He was frequently described as a model landlord – 'a thoroughly good landlord who took a very personal interest in the welfare of his tenants'. 'Anything which would promote the happiness and welfare of the villagers around Eridge found in Lord Abergavenny and his family generous supporters', wrote the Courier obituarist who also recorded that the Marquess attended many of their weddings and funerals. He built the Village Hall, in which two generations of his family were to entertain the villagers with their 'Theatricals, Concerts, Humorous Songs and Impromptu Verses'.

He gave Balls for Trade and Tenantry in a marquee on the Castle lawns. He organised cricket matches between a Married team, a Singles team, an Estate team and a Castle team; 'bountiful' teas which the Marchioness 'superintended' as well as 'ample supplies of tobacco and nut-brown ale' for the men; dancing on the village green; and in cold winters such as 1879, cricket on the ice of Eridge Lake, followed by illuminations and fireworks. All in all, he seems to have been a very benevolent patriarch.

Eridge Castle was also the scene for many major political events, to the extent that it was often called 'the Carlton Club in Kent' (although Eridge has always been in Sussex). The 'Kentish gang' of politicians met there regularly. Disraeli was a great friend and frequent visitor – he loved venison and strawberries, both of which were in ample supply at Eridge. The regular shooting parties also served another purpose as a forum for political discussion and debate. There were also regular meetings of The Primrose League and perhaps the largest political demonstration ever held up to that time in the South of England, was that organised by the Marquess of Abergavenny on August Bank Holiday 1888, when 30,000 representing over 200 Conservative Associations of the Home Counties crowded into Eridge Park.

He was the subject entitled 'The Tory Bloodhound' of one of the celebrated 'Vanity Fair' cartoons by 'Ape' ('Statesmen No. 267' in 1875) which showed him wearing the Abergavenny check trousers for which he was famous. The commentary to the cartoon speaks of his 'considerable influence in the preservation of privileges in which the people of England retain confidence'. An early epitaph to a born-again Tory.

❖ ❖ ❖ ❖ ❖ ❖

The Tory Bloodhound.

George Evan Macbean (1860-1902) was Abergavenny's Land Agent for the Eridge Estate, which included the Home Farm Estate, until his death from a stroke in 1902 at the early age of 42.

Macbean was unmarried and lived at The Cottage, Eridge Green (a 'tied' house which was taken over by his successor, Ernest Gaisford), and according to the 1901 Census, was looked after by a married couple, who were butler and cook, and a groom. He was the second son of Colonel Forbes Macbean of the 92nd (later the Gordon) Highlanders and was not surprisingly born in Scotland. While Agent for the Marquess, he was also Secretary of the Eridge Hunt; an active member of the Executive of the Tunbridge Wells and South-Eastern Agricultural Society; and a Captain in the Imperial Sussex Yeomanry, a Territorial Army unit which had been founded by the Marquess in 1900, no doubt as a consequence of the Boer War.

George Macbean's tombstone.

He died, while in what was described as 'the most robust health', from what was then called a paralytic seizure on Thursday, 11th December 1902 – leaving an estate of £1,183-15s-3d. to his widowed mother. He is buried in the churchyard at Eridge Green, with a Celtic cross as his tombstone and *within* the Abergavenny family plot, which must indicate the family's regard for him.

The Courier said that he would be 'remembered with gratitude for many acts of kindness to the

The Abergavenny Family plot in Eridge Churchyard.

poorer tenantry, while by one and all he was esteemed as a painstaking agent to the noble house which he represented, also as a good sportsman in connection with the secretaryship of the Eridge Hunt, which he so ably filled'.

This high regard was confirmed at his funeral. Large crowds lined the route from the Castle to the Church and the funeral 'was held among widespread manifestations of regret, and with impressive solemnity, accompanied by military honours and weather of a most adverse nature'. The church (which held 300) 'was filled to its uttermost capacity, many having perforce to remain outside during the service'. His coffin was draped in the Union Jack and the cortege was flanked either side by the 32 members – Officers, NCO's and men – of the Eridge Troop of the Sussex Imperial Yeomanry, while his favourite horse 'Tommy Atkins' followed immediately behind the hearse.

At the conclusion of the funeral, his elder brother, Colonel Forbes Macbean[14], addressed the Eridge Troop of the Sussex Imperial Yeomanry expressing his gratitude and afterwards he entertained them at 'The Gun' (now 'The Nevill Crest & Gun').

The Marquess did not attend the funeral. The Marquess was of course 76 and it was a very wet and cold December, so his absence is entirely understandable, but it was also protocol that the Marquess should not normally attend, but would send his carriage and his sons to represent him.

This he did in the case of a previous Steward/Agent, William Delves, who died in 1886. But on this occasion, there was surprisingly no carriage, although the family was strongly represented by at least six members – Lord and Lady Henry Nevill, the Marquess and Marchioness Camden[15], and the Hon. T.A. and Lady Idena Brassey

---

[14] His elder brother, also Forbes Macbean, followed his father through the Gordon Highlanders, serving in the Second Afghan War (1879-80) including the March from Kabul to Kandahar; in the Transvaal campaign of 1881 and in the South African War from 1899-1902. At the time of his brother's death, he had just returned from South Africa where he had been the Colonel commanding the 1st. Battalion, The Gordon Highlanders from 1900 (until 1904). He was awarded the CB in 1900, the CVO in 1905 and was appointed an ADC to King Edward VII in 1907, an appointment which he held until the King's death in 1911. He retired as a Major-General and died in 1919 at the age of 62.

[15] 4th Marquess (title created 1812). Succeeded to title at birth in 1872. Married Joan Marion, daughter of Lord Henry Nevill and grand-daughter of 1st Marquess of Abergavenny, in 1898. Lived at Bayham Abbey, Lamberhurst and owned about 18,000 acres (cf. Abergavenny with about 30,000 acres). He would have been too young to have been responsible for the development of Camden Park in Tunbridge Wells.

(daughter of 1st Marquess). Other notables among the mourners included Sir Frederick Milner, MP, and Mrs. Milner (presumably his mother); W.C. Cripps, the Town Clerk of Tunbridge Wells; and Augustus Drake of Drake & Lee of Lewes. Mr. William Roper, who was also Secretary of the Agricultural Society, was unable to attend.

There is as yet no record discovered of when Macbean took office, nor is there a clear distinction between the role and title of Steward, which William Delves held until 1880, and that of Land Agent, which Macbean seems to have taken on afterwards. Obviously Agent (which title Delves also seem to have used later on) is a wider role with more autonomy than Steward and this may be a reflection of changing circumstances. But it is not clear whether Macbean was Delves's successor, although this seems unlikely since Macbean would have been only 20 when Delves retired in 1880.

Macbean had as a subordinate in his office, Andrew Williamson, who only features in correspondence. George Macbean was succeeded as Agent by **Ernest Charles Gaisford**.[16]

Macbean originally commissioned:

William Brackett, FSI, the surveyor, valuer and estate agent, who lived at Roxwell, 9 Guildford Road and had his business premises at 27-29 High Street. He was well-known and regarded and was to be Chairman of the Tunbridge Wells Tradesmen's Association (later to become the Chamber of Commerce) in 1896. He was a shrewd businessman and had produced since 1849 a monthly Tunbridge Wells train timetable, which naturally listed the specifications of all the properties that he had to let, or for sale.

Mr. William Brackett, FSI.

Brackett produced the first detailed survey of the Home Farm Estate on

---

[16] Gaisford was sufficiently well thought of by the 1st Marquess to be left £200 in his will in 1915. He was to remain the Marquess's Agent and (according to the 3rd. Marquess's will) to be the friend of the 3rd. Marquess for many years. After his retirement, he was to be one of the Executors of the 3rd. Marquess's Will in 1938. Gaisford died in July 1943, leaving an estate of £53,389-1s-9d.

11th November 1893. He does not seem to have been involved much in the Home Farm development for some time after his report, possibly because in the covering letter to his report, he suggested that he could provide a purchaser for the Estate – "I would be glad to place before His Lordship a gentleman of means who would, we believe, be prepared to treat for it at once". Later evidence suggests that this was seen as interfering and was resented by George Macbean. Nonetheless, Brackett repeated the offer on 11th September 1895 indicating that he had 'an applicant to whom we would like to offer the whole of the available building land'. His offer was answered by Macbean the following day, very swiftly and curtly in $1^1/_2$ lines: "Please send all applicants to the Eridge Estate Office who will handle all matters". In retrospect it was a great pity that his offer was refused since Warwick Park might have been a more successful development if it had been carried out by one person. Despite the refusal, Brackett was used to produce a report in February 1897 on Ground Rents for the Estate. This report was produced in conjunction with:

William Roper, FSI, Auctioneer, Surveyor and Valuer who seems to have worked from home at 49 Mount Pleasant Road. Roper had been corresponding with Macbean as early as 1895 and had prepared the detailed road and sewage construction plans for the Warwick Park Estate in 1896, so it is possible that Roper brought Brackett back in, rather than the other way round. It is not surprising that Roper acted as the surveyor in the building of the Nevill Ground (see Chapter 6).

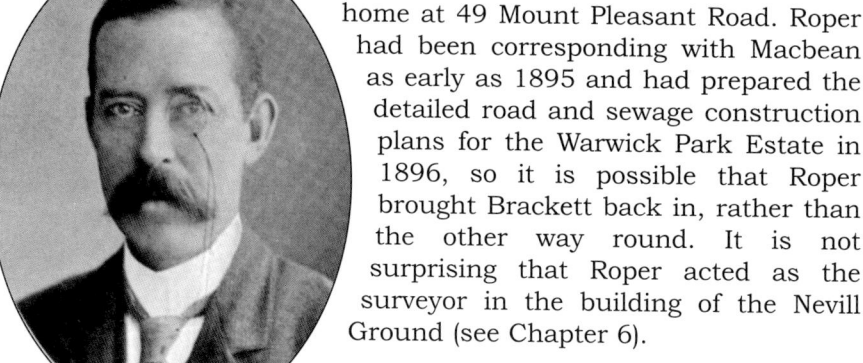

Mr. William Roper, FSI.

Despite the refusals of his offer, Brackett seems to have recovered his position since he went on to get the largest share of the Estate Agents' commission for Warwick Park in the early 1900s (but that of course was after Macbean's death).

✪ ✪ ✪ ✪ ✪ ✪

Augustus Drake of the solicitors Drake & Lee of Castlegate, Lewes who were the solicitors for the Trustees of the Abergavenny Estates. Augustus Drake was instrumental in recommending as early as 23rd.

November 1893 (i.e. less than a fortnight after the Brackett report was presented):

Henry Currey, one of an architectural practice of two brothers, Henry & Percivall Currey, of 37, Norfolk St, London WC. Henry Currey is probably best known for the design of the six-blocked St. Thomas's Hospital (1868-1871) which faces the Houses of Parliament across the Thames. Henry Currey had been appointed the Duke of Devonshire's architect in 1859 to lay out the Duke's estate in Eastbourne for residential development and had produced much which is admired to this day, including the Winter Garden, Meads and the Western Parades.

Currey had been a student of Decimus Burton and had worked with Joseph Paxton on the Great Conservatory (1837) at Chatsworth, the Devonshire seat in Derbyshire, which had a significant influence on the design of the Winter Garden at Eastbourne (1874).

Burton had been commissioned in 1838 by the Duke (when he was the Earl of Burlington) to draw up a plan for the new town of Eastbourne, but nothing seems to have come of it. It is not known what ideas his pupil, Currey, may have brought with him to Eastbourne when he was appointed in 1859. At the time of his appointment, it was recorded that Currey was a relative of the Duke's solicitor, although we do not know whether Drake was the Duke's solicitor at that time.

Whatever the relationship, Currey was known to Augustus Drake who described him as 'a different class of man altogether from the other two' (Whitley [see below] and another) 'and in his hands, we should think his Lordship and the other Trustees might safely leave their interests'. Drake's recommendation was accepted and Henry Currey was to prepare the first layout of the Home Farm Estate in 1894.

Henry Michell Whitley, was 'Mr. Gilbert's surveyor at Eastbourne' and was also highly regarded by Drake, despite Drake's belittling comparison of him with Currey.

John Davis Gilbert and the Duke of Devonshire between them owned most of the land of Eastbourne and were instrumental in developing it as a town, from a population of 3,433 in 1851 to 43,344 in 1901. Gilbert appointed Nicholas Whitley (1810-1891), a surveyor and civil engineer who was born and seems to have lived all his life in Cornwall, to be his architect in 1862 and the first comprehensive design for the

Gilbert estate was complete by 1870.

Henry Michell Whitley (b.1845) was the son of Nicholas Whitley. He was appointed Mr. Gilbert's surveyor in the 1880s, but is more usually called a civil engineer. He was to offer much advice on the Warwick Park Estate. He was also given some form of official appointment, apparently with the Borough Council, since a letter from Cripps to Macbean of 15th July 1896 says somewhat ambiguously that 'the Chief Clerk has appointed Whitley as Surveyor' (but of what is not clear). Unless of course 'the Chief Clerk' is a sarcastic reference to his fellow solicitor, Augustus Drake, who acted for the Trustees, in which case the appointment would be for the Home Farm Estate.

✪ ✪ ✪ ✪ ✪ ✪

The newly-created Borough Council had two main players:

W.C. Cripps

William Charles Cripps (1855-1952): Solicitor, and also first Town Clerk of Tunbridge Wells which he was for 36 years, from its Incorporation in 1889 until 1925. He lived at The Lawn, 5 Camden Park. As was common with many Town Clerks at the time, he carried on his practice as solicitor and amongst others, advised the Eridge Estate.

He seems to have been adept at avoiding conflicts of interest and it is clear that he and George Macbean, who was five years his junior, were friends. In private handwritten correspondence, he addresses Macbean as 'Dear Bean' and Macbean replies 'Dear Cripps', although when the typewriter was introduced into the Town Hall in 1894[17], a more formal 'Dear Mr. Macbean' takes over when the letter is produced by a 'Shorthand & Typewriter clerk', clearly a forerunner of the modern (but now largely-defunct) secretary.

His closeness to Macbean is best illustrated by a letter written on 29th February 1896. The matter to which it refers is not entirely clear – it could be the Settled Land issue, or the Sewage issue, or the issue of diverting the highway – but it clearly indicates a degree of co-operation bordering on collusion between the two. Cripps wrote: "I enclose a draft of a letter which I think I ought to write to you and which if so willing, you should show to the Marquess. Let me know what you wish. I am a bit worried about the thing for fear that it might go wrong and you get blamed for what really couldn't be your fault, you not having had proper facilities".

His practice, which included his son, was known as W.C.Cripps, Son & Daish and was situated at 84, Calverley Road. It was to develop in due course into the well-known and leading Tunbridge Wells practice of Cripps, Harries Hall. On retirement from being Town Clerk at the age of 70, he became a Freeman of the Borough, and subsequently a Kent County Councillor at the age of 74, and Alderman at the age of 85. His wife died in 1904 when he was 49 and he never remarried. His lifelong hobby was listed as 'shooting' (what was never specified) and he was for many years the President of the St.Peter's Rifle Club which is still situated at the top of Warwick Park and which was the successor to the Pantyles Rifle Club. When he died in 1952 at the age of 97, his estate was probated at £104,367-3s-2d.

The other key person in the Town Hall was:

Thomas Edward Wheatley Mellor, Borough Surveyor. He lived at Oakley Road, Boyne Park, Tunbridge Wells in what was then called 'a joint tenement' with his sister, Sarah Mellor. He does not feature strongly, but he was of great technical importance on the major issues of the road lines, the sewers, footpath diversion and overall planning permission. He would seem to have been provided by the Council with

---

[17] The first extant typewritten letter from Cripps to Macbean is dated the 16th October 1895 but the Town Hall was 'mechanised' with one typewriter (naturally kept in the Town Clerk's office) in 1894. When it was proposed to replace this machine with a new one in 1898, Alderman Clifford criticised it as an expensive luxury and Alderman Delves defended the proposal, saying that it had been in use for four years and needed repair and it was to be exchanged for one of an improved type for £15 and the old machine.

the use of a horse, and a horse and carriage – no doubt the then-equivalent of a company car.

In April 1899, he fell ill and was granted sick leave which was extended at three month intervals until he finally resigned on the grounds of ill-health in April 1900.[18] Mellor was clearly concerned about the impression his resignation might give, since he requested in May 1900 'a written testimonial as to the nature of his services and the circumstances which had compelled his resignation'. The Council therefore resolved unanimously that 'This Council desires to place on record its high appreciation of the integrity, marked ability and invariable courtesy displayed by Mr. T.E. Mellor, AMICE, and its great regret that the state of his health has necessitated his resignation.'

In the more cynical 21st century, one can only wonder what was it all about?

✦ ✦ ✦ ✦ ✦ ✦

The first two groups of players – the Marquess and his advisers, and the Borough Council – were obviously involved from the very beginning of the Warwick Park development in 1893-4. The third group – the developers and builders of the houses in Warwick Park – were not to be involved until much later, from 1897 onwards, but they were to have an important *and contrary* influence on the style of Warwick Park.

The leading builder was **Louis Stephen Beale** (1853-1939). In his obituary in the Courier of 3rd. February 1939, Louis Beale is described as 'a man of wide interests, but always a family man.' The 'but always' is somewhat intriguing. He had five sons and five daughters and he seems to have had a penchant for giving them unusual Christian names – for example, Louis Bernhardt Beale, Bertram Saxon Beale, Donald Olaf Beale, as well as Miss Daisee Beale.

The wide interests included 'globe-trotting' which he took up when he retired in 1910 at the surprisingly early age of 57. This was an unusual hobby for that time, and took him twice round the world, visiting

---

[18] His successor, William Maxwell, was appointed in 1900 at a salary of £380 a year rising by annual increments of £20 to £500; and it was specified that his whole time was to be devoted to the Council, which implies that this was not the case with his predecessor. For comparative purposes, the Chief Constable of Tunbridge Wells was appointed in 1893 at a salary of £200 a year, rising to £225 after 5 years, and £250 after ten years, plus a uniform allowance of £13 a year.

practically the whole of Europe, Northern Africa, North America (including Alaska) and South America, India, China, Japan, Australia, New Zealand and Russia. "He gained an intimate knowledge of native manners and customs in practically all of them ... he also collected many curios." One wonders what these were.

Louis Beale was born in Frant on 20th November 1853, the son of Stephen Beale, a carpenter, and Frances Charlotte Beale, née Cheeseman. Stephen Beale (1819-1888) was the son of Stephen and Sarah Beale, who were listed as a 'butcher' and 'butcheress' of Bells Yew Green in the 1851 Census returns. He married Frances Cheeseman in 1845 when he was 26 and she was 25. Their first child, Louis Stephen Beale, was not born until eight years later.

When Louis left school in 1867 at the age of 14, his father was still listed in Mathieson's Directory for Tunbridge Wells as a carpenter in Frant Road. However over the next 20 years, and without doubt with the help of Louis, they became builders and were listed under that category as Stephen Beale & Son of The Derry, 4 Birling Road. By the time Louis's obituary was written in 1939, this part of the history had been rewritten and the obituary reported that he left school at 14 "to join the family firm of Messrs. Beale & Sons [its name from only about 1889, by which time Louis was in charge]. The obituary goes on "and as an ordinary employee went through all the various departments, eventually becoming the head of the firm whose skilful work has made many valuable contributions to the architecture of the town... Mr. Beale introduced many distinctive designs and perhaps most notable are those residences in Kingswood Road, Madeira Park, Pembury Road, Linden Park and Warwick Park."

The premises of L.Beale & Sons Ltd were at 'The Derry', 4 Birling Road (a building which is still there with its builder's yard behind), and the Madeira Park

Louis Beale

Estate Office was at 6 Madeira Park[19], which was also the private residence of Louis Beale and his family.

Beale was a prominent Freemason and over time was the Worshipful Master of five local Lodges, as well as holding 'many Provincial honours'. He was at one stage the Prime Warden of the Worshipful Company of Blacksmiths 'an honour which brought with it the Freedom of the City of London'. In 1896, he was the President of the Tunbridge Wells Tradesmen's Association. He was also involved in many local associations and in the Borough Council, but he was a Councillor for the West Ward for only five years from around 1900[20]. He died in 1939 at Cumberlands, Cumberland Walk, leaving £91,245-9s-1d (worth about £2,750,000 at today's values), considerably more than his two closest rivals in Warwick Park, Henry Wild and Thomas Bates. Beale was very generous to all his children and he helped them financially either in their businesses or with gifts. His family estimate that he gave each of his ten children £8-10,000 in this way while he was alive, so his real worth (and his achievement) was almost certainly double what he left in his will.

Henry Vaux Wild (1838-1926) was born in London on 5th December 1838 at 28, Hyde Place, Hoxton Old Town. He was the son of Joseph Wyld/Wild, a goldbeater, and his wife Sarah, née Fordham. Henry's progress can be traced through the UK Census returns and the General Registrar's Office (GRO). He married Annie Tibbitt in 1870; was listed as a goldbeater in the 1871 Census, as living in Lavender Grove, Hackney with a wife, a son and an 18 year-old 'general servant'. By 1881, while still living in Lavender Grove but in a different house, he had become a 'House Agent & Decorator', with the same wife, but two children – son and daughter – and a different 17 year-old 'general servant'. We have not yet been able to identify his whereabouts in the 1891 Census.

How he came to Tunbridge Wells is as yet unknown; when he came, is also far from certain. The earliest known record of him in Tunbridge Wells is from Kelly's Directory of 1892 when he would have been 54, and which shows him living at 3 Norfolk Road, Tunbridge Wells.

---

[19] No.6 is now called Milward House and is a Pilgrim Homes retirement home.
[20] His eldest son, who became Sir Louis Beale, KCMG, CBE (1879-1971) and was the UK Commissioner-General at the New York Trade Fair in 1939, lived at Ellerburne, Warwick Park (now No.36) from 1901, when he would have been only 22, but presumably married. His second son, Capt. Bertram Beale, MC, ran the family firm of Beale & Sons, which no longer exists.

Norfolk Road was and is a pleasant but modest road of terraced houses off Claremont Road which in the 1891 Census had Heads of Household who were typically a Railway Engine Driver, a Railway Guard, a Railway Booking Clerk, a Grocer's Assistant, a Pastry Cook, a Commercial Traveller, a Printer/Compositor and a Strict Baptist Minister. All of which suggests, if his neighbours are any indication, that Henry at that time was certainly not rich.

What is undoubtedly significant is that his next door neighbour at No.5 was a certain **Thomas Bates**, some 26 years younger than him, who was at that time a carpenter working for Louis Beale. They were to remain neighbours for five years, until Henry moved to a very much more substantial detached house, No.4, Eden Road, and called by him Kinnellar, where he remained until 1917. What enabled Henry to 'move up' relatively late in life to become the neighbour of a retired Judge and Knight (at No.3), is a matter for speculation, since his occupation and source of income before 1898 is unknown. There is no record of him in the commercial life of Tunbridge Wells as recorded in the very comprehensive Directories of the time. But his entry in the 1901 Census records him as a 'retired builder' and his two unmarried children, now aged 29 and 22, as being of 'independent means'. Some transformation!

Thomas Bates however was a carpenter by trade who worked for Louis Beale in the 1890s but he was to develop into one of the leading builders in Tunbridge Wells. The exact relationship of Henry Wild and Thomas Bates over the next 10-20 years is difficult to gauge. Was Henry Wild a property developer and/or the mentor of Thomas Bates, who encouraged Bates to go independent and gave him projects to build? If so, where did Henry Wild suddenly get his money since he presumably did not have the capital to do so, when he was in Norfolk Road? Was Henry Wild the partner of Thomas Bates when he went independent?

But where did the money come from? It is possible that he inherited it – after all, his father and he had been goldbeaters which was a skilled occupation which no doubt provided opportunities for accumulation. It is possible that he made it in a profession/ occupation in Tunbridge Wells or London which was not recorded in Kelly's Directory. We only know of him from a commercial point-of-view from 1898 (when he would have been 60) as the developer (not builder or architect) of many of the houses in Blatchington Road and the immediate environs. He seems to have been treated with some suspicion by the Abergavenny

Estate Office, as a late payer of rent and a demanding lessee.

Thomas Bates was to become one of the principal builders of the Estate and Wild was probably the person who encouraged Bates to leave Beale and set up on his own. Certainly Bates was to be the builder of all the houses which Wild developed. The last houses which Wild developed were in 1910, when he would have been 72.

Wild took the only extant photographs of the Home Farm and the New Road on 2nd. January 1899, no doubt because he was to develop part of the farmyard as Cliff House (now Nos.67 and 67b) the following year. He lived at 'Kinnellar', 4 Eden Road until 1917, then at 42 Claremont Road until 1923, and finally at 21 Madeira Park where he died on Boxing Day 1926 at the age of 88. The Courier which was normally very generous with its obituaries, made no mention of his death in their issue of 31st December 1926 except for a paid two lines in its Births, Deaths and Marriages classified advertising. Perhaps the Courier's usual attention was below par as it was New Year's Eve or maybe the death of an old man at 88, who had been out of the business of the town for nearly 20 years, passed unnoticed. He left £9,836-9s-0d which was not inconsiderable in its day.

Thomas Bates (1864-1930) was born in Newick near Uckfield, Sussex, the third son and sixth child of his parents. He trained as a carpenter and there is a widely-held legend in the family that he worked initially in a Tunbridge Ware factory on the Frant Road before going to work for Louis Beale. This would fit in with the Henry Hollamby Tunbridge Ware factory in Frant Road which was burnt down in 1891, putting 40 workers out of work.

Since Thomas Bates also married in April 1891, he would have been under great pressure to find work and therefore it is not surprising that as a carpenter, he would switch to building and go to work for Louis Beale. He worked for Louis Beale for probably about seven years before setting up on

Thomas Bates

his own in the late 1890's. He lived at 5 Norfolk Road from 1892-1898, so it is probable that his move to 6 Nevill Terrace, which is off the Eridge Road and by the Tunbridge Wells West railway station, coincided with his setting up on his own. There is a very strong suggestion that Henry Wild played an important part in Thomas Bates 'going independent'. Certainly Bates in 1898-9 was building houses for Wild in what became Blatchington Road and continued to build for Wild until 1910[21].

Initially it is quite clear that he was not a developer as such, but a builder for other developers. His earliest buildings were large houses particularly in or near Roedean Road, but he subsequently became a developer in his own right. When he died in 1930 at the age of 66, he left £10,969-8s-9d, a slightly larger but fundamentally similar amount as his 'mentor' Henry Wild.

Samuel Edwin Haward was a successful local ironmonger and engineer. He lived at Yotes Lodge, Culverden Park and traded as S.E.Haward & Co.Ltd at 44-48 Goods Station Road and 29 Mount Pleasant, Tunbridge Wells. William Henry Delves (the son of William Delves, Abergavenny's Steward) who was an Alderman and in 1900-1 Mayor of Tunbridge Wells, was also a Director of S.E.Haward & Co.Ltd. This is another example of how Tunbridge Wells was a small and close-knit community. Haward, as the landlord of one of the houses he had built, was to be involved in a legal dispute with the Marquess in 1900.

✡ ✡ ✡ ✡ ✡ ✡

In a small town such as Tunbridge Wells, everybody knew everybody else and they met on what might generously be called an almost equal footing. The Mayor's Reception, given by the Mayor, Major C.R.

---

[21] Thomas Bates generated a great deal of ill-will when he moved to 6 Nevill Terrace in 1898. The Terrace was eight terraced houses intended for ' private dwellings for letting apartments'. However Bates immediately built a workshop in his garden which led to complaints from his neighbours about the 'hand-sawing and hammering going on almost incessantly from 6 in the morning till the evening'. Eventually in 1902, he was given permission by Abergavenny's Agent, Macbean, to have a shed 'for storage only' and Wild wrote to Macbean thanking him for this and promising that he (Wild) would make sure that ' the privilege is not abused', which indicates Wild's close involvement with Bates. However Bates continued to ignore the restriction and the complaints continued without, it seems, any redress until at least 1907, by which time the neighbours were giving up and leaving and Bates took over Nos. 6, 7,and 8 as offices for his expanding business. Bates eventually acquired the freehold of Nevill Terrace from the 2nd. Marquess in 1924. He also acquired land as a builder's yard in Eridge Road (behind Nevill Terrace), as well as 14 Eridge Road (formerly Richmond Lodge) and stabling at the rear of 21-22 Eridge Road.

Fletcher Lutwidge, was held at (what was then called) the Bishop's Down Spa Hotel on 31st January 1896 and included most of our main players among its guest-list of nearly 700 (which was quite a high proportion of the town or neighbourhood, when the town only had a population of about 30,000):

The Marquess of Abergavenny	Marquess Camden
Lord & Lady Henry Nevill	
Lord & Lady William Nevill	Lord & Lady George Nevill
G. E. Macbean, Esq.	
Alderman & Mrs. Delves	Mr. W. and Miss Brackett
Mr. W.C. and Mrs. Cripps	Mr. A.W. and Mrs. Brackett
Mr. T.E.W. Mellor	Mr. W. and Mrs. Roper
	Mr. L.S. and Mrs. Beale
	Mr. S.E. and Mrs. Haward

There was however, according to the Tunbridge Wells Courier, 'a fog outside of unusual volume' on the night of the Reception, and so they could not tell their readers (and so we will never know) which, or how many, guests had failed to attend.

It is however illuminating of their real social relationship to learn that, when it came to the Eridge Hunt Ball which The Courier described as 'the great fashionable event of the year' and which was held at the Pump Room in the same month of January, only the Abergavenny family and Macbean and the Cripps attended. Tradesmen and those in commerce instinctively knew their place and kept to it.

CHAPTER 4

THE ORIGINS OF WARWICK PARK

Before Warwick Park and its ancillary roads were developed, the land was called the Home Farm Estate of the Marquess of Abergavenny. The name Home Farm did not, however, have any particular significance (as it usually does), in relation to Abergavenny's seat, Eridge Castle (now Eridge Park), which is some three miles away.

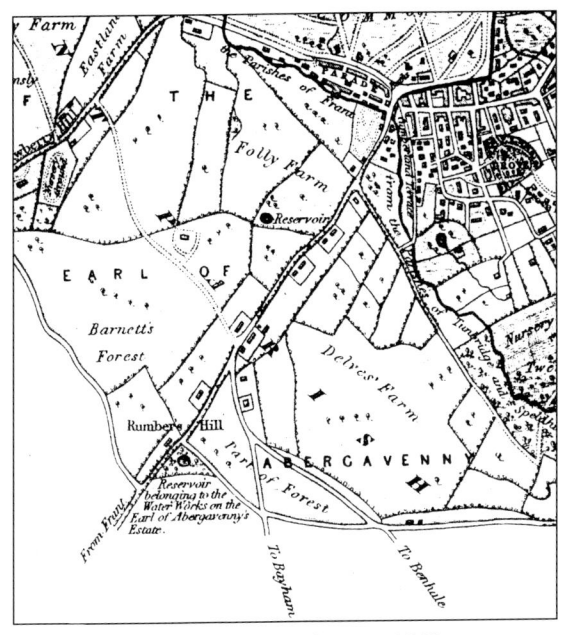

The Home Farm Estate included all the land from Nevill Street by the Pantiles in the west, up to Forest Road in the east; and from Frant Road in the south, to beyond the Hastings railway line (the SER at that time) in the north.[22]

It is not clear whether the farm had always been called Home Farm. Certainly it was called that in the 1851 Census and also in the Burgess Rolls of 1873 and later. But it is also recorded on Stidolph's map of 1838 and Colbran's maps of 1838 and c.1853 as Delves' Farm. It is also referred to, on a Parish Boundary map of 1894, as Forest Farm, no doubt because of

Detail from Stidolph map, 1838

---

[22] Until 1894, the whole of Warwick Park from the Home Farm site down to the Pantiles would have been in Sussex. This was because the Grom brook now largely underground but mainly overground in the 18th and 19th centuries, which flowed from the Home Farm site down to the Pantiles, was the county boundary; and since it turned to flow south at its junction with the Church of King Charles the Martyr, this meant that the eastern side of the Pantiles was also in Sussex. But the creation of the Broadwater Down parish (in Kent) meant that the boundary was moved back in 1894 from the brook to Forest Road, and subsequently in 1900 to beyond the cemetery. This took the Sussex boundary about a mile further east and the Home Farm Estate became completely Kent. The change of boundary is not thought to have had any influence on the development of the Warwick Park Estate.

49

Forest Road which had run along its eastern boundary for centuries. But we shall refer to it as the Home Farm Estate, since it is by this name that it was universally known during the time of its development at the turn of the 20th century.

Home Farm, which was essentially pasture, would seem to have been leased by the Delves family since at least 1800 when W. Delves is recorded in the 1800 Terrier (the map and specification of lands held) of Frant Parish, as leasing 259 acres including Home Farm. They may well have held the lease (although there is no factual evidence) since the 18th century when they arrived in Tunbridge Wells.

Their name is unlikely to have been used on the maps unless they were long-standing

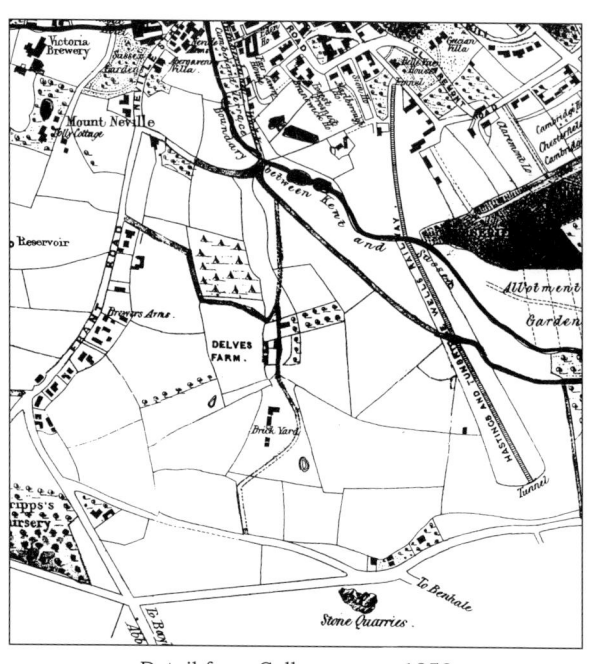

Detail from Colbran map, 1853

and well-established tenants of the farm. And this would fit their circumstances, since they started as butchers who would have needed pasture to keep their livestock before slaughter (and the closer it was to their shops in the Pantiles and Chapel Place, the better). Their business interests expanded over time into other areas – wholesale and retail trade, property and House Agency, the forerunner of Estate Agency – but they also remained butchers until late in the 19th century.

The fact that they were principally butchers and also leased the nearest pasture farm to their shops cannot be coincidence. Until the development of the railways and refrigeration, all meat would have been from a local source. Animals would have been kept alive until they needed to be slaughtered and Home Farm would have been a very convenient and central pasture for the Delves.

However meat supply started to change from the 1860's onwards. Smithfield Market in London changed from a live animal market to a meat market; railways could provide swift delivery; refrigerated ships brought cheap meat from North America and Argentina; and refrigerated storage in Britain reduced the need to keep livestock alive, so the need for Home Farm as a 'fattening pen' was reduced.

All of this, coupled with the fact the Farm had been divided by two railway cuttings (the Tunbridge Wells-Hastings line in 1847 which cut off about a fifth of the Farm from the rest; and the Central Station-West Station loop-line in 1866 which divided the remainder) probably made the Farm less necessary, less manageable and less economic and this is the most likely reason why Delves surrendered the lease of Home Farm in about 1870. It is also probable that the Delves family had advanced sufficiently in status for them to give up being butchers. William Delves giving up his lease would have provided the opportunity for the break-up of the Estate as a single unit and the leasing of separate parts of the Estate to a number of smaller tenants.

William Delves was one of Tunbridge Wells's leading citizens. (See box below for family details.) He became the Marquess of Abergavenny's Steward in 1844, when he was 37, and was to remain so until 1880, although when he witnessed a Codicil to the Marquess's will in 1868, he was described as Land Agent.

Home Farm, from Warwick Park road, 2nd January 1899

It is clear that William Delves was far too grand to have lived at Home Farm itself while he held the lease. (In fact, he lived until his retirement in 1880 at Hargate Lodge on Broadwater Down, which belonged to the Marquess, and subsequently until his death at 1, Montacute Gardens.)

In the 1851 Census, the farmhouse was occupied by James White, Delves's bailiff, and his wife Ann and their three sons and three daughters. In the 1871 Census, it is occupied by John Sanders and his wife, Susanna, and daughter, Fanny. He is described as a Farm Foreman, which suggests that William Delves might still have the leasehold. But by 1873, the Burgess Roll shows the Home Farm tenant as James Harris with three votes as a ratepayer on a farm with a Rateable Value of £148 a year.

By the 1881 Census, the occupant Thomas Hooper (with his wife and widowed mother) is described as 'a farmer farming 74 acres and employing three men and a boy' and is clearly the leaseholder. From the Burgess Rolls, it would seem that Hooper was the tenant from 1874 to 1882.

The farm was leased for a few years in the 1880's by W.B. Dick who ran the Spa Hotel but by 1889 the lease was held by William Gladman, followed very shortly by George Gladman, who was presumably his son.

In 1893, the Home Farm itself with some 77 acres still had just over half of the Estate, and was leased to George Gladman on an annual basis. The remaining 58 acres were leased to some 15 tenants, mostly on a weekly, quarterly or annual agricultural basis, but there were five tenants, all of residential property, who had leases ranging from 21 to 80 years (the last due to expire in 1963).

It is clear that since William Delves gave up his lease in about 1870, the Home Farm Estate had been slowly eroded, but it is also clear that there was no concerted thought about developing the Estate en masse until the 1890's. All the erosion had been small scale: 15 short-term 'agricultural' leases totalling 58 acres; three residential leases, totalling 6.6 acres and all given in 1883-5 to the same lessee, Mr. E. Thorns: a lease for Wyborne Grange (4.6 acres, at £30 p.a. for 80 years, from 29th September 1883); with an adjoining cottage (a quarter acre at £10 p.a. for 78 years from 29th September 1885); and The Hermitage (1.8 acres at £25 p.a. for 40 years from 29th September 1885). The Hermitage had formerly been a Convalescent Home for Children, run by a Mrs. Ladds, whose lease had been set at £18-4-0 p.a.

Home Farm was, and still is, a very hilly site which may have been a further factor in its relatively late development. Its lowest point is on the west where it borders the Pantiles and King Charles the Martyr – a mere 80 metres (262 ft.) above sea level. It highest point is on the east side – the Forest Road ridge which is 133 metres (436 ft.) above sea level. So it climbs some 53 metres (174 ft.) from west to east in approximately 1,300 metres (4,265 ft) – one metre up for every 25 metres along (or just a 4% incline.) But in some parts, it is much steeper – what is now Roedean Road goes up 16 metres (52 ft.) in approximately 200 metres (650 ft.), which is a more strenuous 8% incline.

'Milkmaid' at the Home Farm gate, 2nd January 1899

The Home Farmhouse and yard had three entrances:

– from the Frant Road down a cart-track which later became Roedean Road;

– from further west on the Frant Road down Nevill Lane (also known as Cut-throat Lane and later renamed Rodmell Road) which petered out into the track to the farm which in part became the extension, Upper Cumberland Walk, but which continued beyond to the Home Farmyard;

– and from the Birling Road down a track whose line has been more recently altered to allow the development of Birling Park Avenue, but whose original line is still to be seen in the road-wide footpath, called locally The Twitten, which runs from Warwick Park opposite Nevill Gate up to Birling Park Avenue.

The Home Farmhouse and yard were virtually in the centre of the land it held and were broadly equidistant from Nevill Street and Forest Road. The site of the Farmhouse and yard (Plots 43 and 44) is now occupied by Nos. 63, 65, 67 and 69 Warwick Park.

William Delves and the Delves family

William Delves (1807-1886) belonged to a Sussex family which first settled in Tunbridge Wells about 1750. They were a substantial local family in every respect – both in number and branches, and in their business interests and local government involvement.

They started as butchers and this continued to be part of the family business until the late 19th century, but they also expanded into other areas of retail and wholesale trade and into property – particularly lodging houses for the summer visitors.

When William's great-grandfather, Richard, died in 1804, his estate included eleven farms with a total of about 600 acres. When William's grandfather, Joseph, died in 1827, he left £18,000 which was divided among his seven children. Despite his inheritance, William's father, Richard, was to be declared bankrupt at the end of 1830.

William was at first a butcher with premises in the Pantiles. In 1828, he married Elizabeth Jane, the eldest daughter of John Nash, the Pantiles bookseller and postmaster, and a year later, their first child was born – William Henry, who was to be the Mayor of Tunbridge Wells in 1900 at the age of 71.

Elizabeth Jane died in 1833, possibly following further childbirth, and William married again – to Sarah Amoore. William was to have in total seven children, three sons and four daughters.

William became the Steward of the Earl of Abergavenny in 1844 at the age of 37 and was to remain in that post until he retired in 1880 at the age of 73. This did not prevent him from holding other responsibilities and carrying out other duties. Until his death, he was a Director of the Gas Company which had been formed in 1843; and from 1860, one of the 24 Commissioners who ran the not yet (until 1889) incorporated borough of Tunbridge Wells. For over 50 years, he had held the post of parish officer for Frant as either churchwarden, overseer or guardian. He was truly 'a pillar of society' and according to his obituary in the Kent & Sussex Courier, he was "very highly esteemed by the tenantry for his habitual fairness and urbanity" and without doubt by the Marquess as well, who sent his private carriage and his two sons, Lords George and Henry Nevill, to the funeral. His obituary also records that "Broadwater Down and Hungershall Park were entirely his own creation, and to his active brain, many other improvements are due". He left a personal estate of £6,714-2s-2d.

His eldest son, William Henry Delves (1829-1922) was to become even better known. He trained as a banker with his uncle, Robert Nash, and progressed to be manager of Molineux, Whitfield & Co's 'Old Bank' on the Pantiles. He became a Town Commissioner in 1882, a Town Councillor on Incorporation in 1889, an Alderman in 1892, a JP in 1899, Mayor in 1900 and a Freeman of the Borough in 1910. His particular interest on the Council was finance – he was known as 'the Statistical D(elves)' – and he was Chairman of the Finance Committee for many years. When he died on 4th April 1922 at the age of 93, he was still on the Council – indeed he was going to move the adoption of the next year's Borough Rate at the Town Council meeting on the following day; and he was still a Director (as he had been since 1859) of the Gas Company of which he had been the Chairman from 1887-1920. He left a gross estate of £25,012-12s-2d.

William Henry Delves in 1873, as a sergeant in the Tunbridge Wells Rifle Volunteers.

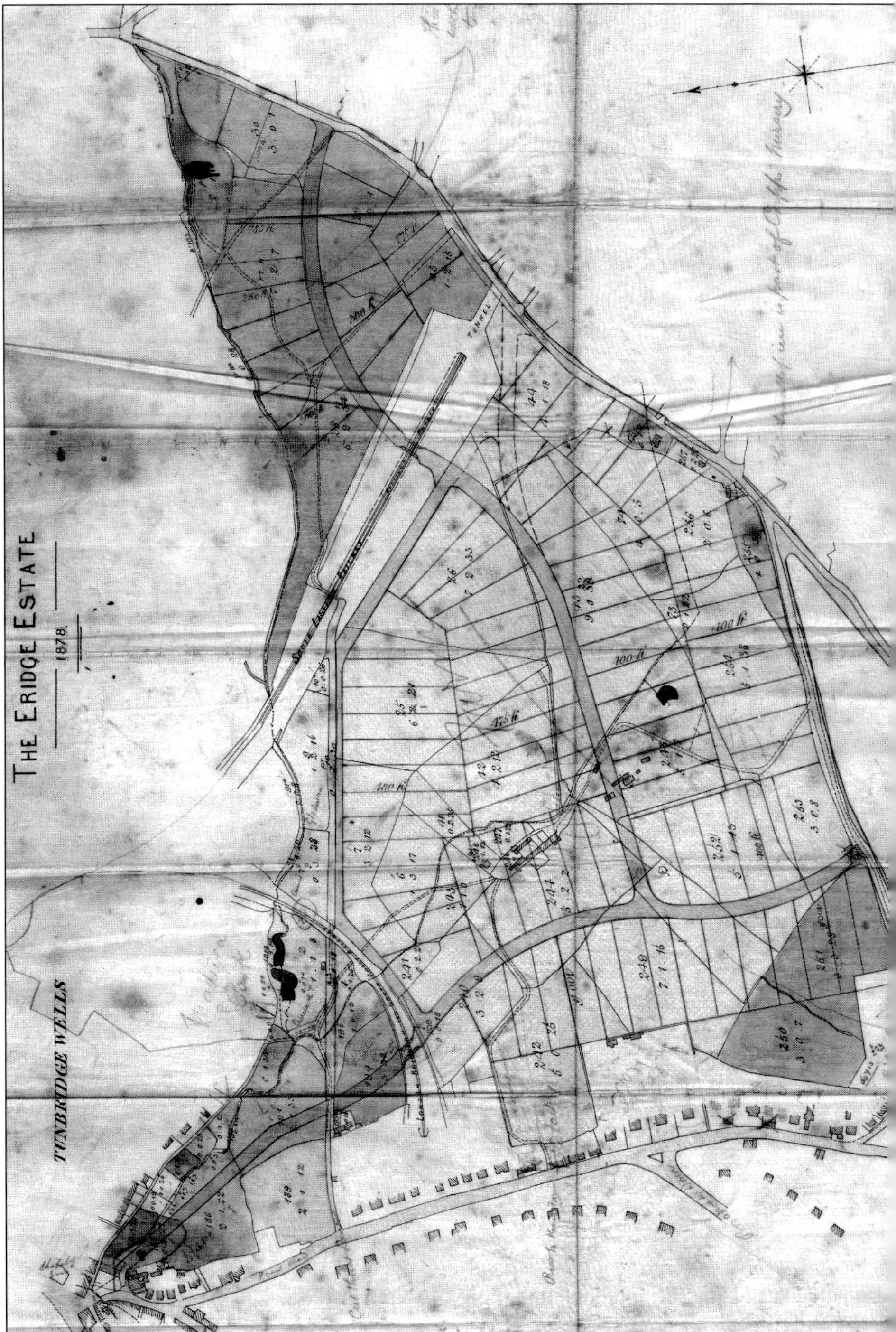
THE ERIDGE ESTATE
1878
TUNBRIDGE WELLS

CHAPTER 5

THE RATIONALE FOR, AND SEQUENCE OF DEVELOPMENT OF THE HOME FARM ESTATE

Several reasons can be inferred for the development of the Home Farm Estate:

- the agricultural depression of the 1890's and its negative effect on Abergavenny's income;
- the consequent need to find/develop other sources of income;
- the recognition that urban rents per acre were considerably higher than agricultural rents;
- the pressure of a town which had expanded considerably since the coming of the railway and was *thought* to be continuing to expand;
- the fact that the Home Farm Estate was the closest land to the centre of the town which was still undeveloped;
- the fact that the Home Farm Estate was less economically viable than before the coming of the two railway cuttings and was also no longer 'protected' by the 'self-interest' of the Delves family.

The first documentary evidence of any plans to develop the Home Farm Estate is to be found in a map entitled The Eridge Estate (but which shows only the Home Farm Estate part of it) and dated 1878. This has been overdrawn probably in the late 1880's or early 1890's to show possible road layouts with 100 plots for development.

For currently unknown and inexplicable reasons, this plan envisaged no development between Nevill Street and the West station railway cutting, and put 79 plots between the cutting and Forest/Birling Roads and a further 21 plots on the northern side of the Hastings railway cutting. All the plots were virtually identical and took little notice of the landscape. Clearly a more professional survey was required and this was prepared and presented on 11th November 1893 by William Brackett & Sons, Chartered Surveyors and Valuers, (established in 1828 and still today occupying the same premises at 27-29 High Street, Tunbridge Wells) to the Marquess, or more specifically to Mr. Macbean of the Eridge Estate office which was at 65 Frant Road.

The Brackett map, 1893

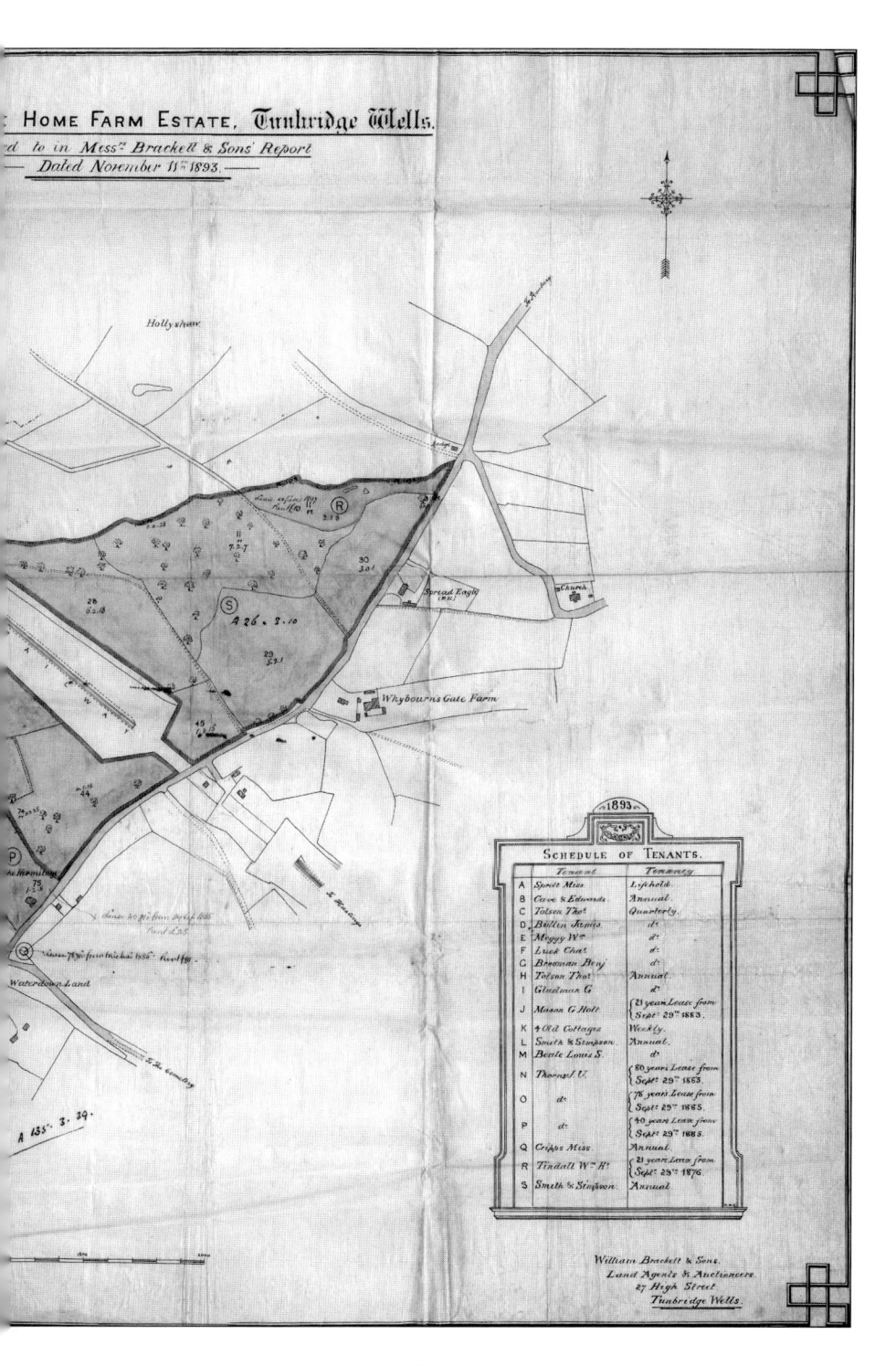

HOME FARM ESTATE, Tunbridge Wells.

...d to in Messrs Brackett & Sons' Report
Dated November 11th 1893.

SCHEDULE OF TENANTS. 1893

	Tenant	Tenancy
A	Sprott Miss	Lifehold
B	Cave & Edwards	Annual
C	Tolson Thos	Quarterly
D	Bullen James	do
E	Meggy Wm	do
F	Lued Chas	do
G	Brooman Benj	do
H	Tolson Thos	Annual
I	Gladman G	do
J	Mason G. Holt	21 years Lease from Sept. 29th 1883
K	4 Old Cottages	Weekly
L	Smith & Simpson	Annual
M	Beale Louis S.	do
N	Thorpe J. U.	80 years Lease from Sept. 29th 1883
O	do	78 years Lease from Sept. 29th 1885
P	do	40 years Lease from Sept. 29th 1885
Q	Cripps Miss	Annual
R	Tindall Wm H.	21 years Lease from Sept. 29th 1876
S	Smith & Simpson	Annual

William Brackett & Sons,
Land Agents & Auctioneers.
27 High Street
Tunbridge Wells.

The Brackett survey estimated the Estate from the Pantiles to Forest Road and from Frant Road to the other side of the Hastings railway line as 135 acres, 3 roods and 6 perches.

The survey divided the Estate into three segments, or Portions as they were called:

Portion I, of just over 15 acres, was the land below the railway cutting (to the now disused Tunbridge Wells West station) down to Nevill Street;

Portion II, of some 93 acres, was from the railway cutting up to Forest Road and from the Frant Road to the Hastings railway cutting;

and **Portion III**, of some 26 acres, was the land on the far side of the Hastings line (now part of the Farmcombe Road Open Space and housing development which took place after World War II).

The survey report recommended the development of Portions I & II as one scheme, which is what was eventually to be carried out.

Brackett's report (hand-written in the days before typewriters were common) contains some interesting background comments. "Owing to the proximity of the Estate to the centre of the town, and the fact that it runs directly into the heart of a thickly populated area, its development for building purposes, when once commenced, is, in our opinion, likely to be remarkably rapid. There is no other tract of land of anything like this extent in the Borough which is situated so near the railway stations, Common and principal shops. Had the Estate been put on the market 20 or 30 years ago, Tunbridge Wells would in all probability have increased on that side as rapidly, if not more rapidly, than it has increased at the north end of the Borough."

Brackett's assessment of the location was entirely logical and reasonable, so it is somewhat surprising that the development of the Estate, when it started some four years later, was not as rapid or comprehensive as he forecast.

Brackett estimated that there was a need to construct 11,000 feet of new roads and to widen certain existing roads. He also advised that in his opinion "21,900 feet of available building frontage can be secured, and in all but few instances would the plots have a depth of less than 200ft., *whilst about 2,000ft of frontage suitable for the Broadwater Down Class would have a depth of 400ft.*"

Brackett also estimated that Portions I & II were worth £38,000, based on estimated Ground Rents (GR) of £1,520 p.a. and a multiplier of 25 years; and Portion III was worth £5,400 with a GR of £216 p.a.

This survey obviously stimulated Abergavenny's interest, particularly in view of the 'cash-flow' problems outlined in Chapter 2. He had the opportunity of developing urban rental incomes which were out of all proportion (up to twelve times more) to agricultural income, but there was a downside. It would require a significant degree of investment but in the long run, the return would considerably outweigh the cost.

It is clear from his archives that he did not intend to develop the Estate himself. But if he wanted to benefit from the development, he had to put in the infrastructure of roads and drainage, which would enable builders to develop one or several plots which could then be marketed. He had to optimise the number of plots which could be provided consistent with the style of the area – or to go back one stage, he had to optimise the building frontage, which meant that he had to optimise the number and/or the lengths of roads which could be developed on the Estate.

The Sequence of Events

Despite Drake's recommendation of Henry Currey and the Marquess's swift acceptance (23rd. November 1893), Henry Currey was to prove 'not immediately available'. Drake briefed him on 1st. December 1893 but nothing happened until three months later when Currey wrote a letter on 5th March 1894, apologising for the delay in visiting the site 'due to being invalided'. A visit was made to the site on 19th March 1894 and Currey submitted on 11th June 1894 a Report and Plan in which he stated " Some of the roads may be a little steep but this is not a material objection in an Estate of this character. The land has a picturesque character with very considerable undulation and is well adapted for residences of a superior nature."

This plan increased enormously the number of potential plots – from 100 on the 'Eridge Estate Plan' to a total of 248 plots – 31 in Portion I; 167 in Portion II; and 50 in Portion III. Currey emphasised that his plan was only an outline to establish how many plots could be put on the site.

With his plan, he estimated that there were 25,450 ft. of building frontage (which implied road lengths of about 12,500 ft.), producing a

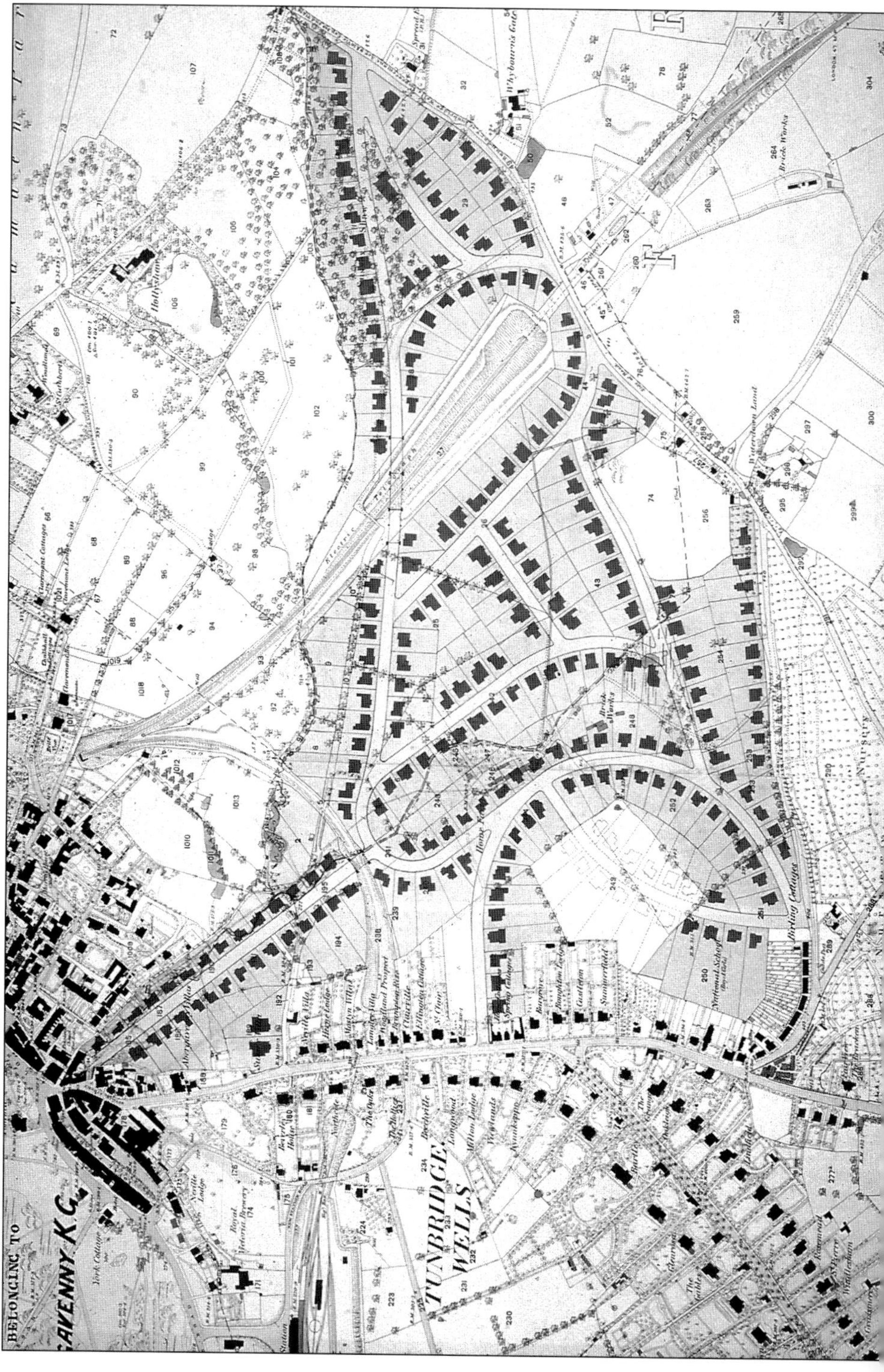
BELONGING TO
TUNBRIDGE WELLS
Brick Works
Station

GR of £5,000, or worth £150,000 at 30 years' purchase (i.e. a multiplier of 30). Against this income/value, should be offset the cost of developing the site, which Currey estimated at:

Cost of road-making	£50,000
Cost of two bridges	£10,000
Interest & Management	£15,000
	£75,000

leaving a balance (notional profit) of £75,000.

Currey went on however in his report to say that it would probably take 20 years to develop and that the value of "this balance of £75,000 deferred 10 years (the mean) would be £56,250 as the present value of the Estate, equal to about £400 an acre".

While this was a distinct improvement on the values estimated by Brackett (£43,400), the cost of development and the associated risk must have been somewhat of a shock. It also did not fit in with how the Marquess and/or his agent saw as the nature of this new estate. We must assume from subsequent developments that that they felt that the number of plots was excessive and out of keeping with the style of development they had in mind. We must also assume, in the absence of documentary evidence, that the style they were looking for, was to emulate that which had already been created for Eastbourne, which was much admired in its day.

The Marquess and Macbean were no doubt influenced by their advisers. Augustus Drake had acted for both the Duke of Devonshire and John Davis Gilbert in the development of Eastbourne; Currey and Henry Michell Whitley had also been directly involved on their behalf.

It is reasonable to conclude that Eastbourne as an upper middle/middle class estate was an acceptable and successful 'role model', not only for the Warwick Park Estate but also for Tunbridge Wells in general, and the nature of Eastbourne was not in any way at odds with the upper middle/middle class aspirations, or the general character, or nature of Tunbridge Wells. Although Tunbridge Wells had existed longer than Eastbourne, Eastbourne had grown faster and larger and had become a municipal borough a significant six years before Tunbridge Wells.

Everyone (Abergavenny, Macbean, architects and surveyors with the possible exception of Brackett) seems to have thought of the Warwick

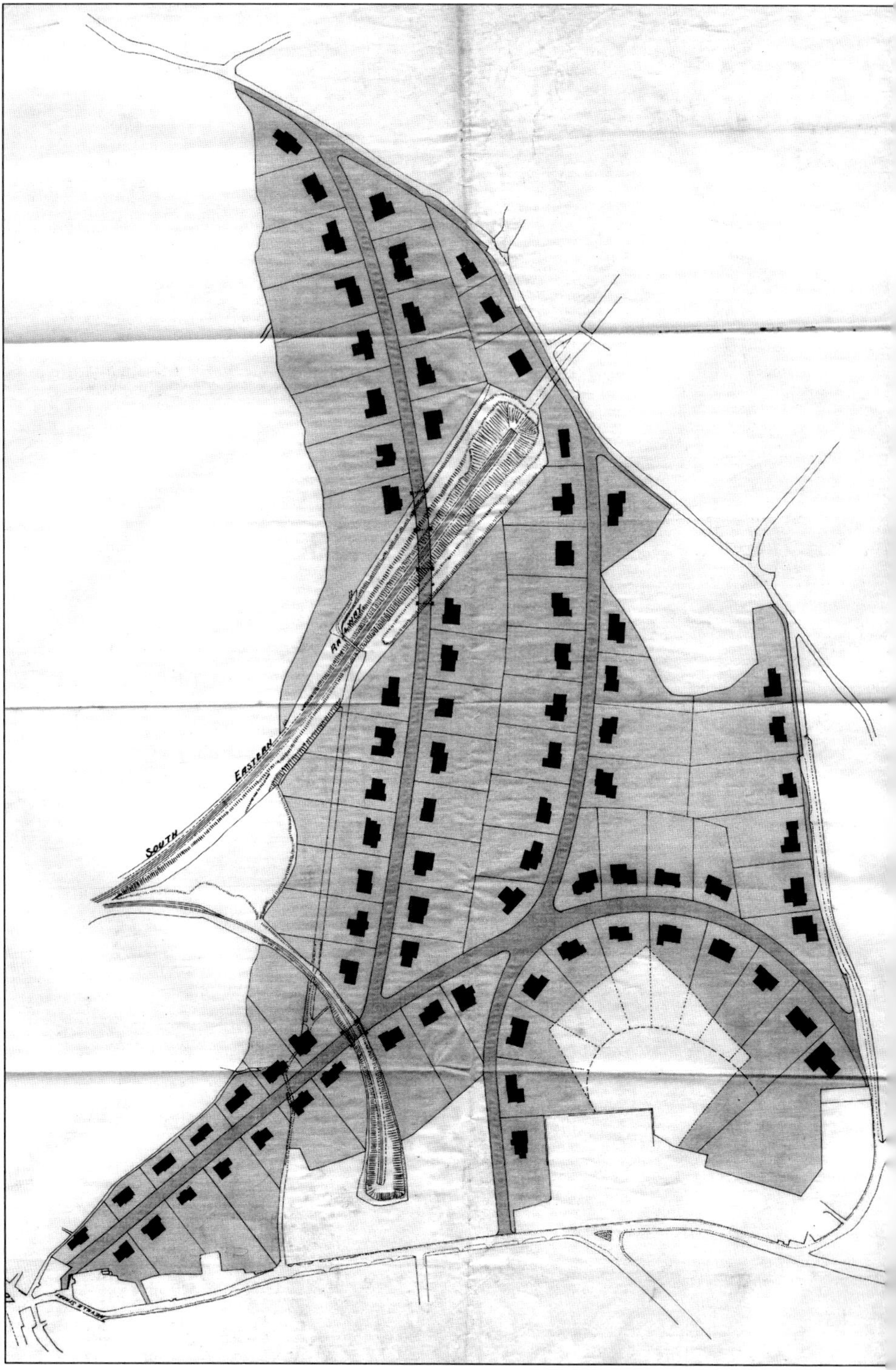
SOUTH EASTERN RAILWAY

Park Estate in the Eastbourne mould and possibly as another Broadwater Down. This was a Nevill development of the 1860's of large houses in extensive grounds without the enclosed nature of the earlier Calverley Park (1828-1838) or the slightly later Nevill Park (1845 onwards). Broadwater Down was only about 200 yards away from the Warwick Park Estate boundary, so the comparison was not unrealistic. Brackett was possibly the only one to see at least the lower reaches of the Warwick Park Estate as sub-Broadwater Down, although he felt that the higher reaches could or would match it.

It is clear from correspondence that Currey's first proposal was unacceptable as over-development (although the reasons are not specified) and he was asked to think again. As a result, on 25th July 1894 (only six weeks after his original proposal), he submitted two alternative plans, labelled B and C, which proposed many fewer but larger building plots.

He expressed a preference for Plan B, which allowed a total of 84 plots over the three Portions, or 68 in Portions I & II alone.

Plan C allowed only 57 plots over the three Portions, or 45 over Portions I & II. These would seem to have been much more acceptable to the Marquess and his Agent, but little or no action seems to have been taken by them for almost a year following this, probably because they were involved in the negotiation about a major development which would affect how the Home Farm Estate could, or would, be laid out.

This was the creation of the Nevill Cricket and Athletic Ground, which is dealt with in more detail in the next Chapter. Suffice it to say in this Chapter that as a result, on 30th July 1895 (a whole year after he had submitted Plan B and C), Currey submitted a further survey report and revised Plan C, which included a proposed site for a cricket field of some 10 acres, with a suggested ground rent of £10 per acre. To offset the loss of building development implicit in the cricket field, he included 'a range of small dwellings in the rear of the Cricket Field suitable for Coachmen or Gardeners on the Estate.' This was to provoke Henry Michell Whitley into his 'One Great Objection to cottage property' which is detailed below.

Currey's original plan of 1894 (hereafter called Plan A) was for 198 detached houses on the site south of the Hastings line (i.e. with a boundary of the railway line, Forest/Birling Road, and the Home Farm boundary with both the Frant Road and the Pantiles), plus a further 50 detached houses on the northern side of the railway line.

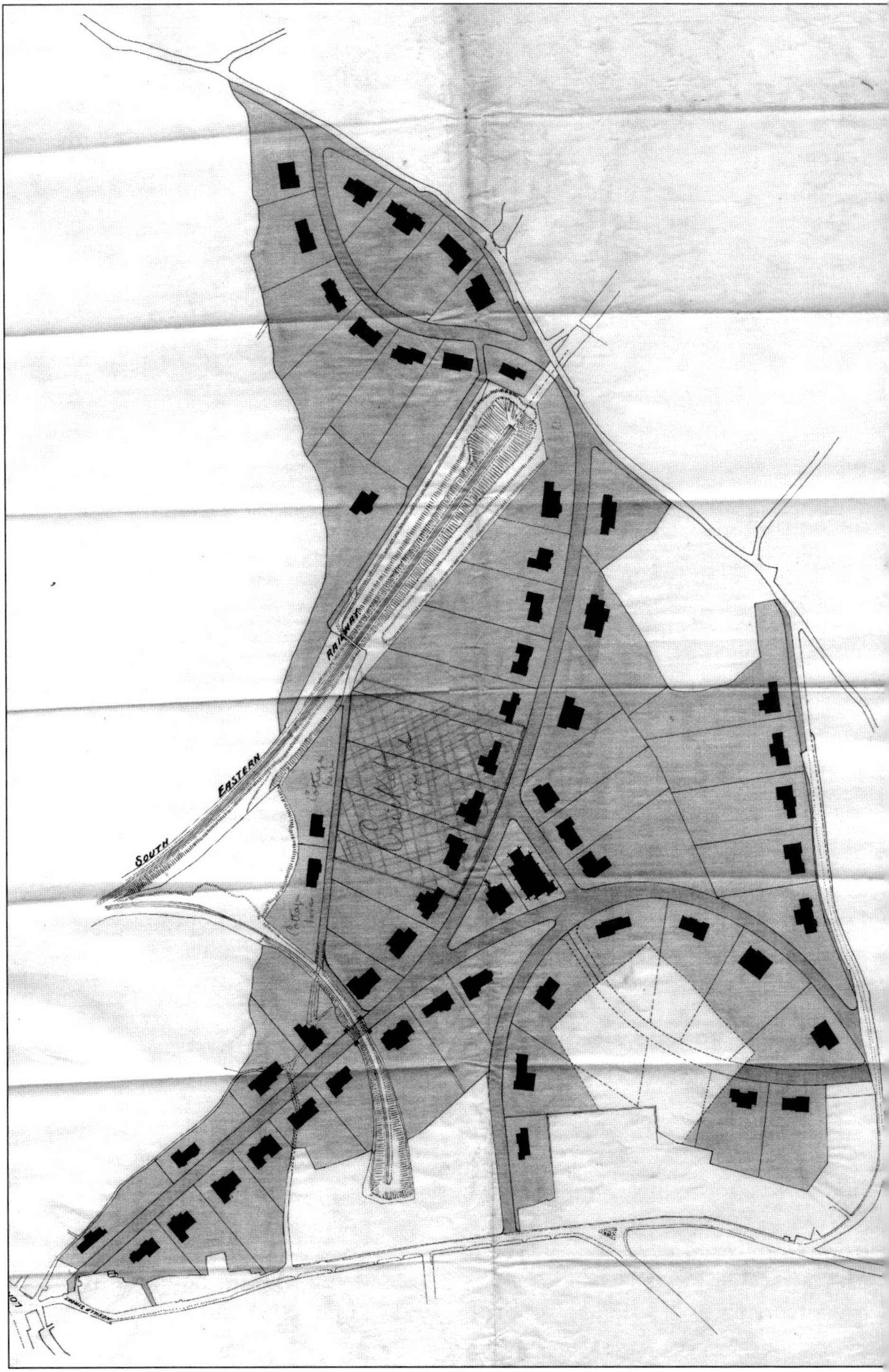
SOUTH
EASTERN
RAILWAY

This plan called for what is now Warwick Park going east to divide into two roads just beyond what is now the junction with Roedean Road. The right-hand fork would curve off to join the Birling Road; the left-hand fork would shortly subdivide with a further road to the left which would subdivide again with one fork crossing the railway line to reach Portion III and the other fork following the railway line to join Forest Road at the top. The first subdivision would also continue up the hill but would curve round to meet the top of Birling Road and there would be two roads connecting this with the road which ran along the side of the railway to Forest Road.

With the B and C versions, this road structure was continued, but the plot sizes were increased (i.e. the number of plots were reduced). It is a complicated formula to offset plot size against income, since every plot is potentially different in its appeal. Obviously the criterion is to optimise building frontage and minimise development costs. One part of the proposal after the idea of the Nevill Ground was accepted, was to include cottages between the Hastings railway line and the Cricket Ground. This was however advised against by Henry Michell Whitley writing on 26th March 1896 to Mr. Macbean from the Manor Office at Eastbourne: "the suggested proposed cottages facing the Cricket Ground should be omitted. One Great Objection to cottage property is the laundry linen drying in the gardens, which is unsightly when seen from the windows of the better class of houses".

Henry Michell Whitley did however have some suggestions which would still be considered sensible today. He advised that the development of the Estate should 'work steadily forward, plot by plot' and not allow random development. In the event, his advice was never followed. If it had been, there is no doubt that the development would have been more coherent and compact. That his advice was not taken is somewhat surprising since he was to be appointed Surveyor of the Home Farm development in July 1896.

At Macbean's suggestion, Whitley also prepared a proposal for an Ornamental Garden which was never carried out, probably because Abergavenny wanted the Council to agree to maintain the Garden but the (relatively) new Borough Council remained totally and uncharacteristically indecisive. Whitley proposed that since the land 'between the new road on the west and Patty Moon's Walk (*now Cumberland Walk*) on the east is not suitable for building over' because of 'its low-lying position', an ornamental garden should be laid out on the site (the north side of the road between Rodmell Rd and the Church

Hall of Charles the Martyr) with an ornamental lake, two waterfalls and a bandstand; and the Borough Council invited to maintain it.

In his proposal, Whitley wrote 'The advantage of laying out this land as a garden would be: Firstly, it would form an attractive and elegant entrance to the Estate which is a matter of great importance, as a bad access would much deteriorate the letting value of the property, and secondly, it would enhance the value of the property around.'

The failure of the Corporation to co-operate was not that they were antagonistic, but rather confused and uncertain about what they could or should do. They had for a number of years been looking for sites for both a Summer Garden and a Winter Garden (in the Eastbourne mould) and had been in correspondence with Macbean. Their hesitation was due principally to their uncertainty as to whether they were allowed under the Tunbridge Wells Improvement Act of 1889 to establish such gardens and charge (as in Eastbourne) for admission.

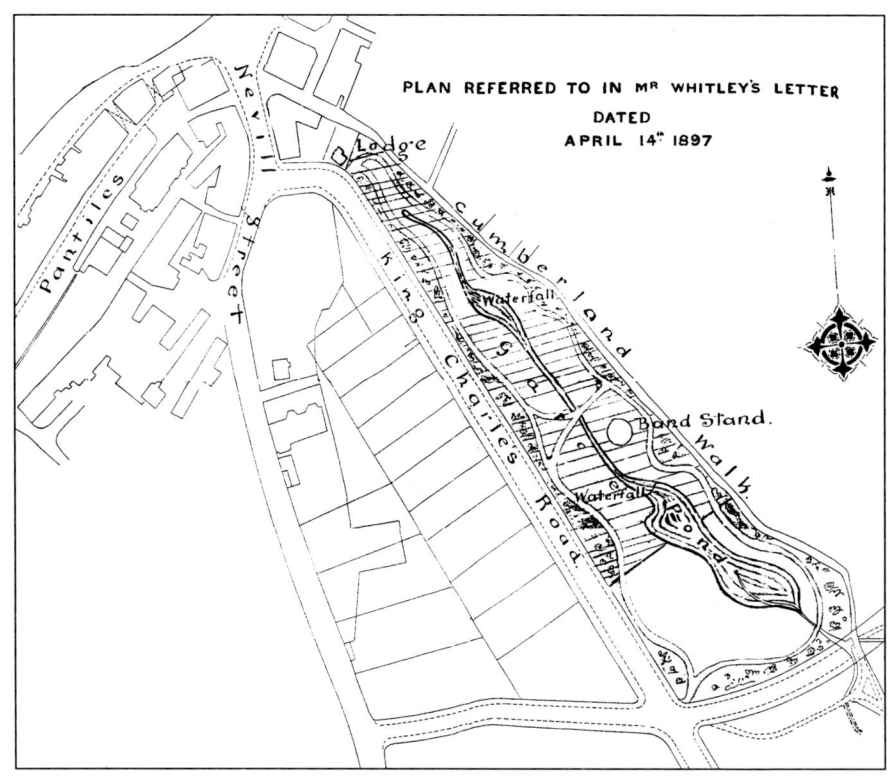

Whitley's Plan for an ornamental garden, 1897.

As early as 1895, the Council had been in discussion with Macbean about a public garden in the Home Farm Estate area, and as late as May 1900, the discussions continued about a Public Pleasure Garden situated between Warwick Park and Cumberland Walk. But the discussions came to nothing and it was not until 1911 that the Council settled on what is now Calverley Grounds, and not until 1921 that this was ultimately achieved. The land between Warwick Park and Cumberland Walk, which was deemed unsuitable for building in 1897, was consequently to remain as pasture for many years, but was eventually developed as Nos.13-29 Warwick Park, long after the Second World War.

Another part of the Plan C proposal somewhat surprisingly allowed for a church and vicarage on an island site created by the road forking, which would have been only 800 yards from the church of King Charles the Martyr at the bottom of the hill. The church and vicarage island site would have been in the area now occupied by Nos.67 and 69 (on the north side) and Nos. 90 and 92 Warwick Park (on the south side). This proposal sank apparently without comment and certainly without a murmur.

The 'Plots For Sale' prospectus which was produced in January 1897 was however quite different from versions A, B and C and was almost certainly influenced by the developments over the Nevill Ground which took shape during 1895 and for which a construction contract was signed in April 1896.

Portion III was abandoned presumably because it would require extra costs in building a road bridge over the railway cutting where previously there was only a footbridge and the number of plots it would reach was thought to be uneconomic; and Portions I and II would contain only 65 plots for detached houses. As a plan it resembles fairly closely the Warwick Park area as we know it today, but it contained a number of new roads which have never been built. One of these followed the cart-track which ran from Home Farm to Birling Road, the other went behind the Nevill Ground and joined Warwick Park near its junction with Forest Road.

Comparison of alternative plans.
A side-by-side comparison of the alternative plans produced for the development of the Home Farm Estate suggests that Abergavenny and Macbean did not start with a very clear idea of what they wanted and they moved somewhat pragmatically and empirically towards a

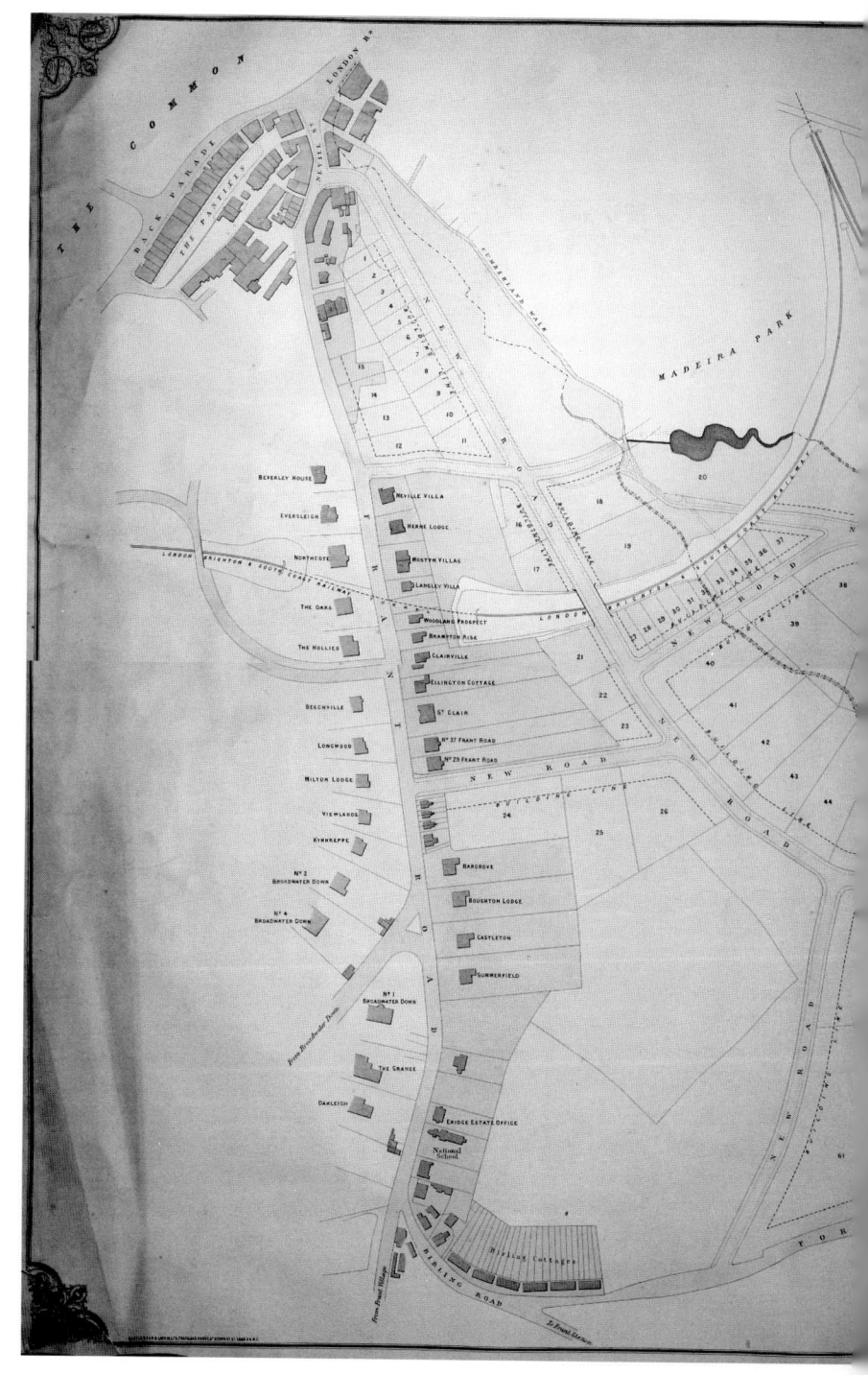

'Plots for Sale Prospectus' map, 1897

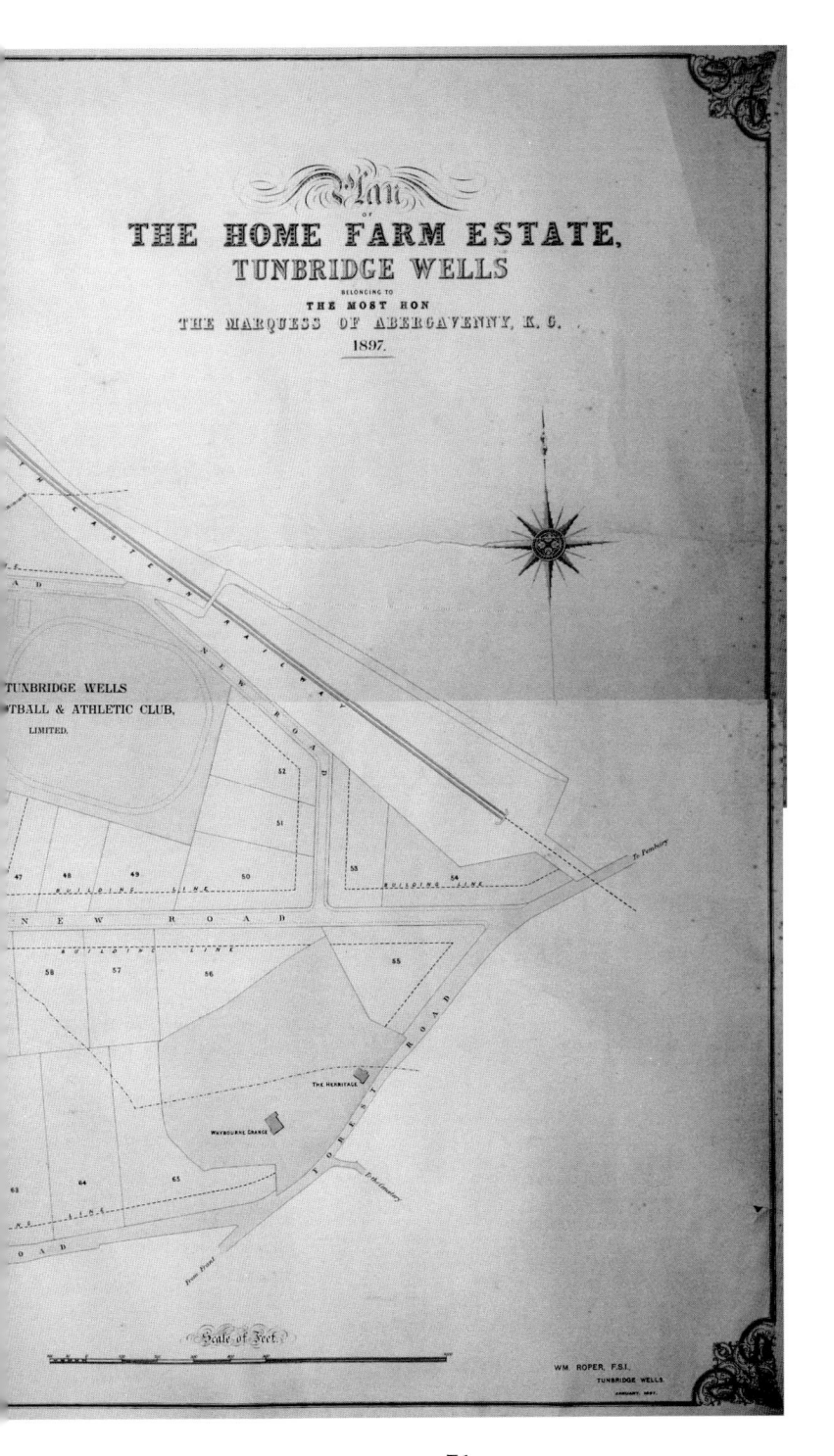

Plan of
THE HOME FARM ESTATE,
TUNBRIDGE WELLS
BELONGING TO
THE MOST HON
THE MARQUESS OF ABERGAVENNY, K.G.
1897.

WM. ROPER, F.S.I.
TUNBRIDGE WELLS.

solution, more often dictated by practical and immediate, rather than aesthetic and long-term considerations.

They started with the Eridge Estate Plan which was clearly a first stab at what might be possible and which suggested that 100 plots could be feasible. The Brackett report of 1893 which followed was a precise calculation of new road lengths and property frontages with potential rent estimates, but it is interesting that the report avoided any estimates of the number of plots or any indication of road lines. Possibly Brackett did not wish to commit himself at this stage because of the hilly terrain or because he hoped to do this as a second stage. Brackett was not however to be given a second chance. The job of proposing road lines and number of plots was given, within three weeks of Brackett's report, to Henry Currey on the recommendation of Augustus Drake. Currey's appointment does not seem to have been pre-planned and only came after Drake had seen the Brackett report.

Currey was slow to start and clearly got the number of plots wrong as far as Abergavenny and Macbean were concerned. His original proposal (Plan A) was for a total of 248 plots (an average of just under half an acre a plot). It may be that he was encouraged to think big by the Eridge Estate Plan (although there is no evidence that he saw it). It may be since he was briefed apparently by Drake, that Drake was out-of-touch with Abergavenny's and Macbean's views and feelings. It may be that he judged that 248 plots were what the site of 135 acres justified (and subsequent events suggest that he may have been right). But it was not acceptable and he was asked to re-think with a lower density.

Within about a month, he quickly produced Plan B with 84 plots, and Plan C with 57 plots. The fact that he produced two alternatives suggests that he was unsure and uncertain and wanted to please, by covering what he saw as the spectrum of alternatives. These alternatives seem to have been acceptable insofar as there were no further revisions for about a year, when Plan C was revised to incorporate a cricket and athletics ground. Clearly there had been a hiatus in planning direction caused by the negotiations about what would subsequently become the Nevill Ground. Even with the revised Plan C, Currey's proposals seem to be acceptable. But Currey vanishes from the scene at this point.

We do not know whether this was his choice, or the Marquess's, or other factors such as Currey's age, since Currey must have been about 70 by this time. But the next layout of the Estate published in January 1897 was a radical change – a change almost certainly dictated by both the access needs of the Nevill Ground and the fact that the Ground cut across some of the previously planned roads. The 1897 plan was prepared by William Roper – a local surveyor who had detailed local knowledge and who had been appointed surveyor for the Nevill Ground development in February 1896 – probably with the assistance of William Brackett. It was the plan which was to be implemented with a couple of important changes. It was essentially the plan of Warwick Park as we know it today. It specified 65 plots and eliminated any in Portion III – the 26 acres north of the Hastings railway line.

The development of the projected number of sites over time is summarised below:

	Portion I	Portion II	Portion III	Total Est. Acreage	Building Frontage
Acreage	15	93	26	135	–
No. of plots	**No.**	**No.**	**No.**	**No.**	**Feet**
Eridge Estate Plan	–	79	21	100	–
Brackett Survey 1893	—	–	–	–	21,900
Currey Plan A 1894	31	167	50	248	25,450
Currey Plan B 1894	14	54	16	84	–
Currey Plan C 1894	10	35	12	57	–
Plots Map 1897	19	46	–	65	–
As developed by 1999	21	44	–	65	–

It must be emphasised that these figures are plots, not houses as such. As will be seen later, a number of plots were subsequently to be split and more than one house built on each of them. But the table does illustrate the relative schizophrenia which seems to have affected the Warwick Park development, both initially and subsequently. The total number planned yo-yoed initially between 248 and 100, which clearly indicates confused thinking about, and assessment of, the site and its target potential. The number then stabilised at a much lower 57-65. However the irony is that while the number of plots appears to have stabilised at 57-65, in reality the number of houses increased to about 120, largely because of the number of houses built subsequently on split plots, and this was certainly not what was envisaged originally by the Marquess and his Agent.

CHAPTER 6

THE NEVILL GROUND

Cricket has been played in Tunbridge Wells since the earliest days of both cricket and Tunbridge Wells.

Cricket on Tunbridge Wells Common in the late 18th century.

The earliest printed record is probably in the Sussex Weekly Advertiser which on 2nd. September 1782 reported "On Friday se'nnight a game at cricket, which had been depending three days, between eleven gentlemen of Tunbridge Wells and the same number of Groombridge, ended in favour of the latter, who won the game by four notches only."

For the first 100 years or so, the Common was the focal point for cricket in Tunbridge Wells, but there was only one pitch. The demand for matches to be held on the Common led to the creation in 1885 of a second pitch – the Lower Cricket Ground – just as the Upper or Higher Ground lost some of its status by ceasing to be a venue for County matches.

Upper Cricket Ground on the Common, c.1880.

County matches were played on the Common from 1845 when Kent first played Sussex there until 1884, when Kent moved to Tonbridge and Maidstone for the annual Sussex match. The reason for this was the increasing complaints about the condition of the Higher Ground, which was aggravated by it being part of the Common and therefore open to the public and grazing animals.

There is no doubt that the loss of the County matches had an effect on the town's trade and it was soon suggested that a new cricket ground suitable for County matches, should be found. The proposal came initially from the Tunbridge Wells Tradesmen's Association, but they were soon joined and supported by other town organisations, such as the Borough Improvement Association and the Ratepayers' Association.

The first sites suggested in 1890 were in St. John's Road and in Camden Park, but negotiations for these fell through because St. John's Road was thought to be too expensive at a price of £450 per acre, and too many restrictive covenants were demanded for Camden Park, the freehold of which was owned by Marquess Camden.

The failure to negotiate on these two sites left no apparently suitable site since three prime considerations for a cricket ground were a level site, a reasonably central position and good access. Certainly the Home Farm Estate would not have been considered in its undeveloped state since it was certainly not a level site and did not have adequate access.

But the decision of Abergavenny to develop the Home Farm Estate changed the situation. The Estate would have a spine road (now Warwick Park) which would provide direct access to any Ground on the Estate and the Estate was reasonably central, the western edge of it being only 50 yards from the Pantiles. That still left the problem of a level site, but it would seem that at least initially this was not thought to be a major problem.

There is no known record of which side initiated discussions, but it is the opinion of the author that it was more likely to have been the Tradesmen's Association and its associates, since William Brackett and William Roper were both surveyors connected with the development and both were active in town organisations. Indeed William Roper, although not a tradesman as such, was the President of that Association, retiring from that office in January 1898.

By comparison, Abergavenny and Macbean would have been more detached from and less knowing about town affairs; and the fact that the first three Plans A, B and C contained no mention of a cricket ground suggests that it was an afterthought which was hurriedly inserted into a revised Plan C.

What is clear is that the Nevill Ground arose from the development of the Home Farm Estate, and not vice-versa. There can however be little doubt that once it was proposed, the Marquess and Macbean must have seen that it could be a very useful means of creating awareness and acceptance of the new Estate.

This led to discussions starting in 1894-5 between the Tradesmen's Association and the Abergavenny estate for a ground on the Home Farm Estate. But before negotiations could develop, there was a need for a formal organisation to exist to conduct the negotiations on behalf of the 'town' and for money to be raised to fund any agreement. It would seem that at this point the initiative was taken out of the hands of what can be broadly called 'town trade' and passed to the town and county elite.

A limited company was set up – the Tunbridge Wells Cricket, Football and Athletic Club Ltd. with an authorised capital of £10,000 (1,000 shares of £10 each). The Prospectus for the Company dated October 18th, 1895 indicates that the Marquess was going to be the President of the Club and that there was a Committee of 14 (of whom 12 would be appointed as the first Directors). The Committee was definitely the local elite – led by Lord Henry Nevill, the Marquess Camden, Sir David Salomons Bt., A.S.Griffith Boscawen MP, Col. Trevenen Holland CB, Maj. Lionel Spens, F. Wadham Elers, W.C.Cripps (the Town Clerk) and

Major Fletcher Lutwidge.    F. Wadham Elers.    Major Lionel Spens.

three who had been or would be Mayors of Tunbridge Wells (Major Fletcher Lutwidge, Frank Stone, and J.Stone-Wigg). Messrs. Molineux, Whitfield & Co. (of whom William Delves was Manager) were appointed as the Club's Bankers.

The Prospectus proposed to lay out and make 'a thoroughly good Cricket Ground with a provision for a circular Cinder Track'; to form a Football Ground 120 yards by 75 yards; to lay out and make six Lawn Tennis Courts; to erect a Cricket Pavilion 'with all the usual accessories'; to erect a Bandstand (which was never built) and other covered stands and buildings for spectators; to fence in the whole area; and to establish a Club and furnish and maintain the Pavilion or other Club House. The cost of levelling the Cricket Ground had been estimated by a Surveyor (William Roper) at £1,500 and the levelling of the Football Ground, since it was at a lower level than the Cricket Ground, was not anticipated to be a costly matter. In all, it was estimated that an immediate expenditure of at least £5,000 was required to carry out the above tasks.

The Prospectus listed 28 'gentlemen' who had agreed to take a total of 413 shares with a value of £4,130 and said that Mr. J.Stone-Wigg and Col. Holland 'have kindly offered to take 50 shares each, provided that 8 other gentlemen will take the same number'. This offer cannot have been taken up, since initially only £7,000 was subscribed by Shareholders.

The Company (or rather its new Directors) approved the draft lease which had been negotiated with the Marquess for a 10 acre site adjacent to the Hastings railway line on a 100 year lease starting from 29th September 1895 ($2\frac{1}{2}$ months before the first Board Meeting of the Company), with a peppercorn rent for the first year and £84 a year for the remaining 99 years. A ground rent of eight guineas (£8-8-0) an acre was no doubt thought very reasonable and was certainly less than what was being charged for residential property in Warwick Park, but in reality and in the long-term, it was nearly twice what had been asked for the purchase of the St. John's Road site. But £84 a year sounds a lot less than a lump-sum of £4,500, even if it is for 99 years. Nonetheless, the Marquess was showing public-spiritedness in charging a less-than-commercial rate.

By the terms of the lease, the Marquess had to have built Road No.1 (Warwick Park) before 13th January 1897 and the lessees covenanted to build a road (now Nevill Gate) from Road No.1 to their grounds, on which they would construct a cricket field surrounded by a running and cycling track of three laps to the mile, and a football pitch and six tennis courts.

Tenders for all the roads on the new Estate were invited by advertisement in the Courier of 17th February 1896, to be submitted not later than 29th February 1896, but the road was not to be completed by 13th January 1897 as specified; and it was still being built in April 1897.

At the same time, the Tunbridge Wells Cricket, Football and Athletic Club Ltd seems to have been having its own problems.

The first was that not all the shares had been taken up. Indeed only 60 people (including the Directors) had become shareholders. There were still 188 £10 shares unallotted, so the Company was short of nearly £2,000 of the original authorised capital of £10,000. It was clear that 'the Railway Companies, the Town and Trade of Tunbridge Wells and a large number of the residents of town and neighbourhood' had not subscribed.

The reason for this lack of support is not known: there might have been some resentment at the project being taken over by the elite, but it is much more likely that the price of the shares (at £10 each) was (wittingly, or unwittingly) set too high for trade or popular support. Why the shares were not £1 shares will probably never be known. £10 in 1895 was the equivalent of approximately £500 today and the implied minimum for a shareholder was ten shares, so the 'suggested' investment was about £5,000 at today's values. It is not surprising that the uptake was so sparse.

The second was that the costs incurred (finally £13,943-3s-10d) had exceeded all estimates by an astonishing 180%, and even if the share offer had been fully subscribed, there would have been the need for a further call for capital. Indeed, before the Board realised the full cost and because of the share subscription shortfall, the Board had already decided, *before the ground was even opened*, to issue £5,000 4% Debentures to shareholders in the first instance, and to anyone else who could be persuaded.

The cause of the over-expenditure was that the levelling and preparing of the Ground and running and cycle-track had proved much more expensive than anyone expected. It can be argued that anyone looking at the Home Farm site should have known that there was not a level 50 yards anywhere on the site.

So how was it that the estimates of cost were so wildly wrong?

Was it incompetence? William Roper was an established and respectable/respected surveyor, who was Chairman of the Tunbridge Wells Tradesmen's Association. It is difficult to understand how his original estimates of cost could be so inaccurate. One can only assume that he failed to assess the problems fully. Some levelling had been expected, but not to an average depth of 14 feet of soil over a large part of the ten acres.

Was it under-pricing by a sole contractor? Initially the contract was not formally put out to tender. The first quotation to be accepted was from John Jarvis [for £1,296 + £171 for drainage] and was withdrawn 'on the ground that he had made a serious mistake in his figures'; the second by a Mr. Kavanagh was for £2,322 and was also subsequently withdrawn. So advertisements were published, inviting tenders. Six were received, including the highest one from Mr. Kavanagh for £3,854. The lowest bid was a clearly unrealistic £1,988, but there were also two within £1 of each other at £2,495 and £2,496; and a further two within £2-1s-0d of each other at £2,900 and £2,897-19s-0d. As events were to prove, all these quotations were wildly under the final cost. The contract was given to John Charlton, not because they quoted £2,897-19s-0d, but because they also submitted a letter offering to carry out the work at a charge of 10% on the cost, such a percentage to include the necessary plant and personal supervision of the work. Charlton's letter was supported by William Roper, who attended the Committee in his capacity as Surveyor.

Was this collusion? William Roper and Arthur Charlton (the actual head of the contracting company) must, in a small town such as Tunbridge Wells, have known each other quite well and no doubt Roper would have had a professional view of the competence of each tenderer. But there is no reason to suspect any form of collusion.

William Roper was not only the designer of the new roads of the Home Park (sic) Estate but also the surveyor of the Nevill Ground, and he has recorded that the size of the original (now main) cricket pitch was some 500ft from north to south and 600 ft. from west to east – in all some 5 acres – and was surrounded by a banked cycling and running cinder track, which was railed in and was exactly three laps to the mile.

The ground on which the cricket pitch was created, had originally had a fall of 27½ft. which was levelled by slicing off the higher half and infilling the lower half with the soil from the higher part. On the north side, there was also a hollow which had to be filled up to a depth of 22ft. The result was a pitch which was, according to Roper, 'as level as a billiard table'.

The football pitch, together with six tennis courts, was planned to be on the west of the cricket pitch and the site had a further fall of 13 ft, and the same slicing and infilling was done.

So the Ground had a total fall of some 40 feet and to level it, required that 60,000 cubic feet of earth had to be moved, all of it by a combination of manpower and horsepower since bulldozers did not yet exist. The Courier reported that Mr. Roper's calculations were so accurate that on completion, no soil had had to be removed from, or brought into, the Ground (a claim which can only have originated with Mr. Roper).

It was originally intended that there should be 'a double-faced grandstand' pavilion which would serve both the cricket and the football pitches i.e. it would be on the west side of the cricket pitch and east side of the football pitch. But there would be a drop of about 13 feet between the two levels of pitch. This pavilion was never built, probably because of the lack of money for it, but it could also be that it was soon realised that it was not practical to have one pavilion serving two pitches on different levels.

The Opening of what was called 'the new Athletic Ground'[23] took place on Whit Monday 30th May 1898 before a crowd of about 8,000 – a sizeable audience for a town of 30,000, but less than the estimated 12,000 capacity of the Ground.

According to the Courier, the Opening programme started with 'a luncheon served in a tent on the Ground' attended by the Marquess, Lord Henry Nevill, Marquess Camden, the Mayor and William Roper, amongst others. W.C. Cripps, the Town Clerk, was unable to attend, since he had become seriously ill the previous week. In his speech, the Marquess said that £10,000 had been raised from ' very few' (whom he

---

[23] It should be noted that to the Victorians the word 'athletic(s) ' had a broader meaning than it has today, and was closer to our use of the word 'sport(s) ' and included all games such as cricket, hockey and football.

The Nevill Cricket Ground, Tunbridge Wells during Cricket Week.

implied were not the inhabitants of Tunbridge Wells), and went on to say that the cost of preparing the Ground had exceeded £10,000 and was more than double the originally estimated cost. As a result, the Pavilion planned had not been erected and he appealed for the money to be raised since ' the Ground was not complete and could never be complete unless a good Pavilion was erected' at an estimated cost of £2,000. The Mayor in congratulating everyone on 'such a splendid ground' and 'such a successful opening', said that he thought that "there was nothing like breaking new ground, and that had certainly been done (here), where the natural level had been altered some 14 feet".

The main event in the afternoon of the Opening Day was a mixture of athletic races (100 yards, half-mile and one mile) and cycling races (half-mile, mile and five miles) and the Marquess fired the starting pistol for the first race, remarking that "he hoped for their sakes that the pistol was properly loaded and the barrels not rusty. (Laughter and applause)".

The weather was fine until rain fell between four and five o'clock, which 'had the effect of greatly diminishing the attendance'. All in all, the event was considered a great success and the Ground a great asset for the town. The only slightly discordant note was struck by the Courier remarking that "it was noticeable that until Lord Abergavenny's new

Cricket Week at the Nevill Ground, 1906.

estate is more developed, an undesirable free list are able to take possession of the neighbouring eminencies (sic) and watch the sport from the wrong side of the fence".

Charlton premises in the Pantiles

When the Annual Athletics Meeting was repeated the following Whit Monday, they suffered even worse weather – the showers of the morning 'developed into an almost continuous downpour during the afternoon' and the effect on attendance was very marked, with only about a third of the previous year's crowd. It was however generally conceded that the arrangements were better than the previous year and 'the prizes were the most liberal ever offered locally, including awards of £10 for the premier place in the principal events.'

The contractor for the construction of the Ground was Mr. Arthur Charlton, the nurseryman who had the nursery at the bottom of Eridge Road and also a shop in the Pantiles (no. 35-37, now

Trevor Mottram, the 'Aladdin's Cave' of a kitchen utensil shop). It is clear that with the formal Opening, the construction of the Ground was considered to be complete, for on 1st June 1898 (three days after the opening), William Roper who was also an Auctioneer as well as being a Surveyor, was advertising in the Courier on Mr. Charlton's instruction an auction to be held on Friday 10th June 'at one o'clock in the afternoon precisely'. The goods were described under the heading 'Completion of Work' as ' the valuable Contractor's stock and plant, comprising seven powerful cart horses, chain and quoiler *(sic)* harnesses, waggons, contractor's and dobbin carts, sectional buildings, a large number of fowls and a variety of miscellaneous articles'. So it would seem as far as the Contractor was concerned, that all the work was finished. However the approach road (now Nevill Gate) was still unfinished and was a source of criticism six months later. There was also the Pavilion.

The Cricket Pavilion was to be built in 1899 by Strange & Sons at a cost of £1,060 from donations specifically given following the Marquess's appeal. This was less than the £2,000 estimate given by the Marquess in his speech, but that estimate was probably for a more expensive 'double-faced' pavilion. What was built was more modest and in line with the amount of money which had been raised. It was also built on the south side of the cricket pitch and provides more shade after midday than the west side would have done.

Early in the morning of Friday 11th April 1913, the Pavilion was burnt down, ostensibly in protest by militant suffragettes. The fire was discovered by the groundsman who 'gave the alarm to a Constable at the Pantiles fire alarm' shortly before 4 a.m. The Courier was just going to press and its first edition carried no

Burnt-out Pavilion

more than the briefest announcement. But it promised and actually gave, according to the following week's edition, fuller details in its second edition. Unfortunately for us, when the Courier was put on microfilm for archival purposes, the second edition was overlooked and so our detailed knowledge is limited to scraps of information referred to in reports in subsequent weeks.

But it seems that everybody at the time accepted that the fire was deliberate and was caused by militant suffragettes, referred to as 'these wild women', and the Mayor declared that Tunbridge Wells was 'a hotbed of militants'. The evidence for their involvement was that Mrs. Pankhurst's photograph was found "pinned on the grass before the wreck of the Pavilion" and "Suffragist 'literature' had been scattered around". No one was ever arrested and a more objective (or possibly more cynical) 21st century view might wonder whether an 'agent provocateur' might have been involved.

Several clubs – Tunbridge Wells Cricket Club, Bluemantles CC, the Post Office CC, St. Mark's CC, the Borough Police CC, the Tunbridge Archery Club – used the Ground and the Pavilion. All incurred losses of equipment burnt and for some, such as the Post Office CC which lost £12 of equipment, the fire threatened the very continuation of the club.

While public opinion was aroused against the Suffragettes (see

Burnt-out Stand

the Box at end of this Chapter), it did not go as far as encouraging the public to put their hand in their pocket for the rebuilding costs. The costs were met largely by insurance, but there was about £300 not covered. The collection taken at the public meeting amounted to just £22-3s-11d. Although this sum was described by the Courier as 'gratifying', it did only amount to an average of just over 2d per head (less than 1p in current money) for the 2,500 who are said to have attended, inside or out. There were other donations and also the Mayor's Appeal, which raised £92-6s-6d by 22nd. May (the largest donation: £25 from the Marquess), but all of this was not enough and the Mayor had to write to the public through the means of the Courier to appeal for more. Eventually the proceeds of two special performances of 'Our Boys' at the Tunbridge Wells Opera House were also donated, but anybody could be forgiven for concluding that the inhabitants of Tunbridge Wells were definitely parsimonious, if not actually mean.

However what was surprising, was that a new replacement pavilion, designed by Cllr. C.H. Strange FRIBA, was built by his family building firm in less than twelve weeks – just in time for the start of the 1913 'Cricket Week' in July. It should however be recognised that the pavilion had *not* been burnt to the ground and the foundations at least were probably intact.

Design of the new Pavilion

The Tunbridge Wells Cricket, Football and Athletic Club Ltd. should not be confused with the Tunbridge Wells Cricket Club or the Tunbridge Wells Football Club or the Tunbridge Wells Hockey Club which were quite separate organisations. These 'town' clubs were not in any way involved in the creation of the Nevill Ground, although they were subsequently to use it.

The Tunbridge Wells Football Club was to play its first game on the Ground in September 1898; and in December 1899, they hosted at the Nevill Ground the first County Football match to be played in Tunbridge Wells for eleven years. The contest was between Kent and Middlesex, with Kent winning 3-1, despite playing in a deluge, while the Borough Band 'discoursed some excellent selections previous to and during the match' including the somewhat inappropriate 'Sunshine Above'.

But in the long-run, the move of the Football Club to the Nevill Ground was not successful, possibly because of location, but also more likely because of sharing the ground with the Lawn Tennis Club. Consequently the ground served as football pitches from September-April and lawn tennis courts from April-September. This seems to have led to disputes as to when a football or tennis season began or ended, and culminated in 1905 when the football club requested the use of the ground on the first two Saturdays in September and the Tennis Club refused on the grounds that their season ended on 15th September. The dispute and the associated ill-will and probably other problems as well led the Football Club to hold their last game on the Ground in April 1906. After their departure, the football pitch area which also included six tennis courts at the Upper Cumberland Walk end, was converted to tennis and croquet, and when croquet departed in due course, it became eleven grass and ten hard tennis courts for the Tunbridge Wells Lawn Tennis Club, which it remains to this day.

The Tunbridge Wells Hockey Club was new and was only formed on 14th September 1898, with Lord Henry Nevill as patron and an annual subscription of 10/6d (52$\frac{1}{2}$p). It played its first game at the Nevill Ground on Wednesday 28th September 1898 against Blackheath. The visitors won 3-1. The Club plays there to this day, sharing the pitch seasonally with cricket, without the apparent problems suffered by football and lawn tennis in the early part of the 20th century.

The Tunbridge Wells Cricket Club, which had been founded in 1858, was not to play its first game on the Ground until May 1899. It had held a special public meeting of the Club at the Town Hall on the 16th November 1898 – the Mayor, who was on the Committee, presided – to consider whether the Club should continue to play its matches on the Common, or should move to the Nevill Ground; and by a relatively narrow vote of 15-11, decided on the Nevill.

The Tunbridge Wells Cricket Club had a fixture list of 33 games in 1899 – 22 First XI and 11 Second XI – of which 20 were home games played at the Nevill. However the opening game on Saturday 13th May was a practice match played between two sides chosen on the field. A snippet in the previous week's Courier asked "new and prospective new members to turn up in their thousands"... "The latent power, the inate *(sic)* talent, are what we want to discover. The 'old crocks' are perfectly well-known to us; the young 'cracks' are the special guest for tomorrow". It seems unlikely that thousands turned up, since the Courier the following week reported 14 matches, including the Tunbridge Wells Police Cricket Club, but not the 'practice match'.

The first reported game was the Second XI playing The Leopards (past and present Skinners' School, with masters) 'in the most wretched weather' at the Nevill Ground on 20th May. The match was a draw, The

Leopards scoring 129 and the Second XI 69 for 6 wickets. But in 1899, there was the first initial step towards County Cricket matches being played at the Nevill – the Kent and Sussex 2nd XIs played each other there on July 31st and August 1st. Two years later, the County 1st. XIs were to return to Tunbridge Wells after an absence of 18 years. No doubt an important influence was Major L.T.Spens who was both a director of the Tunbridge Wells Athletic Club Ltd. and a committee member of the Kent County Cricket Club. Lancashire were the opening visitors, followed by Sussex, in Cricket Week, which was to become an annual Tunbridge Wells fixture. Since then, a Kent-Sussex match has nearly always been the highlight of the Week, reflecting the fact that Tunbridge Wells is on both counties' borders.

It is ironic that if the Nevill Ground had existed before 1894 and Kent-Sussex matches had taken place there, those matches would have taken place in Sussex, not Kent, since the County boundary ran along the western edge of the site, putting all of the Ground in Sussex. However the boundary revisions of 1894 pushed the County boundary back to Forest Road and the further revision of 1900 pushed it even further past the Tunbridge Wells cemetery. So the Kent-Sussex match at Tunbridge Wells has always been played in Kent.

Since 1899, the Tunbridge Wells Cricket Club has had a very close association with the Ground, but the financial problems of the Ground were not theirs. They simply used the Ground – they did not run it (nor could they have run it on the income they generated). But they nearly lost their venue in 1901 when the Tunbridge Wells Cricket, Football and Athletic Club Ltd. became at least technically insolvent. By May 1901, the total liabilities of the Company were £2,146. Since inception, their total income had been £13,065, made up of £10,005 subscribed by Shareholders and Debenture Holders, £2000 raised by Mortgage and £1,060 of Donations given especially for the Pavilion. Against this, they had expended £15,211, of which over £13,600 had been spent on the grounds and pavilion.

They had also introduced a membership scheme with a sliding scale of subscriptions. Annual membership, payable on 1st January, was £1-1s-0d (a guinea, or £1.05p) which gave admission to the Ground at all times with use of the Pavilion. There was also a Family membership at £2-2s-0d, which admitted three persons. Then there was a somewhat complicated scale of subscriptions for:

- Playing members of the Tunbridge Wells Cricket Club (£1-1s-0d, but only for the Cricket Season);

- Schoolboys (10/- but for six weeks only and no County matches);
- Visitors (5/- per week and no County matches);
- Tradesmen Players (10/- for the Cricket Season only and no County matches);
- Non-playing Tradesmen (10/- for all Cricket matches, but no County matches);
- Trade employees (5/- with no use of the Pavilion and no County matches);
- Members of the Tunbridge Wells Football Club, Blue Mantles CC, and Lawn Tennis Club admitted to the Ground by special arrangement with those clubs by paying the Annual Member's subscription to the Ground.
- Annual Membership with use of Running and Cycle Track only (10/-)

Somehow, there does not seem to have been many takers for membership, apart from those who actually played at the Ground.

When the first financial crisis came in 1901, the Athletic Club Ltd appealed to the general public to take up the 188 shares of £10 each and the 173 Debentures still not allotted, otherwise 'the Directors will have no alternative but to close the Ground with disastrous results to Athletics in Tunbridge Wells, and the destruction of our hopes that County Cricket Matches may annually take place here.' The threat seems to have been averted since the Ground was never closed, but the Company teetered on the edge for the rest of its life. For example, the week before the Pavilion was burnt down in 1913, the Company held its Annual General Meeting at which it was announced that the Company had made a loss of £52-9s-0d in 1912; and a pattern of small profits and losses seems to have been the norm for the Company.

Nonetheless, the Tunbridge Wells Cricket, Football and Athletic Club Ltd seems to have had a strong instinct for survival, which was to last them until after the Second World War. During the War, the Pavilion was used by the local Home Guard and the grounds were used for exercise and recreation by the XII Corps troops stationed in Tunbridge Wells (including, as he was then, Lt. General Bernard Montgomery, who was living at 'Court Lees', 69 Warwick Park, which backs on to the Ground) . When the War ended, Tunbridge Wells Borough Council took over the lease from the Company in June 1946 and acquired the freehold of 'the 12 acres or thereabouts' from the Marquess for a consideration of £2,850 in July 1951. Since then, the Ground has been managed by the Borough, who must have acquired further freehold land (Plots 50-53 which had never been developed) from the Marquess sometime later, but there is no record of this in the Archives. This land was initially used as a car park for the Ground, but became the second cricket pitch in about 1965.

The Tunbridge Wells Cricket, Football and Athletic Club Ltd. had survived so long through the goodwill of all concerned, including the Marquess, who by 1904 was owed four years' rent (£340 at the then actual terms) by the Club, when the Club had only been tenants for seven years. Similar situations were to continue until the Company was dissolved in the late 1940's. Sadly, since Companies House only keeps records of dissolved companies for 20 years, the full details of the Company's history are lost and we are deprived of an intriguing insight into parish-pump politics. However, the recent discovery in the basement of a local firm of solicitors of the Board Minutes of the Company from its inception in 1895 until 1909, will, when thoroughly analysed, provide an insight into the critical first fourteen years; and no doubt a more detailed and separate history.

Regardless of changes of ownership, the Nevill Ground has continued to be a major feature of Tunbridge Wells. Its reputation is particularly linked to cricket and many a century has been scored in what is regarded by many as a 'batting paradise'. The highest individual score at the Ground was in 1934 when Walter (Wally) Hammond scored 290

The Nevill Ground, 1967.

out of a total of 563 for Gloucestershire. Peak attendance is thought to have been the 14,000 spectators who watched the Kent v. Sussex match in 1946. Sadly attendances now are not what they used to be.

The Nevill Ground in the 1960s.

Tunbridge Wells' Treatment of the Suffragettes

Ill-feeling against suffragettes ran high in Tunbridge Wells as a result of the Pavilion being burnt down.

The Vicar of Christ Church in the High Street cancelled a letting of the Parish Room to the Women's Social and Political Union as they supported votes for women, since the Vicar did not feel that he could 'allow the Hall to be used by a Society the whole policy of which he believed to be morally wrong'.

The WSPU held their meeting instead at the Pump Room where the hostesses at the "At Home" were 'Princess Sophia Duleep Singh[24], an Indian lady, and Mrs. Percy Evans, an American lady living at Rotherfield'. The principal speaker at the meeting was Miss Evelyn Sharp, described as 'a prominent Militant Suffragette' who when asked why Suffragettes attacked the property of innocent people, replied that "no one was innocent so long as they allowed the Government to refuse women votes".

The big event however was the protest meeting on Monday 28th April in the Great Hall, which was organised by the National League for Opposing Women's Suffrage (NLOWS). The Great Hall was packed with many people standing and there was an overflow meeting outside, at which the crowd was estimated at 1,500, and which was by no means as placid as the meeting inside.

Both meetings were addressed by Sir Arthur Conan Doyle (who had played for the Tunbridge Wells Cricket Club) and Miss Gladys Pott, Secretary of the NLOWS, amongst others; and all the speakers were greeted with much applause. The outside meeting had 'frequent interruptions from a posse of young ladies,

---

[24] Princess Sophia Duleep Singh (1876-1948) was the sixth child and third daughter of Maharajah Duleep Singh, 5th and last King of Lahore and Emperor of the Sikhs, who was deposed by the British at the age of ten in 1849 after the Second Sikh War and sent to England to be brought up as a good Christian country gentleman on his large estate at Elveden Hall in Suffolk. At the same time, the famous and priceless Koh-i-noor (Mountain of Light) diamond owned by the Maharajah was confiscated by Lord Dalhousie, the Governor-General, and given to Queen Victoria. Princess Sophia never married and lived in a grace-and-favour house at Hampton Court, granted by Queen Victoria. However, her step-mother (the Maharajah's second wife) was to live in Madeira Park, Tunbridge Wells and die there in 1930. The family history is fully detailed in 'The Maharajah's Box' by Christy Campbell (HarperCollins, 2000).

who thus evinced their sympathies with the cause of Women's Suffrage. They included three prominent local Suffragists and were carrying Suffragette posters and a considerable quantity of literature.' They were booed and severely hustled and their placards torn from them. Eggs 'in a somewhat advanced state of decadence' were thrown at the ladies and their hats were pulled off and their clothes torn.

The Courier described all this as just 'horse-play'. The police then intervened 'and with considerable difficulty rescued the ladies and escorted them to the police station for safety. The procession to the police station was followed all the way by a shouting jeering crowd, who hung about the station for some time hissing and booing, until advised by Chief Constable Prior to go away.' It seems times have not changed.

CHAPTER 7

ISSUES AND PROBLEMS

A number of issues or problems were to arise in the development of the Warwick Park Estate, which could have killed the project, or at least substantially changed it. They can be classified as Issues of Inheritance, Local Council and Existing Leaseholders. There was also at least one issue of Trust and Confidence between the parties which would not have killed the project, but which could have undermined it.

Issues of Inheritance. As described in a previous chapter, the Abergavenny Estates had been put into a Trust many years before and the Marquess was 'a tenant-for-life'. The Trust was necessary not only to minimise or even avoid Death Duties (Inheritance Tax) on the Estate, but also to handle the issue of succession where the heir, Abergavenny's eldest son, the Earl of Lewes, was (in the words of the Briefing given for a Legal Opinion in 1896) 'not capable of giving any consent, he being "non compos mentis", though not found lunatic by Inquisition'.

The existence of this Trust could have prevented any development of the Home Farm Estate since the Settled Land Acts of 1884 and 1890 forbade trustees 'from borrowing money for the purpose of effecting improvements' and it was thought that borrowing money to develop the Home Farm Estate could fall into this category. The Trustees were anxious to meet Abergavenny's wishes if they could do so legally. The question was therefore whether the Trustees could responsibly invest in what might be considered as a speculative development.

Drake wrote to Macbean on 29th February 1896 declaring 'Lord Cranbrook *(one of the two Trustees)* is right. The Settled Land Act provides that capital money may be spent in making streets, roads, sewers and drains necessary or proper with the conversion of land into building land.'

Cripps in *his capacity as solicitor* had also joined in on the issue of whether the Trustees needed to borrow any money for the development. He wrote to Macbean on 26th February 1896: 'Am I right in assuming the Trustees have in their hands considerable sums of money available for the purpose of the development of the Estate, and that these have been produced from the sale of other portions of the Estate, or from fines on the renewal of Leases, or other moneys which ought properly to be treated as Capital? A wire from you "Yes" will be quite sufficient.'

Drake wrote to Macbean on 20th March 1896 saying that the Trustees had 'some £20,000 in Railway Stock and £5,000 on mortgage as well as current cash to a considerable amount.'

But by this time, a Legal Opinion had already been obtained on 17th March 1896 from Mr. Cozens Hardy QC, MP, who opined that 'the Settled Land Acts do not authorise borrowing money for the purpose of effecting improvement' and suggested that it would be simpler and quicker to obtain a Private Act of Parliament to exempt the Estate.

His Opinion caused Abergavenny to be in 'a considerable fume' when he met Drake on 23rd. March[25] and Drake wrote to Macbean saying 'I think nothing further had better be done till you and I have met.' He added 'His Lordship seems rather inclined to do the Home Farm works in sections and not all at once', which suggests that he was looking at ways of spreading the cost over time.

The Private Act of Parliament route does not seem to have been followed. It was agreed instead that an application should be made to the Court for permission for the Trustees to proceed and that a formal and detailed scheme needed to be submitted to the Trustees, so that they could present it in court as evidence of the seriousness and viability of the project when they applied for an exemption.

On 7th April, Drake wrote to Macbean saying 'We shall require a plan of the Estate and a scheme for the execution of the proposed expenditure and their estimated return.' Macbean prepared all the details of the scheme and sent them to Drake on 29th April. In the covering letter, Macbean wrote 'I anticipate the cost of constructing the roads as required by the Corporation together with the bridge over the line will amount to £20,000. The Ground Rents should realise £2,100 including the rent of the Cricket Ground. His Lordship contemplates also building 20 pairs of cottages with a cost of £500 a pair and a total of £10,000. The rental that should be derived from these after making due allowance for repairs is £592 p.a.' (The proposal for 18 cottages

---

[25] The Marquess's general mood may not have been improved by a fire at Eridge Castle on 26th February 1896, which destroyed the Smoking Room on the ground floor. It was discovered by Lord Henry Nevill just before 3am. There was considerable damage, but the fire was put out within the hour, and before the arrival of 'the Steam Fire Brigade' from Tunbridge Wells. The Sun Fire Office paid insurance compensation of £1,085-13s-0d.

was *dis*approved by the Works Committee on 11th March 1898.)

The draft scheme was then prepared by Drake who submitted it on 8th May 1896 to Macbean for his consideration, before sending it to 'Messrs. Cripps for the approval of the Trustees.' It should be appreciated that until the application was heard and approved, nothing could be done about proceeding with the Home Farm development and so at least four or five months had been lost.

The application was heard before Mr. Justice Sterling at 2pm on 8th July. Drake invited Macbean to lunch with him before the hearing at 12.45 p.m. at the Windham Club. While there is no direct correspondence about the judgement in the Archives, the application must have been granted because the issues of diverting the footpaths, settling the dispute over sewerage costs and Council approval sprang once again into life.

Local Council issues. The Marquess needed planning permission for the development and while there was never any real problem about the plans submitted, there were two issues which delayed the granting of permission. The first was the question of who was going to pay for the connection of the Warwick Park Estate sewerage system to the existing town sewerage system. The second was to do with closing what was called the Home Farm footpath from Cumberland Walk to Birling Road and across the railway to Forest Road.

The Works Committee of the Borough of Tunbridge Wells disapproved on 29th November 1895 the plans submitted for new streets and sewers on the Home Farm Estate. Roper wrote to Macbean on 30th .November saying that 'the plans in themselves answer all requirements' but that 'the plans were disapproved yesterday pending a legal undertaking on His Lordship's part to enlarge and deepen the *existing* sewer at his own cost.' Roper was definitively of the opinion that 'it is the duty of the Corporation to do this.'

Drake reacted quickly. On 2nd. December 1895, he wrote to Macbean saying that there had been a similar problem for the Duke of Devonshire and Carew Davis Gilbert in March 1894 and a legal Opinion had been obtained from the two leading experts – Mr. I. H. Balfour Brown QC and Mr. R. Cunningham Glen – who concluded that landlords could compel a Corporation under Section 18 of the Public Health Acts (Amendment) Act 1890 to connect their sewers with the Corporation's main sewers and that it was the duty of the Corporation to enlarge the sewer if necessary. Drake felt that there was no point in wasting time and sent Macbean a copy of what he called 'the double-barrelled Opinion'. Macbean wasted no time in sending it on to Cripps *in his capacity as Town Clerk.*

Cripps may well have suggested sharing the cost for he wrote on 7th December 1895 in a letter marked 'This is confidential between us.' from his home, The Lawn, Camden Park: 'I had hoped to see you about the sewer before I wrote. I shall be sorry if it gets to be a sort of "pull devil, pull baker" instead of a fair "live debate". I had hoped that the matter was going thro *(sic)* pleasantly. What I had suggested about the 'half' was of course quite unofficial and simply for the sake of avoiding a difficulty and smoothing over the awkwardnesses about footpaths and the like. If I am to discuss 'the law' with Drake, I shall have to do so formally as Town Clerk and under the instruction of the Committee. I know that you will understand that I am bound to do the best I can for the Town altho *(sic)* I think I can often serve their interests best by arranging a fair compromise.'

Despite this informal dialogue, Macbean was firm in holding Abergavenny's position. Macbean wrote on 6th January 1896 to Cripps: 'His Lordship thinks it hardly fair or reasonable that he should be called upon to bear the whole cost of lowering and enlarging the sewer and would probably be prepared to meet the Corporation by paying half the cost.'

This issue then went relatively quiet, no doubt awaiting the outcome of the Settled Land issue and the diverted footpaths issue, both of which needed to be settled before agreement could be reached and planning permission granted. The result was a formal undertaking to 'The Mayor, Aldermen and Burgesses of the Borough of Tunbridge Wells', signed on 4th December 1896 (some seven days after the Council had given planning permission) by Macbean on behalf of the Marquess in which the Marquess agreed to pay half the cost incurred of the new sewers and their connection; agreed that all roads would be laid out and completed in accordance with the agreed plan; and agreed that Nevill Lane, Birling Road and Forest Road would be widened in accordance with the Tunbridge Wells Improvement Act of 1889.

The other Local Council issue was relatively minor – almost a formality – and it did have the support of the Council. Nonetheless it seems to have aroused a certain amount of local opposition.

The Home Farm Estate was crossed by two public footpaths – from Cumberland Walk past the Home Farm itself up to Birling Road; and from Cumberland Walk up to and across the Hastings line and out to Forest Road. With the proposed new roads, these footpaths were largely, if not totally, redundant; and they were also impossible to retain with the land being divided up into so many building plots.

On 20th March 1896 – a not insignificant date in relation to the Settled Lands issue – the Marquess gave notice to Tunbridge Wells Council that 'he was desirous of stopping up and diverting the highway on the Home Park Estate'. A special meeting of the Works Committee was called and held on site and a report was prepared for the next Council meeting on 1st. April 1896. The Council saw no problem over the diversion or elimination of the footpaths. The procedure was that the proposed Order to do so had to be published locally and it then had to go before and be approved by the General Quarter Sessions of the Peace for the County. The Order 'for turning, diverting and stopping up Highways known as Cumberland Walk and Home Farm Footpath' was placed in the Tunbridge Wells Courier of 31st July 1896 and the application was to be approved without any opposition on 20th October 1896 at the General Quarter Sessions of the Peace held at St. Augustine's, Canterbury.

But there was some opposition following the publication of the Order. A meeting was held at the Swan Hotel in the Pantiles at which local residents expressed their concern. They decided to request an interview with the Works Committee which took place on 11th September 1896. The delegation consisted of Dr. Adeney (who acted as spokesman), Mr. G. Abbott, Mr. G. Allen and Mr. A. Nicholson, who emphasised that the public right of way (the footbridge crossing the Hastings railway line) should be retained. The Committee decided that the Marquess should be involved and his views were sought. The Marquess (through Macbean) replied that he fully intended to maintain his right of way (which was interpreted as the public's right of way). As a result, the Committee at their next meeting on 18th September, resolved that there should be no change of plan. (As an interesting aside, Cripps as the Town Clerk wrote immediately the same day to Macbean: 'After considerable discussion this morning, the Works Committee decided to instruct me to write to the promoters of the little agitation that they were of the opinion that the plans *(for diversion and elimination)* should stand.')

The irony is that while large sections of the footpaths did vanish, quite

The footbridge across the Tunbridge Wells–Hastings railway line, c. 1850.
The footbridge exists to this day.

a lot still remains today as the building development plans were never fully carried out. So the footpath and railway bridge over the Hastings line is still there as is what is still known as The Twitten – the path from Warwick Park, opposite Nevill Gate, up to Birling Park Avenue.

Existing leaseholders issues. There was never any proposal to buy out existing leaseholders who generally held land on the periphery of the Estate, but there was one small group of six cottages which were part of the Nevill Arms (*now* Thorins, the wine bar and restaurant) at the junction of Warwick Park with Nevill Street. These cottages prevented the widening of the entrance to Warwick Park and needed to be demolished, but the surrender of their leases had to be negotiated first. This was achieved on 10th March 1896. One other relatively short-term lease – a seven acre field behind Emsworth House in the Frant Road – would also cause a problem and lead to the cancellation of one of the new roads on the Estate. It had been leased for 21 years in 1883 and could not be available until 1904.

Issues of Trust and Confidence. One major issue of trust and confidence was that at one stage the Marquess suspected Cripps of overcharging. The Marquess asked Macbean to deal with it and Macbean, no doubt because of his friendship with Cripps, thought the best way to deal with it was bluntly and directly. Macbean wrote to the Marquess on 9th February 1897: 'I thought that the best way to give Cripps a broad hint about his charges was to tell him exactly what you said and there could be no misunderstanding.' Macbean's letter to Cripps of 7th February 1897 read "When with his Lordship before dinner last night, he said 'you must give Cripps a very broad hint that he is not to run up a long bill. He tried to surcharge in some account he has, very much and the Taxing Master had to set him down from 10 guineas to £2-9s-0d in one thing alone. I didn't like this. He ought not to do it. His bill and also Drake's were up at the same time. One was as much too high as the other was moderate. I didn't know this when I spoke to him about the Mineral leases." There you have it straight, the best way I know you will think of getting a broad hint.'

Cripps was astounded. He replied on 8th February 'I can't understand it. Haven't seen the bill and certainly in the claim I sent up, there was no 10 guineas.' He replied more formally on 10th February in a typewritten letter to Macbean which Macbean gave to the Marquess: 'I have not for years had anything occur which has given me more pain and vexation. I hope that you will tell His Lordship that I am exceedingly obliged to him for mentioning the question of these costs to you and thus enabling me to explain a matter which certainly needs explaining. I have now heard from my London Agents... After the bill was prepared, my agent's Chancery clerk, without communicating with me, altered the first item in the bill from 6s-8d to £10-10-0, his explanation being that I had made no charge for perusing the Estates Acts and other documents, plans and papers and he thought that I had omitted to do so. He had of course no right to do so and I have explained my indignation in no uncertain terms. The charge never ought to have been made and I know His Lordship will believe me when I say that I knew nothing of it until I heard from you the day before yesterday.'

Enough said?

CHAPTER 8

ROADS, BRIDGES AND LANDSCAPING

It is probable that the creation of the Nevill Ground was the major factor in changing the road lines which had been originally proposed in the 'Eridge Estate' map and Plans A, B and C. The position of the Nevill Ground made a number of the proposed roads impossible and also made a road bridge across the Hastings line much more difficult. As a result, the roads which were advertised 'for tender' were very different in Portion II and those in Portion III were eliminated altogether.

The plans for the new roads and sewers were approved by the Council on Wednesday 3rd. February 1896. The Tunbridge Wells Courier for 17th February 1896 carried the advertisement which, under the heading 'Eridge Estate New Road' invited tenders 'in connection with the making of New Roads, Sewers, Storm Water Drains, Brick Pavements etc.' to be submitted to Mr. Williamson by Saturday 29th February 1896.

Warwick Park opposite Home Farm, 2nd January 1899. Roedean Rd. to the far left. Note the four white ventilation 'pepper pots' to the right, which can be seen in the other Home Farm photographs.

The Roads

Six roads were specified for tender:

Road No. 1, from Nevill St. to Forest Road. 50 ft wide – road 30ft., paved footpath 10ft wide on each side. 1460 yards in length. Estimated cost £10,935. (This was to become Warwick Park.)

Road No. 2, from Frant Road to Madeira Park. 40ft wide – road 22ft., with footpaths 9ft each side. 260 yards in length. Estimated cost £1620. Note in the Archives: 'This road is really a widening of the existing lane called Cut Throat Lane'. (It was also called Nevill Lane and ran from the Frant Road, but petered out into the cart-track to Home Farm. It is now called Rodmell Road.)

Road No. 3, from where the old (Tunbridge Ware) 'Factory' (and showroom)[26] stood at 27 Frant Road, to Road No.1 – 50ft. wide, road 30ft., paved footpath each side of 10ft., 255 yards long. Estimated cost £2000. (The 'Factory' lease which came up for renewal in 1892 was never renewed, which suggests some premeditation, and the 'Factory' was demolished in due course, to allow for a wider road. This road was on the line of one of the three cart-tracks to Home Farm and is now Roedean Road.)

Road No.4, from a point above Birling Cottages in the Birling Road into Road No.1. 50ft. wide, road 30ft., footpath 10 ft on each side, 378 yards long. Estimated cost £2,825. (The bottom part of this road was eventually to be built 100 years later in 1998, and is now Richmond Place.)

Road No.5, from Road No.1 (Warwick Park) 'leading in a northerly direction to the boundary of the Estate where it adjoins the South-Eastern Railway and thence in a north-westerly direction along such

---

[26] Henry Hollamby's 'Tunbridge Ware' Factory was at 27 Frant Road until it was destroyed by fire in 1891, and when the lease of the site expired in 1892, it was not renewed. (The ground rent was £6-7-6d a year). By the time of the fire, Hollamby who employed as many as 40 men in manufacturing Tunbridge Ware, was in his 70's and after the fire, he decided to retire. He sold whatever stock could be salvaged to Boyce, Brown and Kemp. It is not known whether there was any forward planning considerations by Abergavenny/Macbean in not renewing the lease. The burnt-out building was demolished to widen the entrance of Roedean Road from Frant Road - the line of Roedean Road following essentially that of the cart-track from the Home Farm to Frant Road. Henry Hollamby lived only a few doors down from his 'Factory' - at 'Woodland Prospect' which was between Langley Villa and Fonthill Lodge. Despite its picturesque name, 'Woodland Prospect' was built above the railway tunnel from the West station (or rather the railway was tunnelled underneath the house) and a major part of the 'Prospect' would have been the railway cutting to the Central station.

boundary for 230 yards and thence along the northern boundary of the land coloured green for 280 yards and thence in a westerly direction to the boundary of the Estate where it adjoins a footbridge over the LB &SC Railway.' Total length 670 yards, 40 ft wide, road 22 ft. with 9 ft footpaths each side. Estimated cost £3,000. (This road was never built, but would have started close to the top of Warwick Park and run along the side of the railway down to the footbridge.)

Road No.6, leading from Road No.1 (Warwick Park) to Road No.5. 40ft wide, road 22 ft. with footpaths 9ft. each side. 230 yards long. Estimated cost £1042. (This is now Blatchington Road.)

The specification was for six roads with a total length of 3,253 yards (9,759 feet) at an estimated cost of £21,422. This was considerably less than the Currey 'guesstimate' of £50,000 for approximately 13,000 feet of road-building, but it was also about 1,250 feet less than the original estimate by Brackett of 11,000 feet of roads required. This was principally because the development in Portion III across the Hastings railway line had been abandoned. Portion III does not seem to have been abandoned until late in 1895. It had been from the beginning the least promising in terms of the number of potential plots and this together with the disproportionate cost of a second bridge across the railway is probably the main reason for its cancellation. Certainly no estimates were ever invited for the second bridge and the road beyond it.

It would seem that after the publication of the Invitation to Tender, there was some question as to whether the width of all the roads in the Warwick Park Estate should be reduced to 40 feet in width, which would have saved some money and taken up less land. But this was advised against by the Eastbourne pundit, Henry Michell Whitley, who wrote in a letter of 23rd. March 1896 to George Macbean: "I understand that it is proposed to reduce width to 40 feet. As to this question, I would remark that the standard width of all the roads in Eastbourne is 50 feet and this is not too wide for roads which are intended to be planted with trees, and good houses built along them." At the same time, Whitley advised against land being let at a lower rental than £30 per acre.

In the end, only four of the six roads were built, with only two roads, Rodmell and Blatchington, being 40 feet wide. The two roads which were not built amounted to just under a third of the projected length and just over a quarter of the projected cost, being 1,048 yards (3,144 ft.) at an estimated cost of £5,825. So the real estimate for the four roads which were built, was for 2205 yards (6,615 ft.) – just under two-thirds of Brackett's original estimate – at an estimated cost of £15,597.

Included in that estimate was the cost of providing brick pavements, already a feature of earlier developments in Tunbridge Wells, but also a feature of Eastbourne and other late 19th century resorts. The pavements constructed on the Warwick Park Estate would require over 400,000 bricks. Fortunately most of these still survive, although sadly some have been repaired/replaced in the latter half of the 20th century by less expensive tarmac.[27]

The reason for the two roads not being constructed was that their cost could not be justified by the number of plots which they would serve. *(In retrospect, one might wonder why they were proposed in the first place.)*

In the case of the road running behind the Nevill Ground along the railway line to rejoin Warwick Park, it would only service two plots (Nos. 51 & 52) which could not be serviced from Warwick Park.

The situation was even worse for the road planned to run from Warwick Park to Birling Road. For this road, there were no sites which could not be reached from either Warwick Park or Birling Rd, so there was no economic justification at all. The reason for this was that half the frontage onto this road was not available until at least 1904 – the land on the south-west side of the road which amounted to just over seven acres, had been granted (possibly somewhat short-sightedly) as a 21 year lease which did not expire until 1904 and the tenant, Mason G. Holt, was not interested in shortening his lease.

---

[27] In the context of bricks, it should be recorded that the over-optimistic potential of the Warwick Park Estate development was probably the prime factor in the setting-up of the Forest Brick Works, situated on 20 acres of (Abergavenny) land on the East side (i.e. the other side) of Forest Road, with four tunnel-drying sheds with a capacity of 24,000 bricks. The Works were opened by the Marquess after the usual lunch for such occasions on the afternoon of Thursday 21st.April 1898, just five weeks before he opened the Nevill Ground. In his speech he said that 'he had opened many buildings but had never opened a brickworks before' but that he recognised that building was Tunbridge Wells's major industry. The Works had its own railway siding from the main SER line to Hastings and its entrance is still marked as a footpath from Forest Road. In some respects, the Forest Brick Works which was started by a local architect, W.Barnsley Hughes, had already missed the boat - they were too late for the 400,000+ pavement bricks which would already have been laid and the Warwick Park potential was never achieved. As a result, the Forest Brick Works did not last long. Contrary to local belief, the Works were never intended to supply bricks for railway tunnels on the Hastings line since all of these were built about 50 years earlier.

The road construction contract was awarded to a local company, Walter Arnold & Sons, which was run by a father, Walter Arnold of Frant, and his son, George[28]. They produced an original tender of £15,049-1s-11d, which was negotiated down to £13,292-5s-3d in the contract signed on 23rd. November 1896. Their original tender broke down the costs as follows:

Roads	£9,881- 9s- 4d
Drainage and Pipe-laying	£3,053-19s- 3d
Manholes/Gullies	£ 571-16s- 8d
Subsidiary unspecified work	£1,506-16s- 8d
Maintenance	£ 25- 0s- 0d
	£ 15,049- 1s-11d

The Marquess's Agent drove a hard bargain. The contract is marked with the subsidiary unspecified work of £1,506-16s-8d struck out and an additional deduction 'as agreed' of £250, giving a reduced total of £13,292-5s-3d. This must have been a very tight price and the cost restriction together with the relatively limited resources of a small local firm clearly caused problems. Two years after the original contract, the Arnolds had to agree to a Bond, dated 23rd. November 1898, in which they were 'jointly and severally bound for £1,330' (i.e. 10% of the contract) to the Marquess for satisfactory completion within a proper time and there was to be 'no release from this despite completion.'

It is not entirely clear from the Archive what were the problems about building the roads to the agreed price and within the agreed time. There is an undated hand-written note in the files which reads "Mr. W. *(presumably Andrew Williamson of the Erith Estate office)* has written Arnold giving him notice to remedy defects... We to draft a letter for G.Mc. *(George Macbean)* to write Arnold. Refer to Mr.W's letter giving A. *[Arnold]* notice to carry out the work forthwith or within six weeks....G.E .Macbean's letter to remind A. that he is under a heavy penalty for not completing the works with in the proper time."

---

[28] It is interesting to record that the same Walter Arnold was the first person in Kent to be prosecuted at Tonbridge Magistrates' Court on 28th January 1896 for driving a Horseless Carriage 'at a fast rate' which was admitted to be 8 miles per hour. In giving evidence, PC Head said that he had to run to overtake the carriage, but admitted that both he and the carriage were overtaken by a pony and trap which passed at the time. The witness also testified that when the vehicle was standing, it kept vibrating and a horse passing shied to the other side of the road. Walter Arnold was fined 8/- and costs - a total of £4-7-0d. True to its campaigning character even 111 years ago, The Tunbridge Wells Courier set up a Horseless Carriage Defence Fund.

But whatever the problems were, the 10% Bond was a safeguard protecting the Marquess and as a result, Macbean could reasonably declare on 13th January 1899 to the Council that the roads were ready for dedication. The Borough Surveyor naturally carried out an examination which found a number of things wanting.

It took until 2nd. June for Macbean to respond, in which he said 'that the Borough Surveyor's requirements ... have been largely complied with' and since the owners were willing 'to pay a reasonable sum to complete anything outstanding' he enclosed 'a formal application to declare the following roads to be Highways reparable by the inhabitants at large.' (The 'following roads' were named as Warwick Park, indicating that the name had been chosen by January 1899; a street, 'at present unnamed', which was to be Roedean Road; and a street 'at present unnamed' which is somewhat ambiguously described and could be what would be Rodmell or Blatchington Roads.)

Mr. Macbean attended the Works Committee on 30th June 1899 and undertook to complete (certain) retaining walls; to deposit with the Corporation £500 to complete the making of roads (with any surplus to be returned); and to contribute £100 towards the cost of planting trees (on which later quotations would suggest that the Council made a profit).

The Committee resolved that 'upon the faith of this undertaking, the Council be recommended to declare the following roads to be Highways.' Macbean sent a cheque for £600 on 14th July 1899, and thanked the Committee 'for the trouble they had taken during planning and construction and the consideration they had shewn in taking over the roads as Public Highways'. It is difficult, 100 years on, to judge whether he was being sycophantic, genuine or sarcastic.

One road which was not included in the contract was Nevill Gate. Initially this was a private road. The Secretary of the Athletic Club wrote to the Works Committee on 29th April 1898 stating that 'in constructing a private carriage drive from the new road on the Home Farm Estate to the land include in the Club's lease, they are making a private road to be a carriage entrance, and not a street or thoroughfare.' However, it did become 'a public highway' in 1935, when after having it 'tarmacadamed at a cost of £70 by Messrs. Farrant' (a cost passed on by the Marquess to residents of Nevill Gate as £9 per household and to the Cricket and Athletic Club at £18), the road became public.

No other road building activity is recorded apart from an inquiry in a letter dated 29th June 1906 from Mr. Gaisford, the Marquess's Agent, to the Works Committee asking whether the Council would be prepared to take over a new road in continuation of Blatchington Road if it were laid only 37'6" in width. The Committee resolved an emphatic 'No', stating that such a road must be 40'.

This must tie in with a proposal made to the Committee only a month earlier on 25th May 1906 by Henry Wild, the principal developer of Blatchington Road. This showed a suggested development of building land adjoining Blatchington Road, but the Committee resolved that it was 'not prepared to approve the suggested laying-out of the land in question'. It is not entirely clear what was the land in question, but it was probably the land leading up to the footbridge over the railway. The Council's refusal of Wild's plan probably led to its subsequent haphazard development, plot by plot.

The bridge over the railway

The other major construction tender was for the building of the road bridge over the existing Tunbridge Wells West cutting which separated the bottom 15 acres (down to Nevill St. and the Pantiles) from the rest of the Home Farm Estate. The contract was slightly complex insofar as there were three parties – the Marquess, the railway company (the London, Brighton and South Coast Railway) and the building contractor. The contract was given to Pauling & Co., of 23 Victoria Street, Westminster, for the lump sum of £1,500 (again a much lower cost than Currey's original estimate of £10,000 for two bridges.) A condition, not unusual for those days, was that 'All Iron & Steel of every description must be of British manufacture.' In the agreement signed on 13th April 1897 between the Marquess and the railway company, in which it was agreed that the bridge could and would be built, it was also specified that the bridge would be maintained by the railway company, but the cost of maintenance would be borne by the Marquess.

Trees and Landscaping

The Marquess, no doubt as a means of making the Estate more attractive to potential developers, spent fairly substantially on tree planting, landscaping and fencing.

The three major items were fencing presumably of the road boundaries and of the individual plots, grassing and trees, and road maintenance (the latter despite the road becoming a public highway in 1899). This expenditure up to 1908 can be summarised:

Fencing	£309- 4s-4d
Trees/Planting	£236- 1s-4d
Road maintenance	£500- 8s-6d
	£1,045-14s-2d

Since the road became a public highway in 1899, the Council also incurred some costs. In November 1899, the Works Committee accepted the tender of £11-18-0 from Mr. Hollamby for the supply of 68 lime trees for Warwick Park. One wonders how many of them, if any, survive to this day.

The Abergavenny accounts also record other related expenditure such as:

£3-9s-9d in 1902 for 'Cake for sheep', who were obviously grazing on the undeveloped plots;
£29-17s-6d in 1907 for a half-share of the cost of repairs to the railway bridge;
and £6-10s-6d in 1908 for repainting the Noticeboards.

CHAPTER 9

THE COST AND PROGRESS OF DEVELOPING THE HOME FARM ESTATE

The cost of developing the Home Farm Estate kept reducing over time, partly because the original estimates proved, as all sensible estimates do, to be at the same time, both cautious and excessive; and partly because the Marquess (or his Agent) seems to have kept a relatively tight rein on what, in the end, was done. His attitude is summed up in a hand-written letter from him at Nevill Court to Macbean sometime in 1896. Unfortunately, the day and month cannot be deciphered, but he writes 'I fear that the expenditure in the Home Farm building site will be ruinous and I often wish that I had never embarked in it.'

But the cost was never what he feared. Originally, Henry Currey in June 1894 had estimated £75,000, but this was really a 'guesstimate'. When the detailed scheme paper was prepared for the Trustees in May 1896, the costs were estimated at about £35,000, which proved to be a considerable over-estimate:

Cost of:	1896 Estimate £	Actual Cost £
Bridge	2,600	1,500
Road No.1 (Warwick Park)	10,935	
Road No.2 (Rodmell Road)	1,620	
Road No.3 (Roedean Road)	2,000	15,049
Road No.4	2,825	
Road No.5	3,000	
Road No.6 (Blatchington Rd.)	1,042	
Sewer	150	150
Erection of Cottages	10,000	-
Diversion of Footpaths	100	100
Solicitors, Engineers, Surveyors	1,000	1,000
	35,272	17,799

However the Cottages – originally 20, then 18 – were never built, nor were Road Nos. 4 & 5, so this estimate can be reduced by £15,825 to £19,447. The actual cost was even less – some £17,799 – because further reductions were negotiated on the cost of the bridge and the roads.

But the total cost of the development of Warwick Park turned out to be slightly more expensive. The total cost was eventually some £25,000 – if the audited annual expenditures are accepted. The audited accounts show the following costs for the development of the Home Farm Estate for 1895 – 1908:

1895	£229-13s- 8d
1896	£167-19s- 1d
1897	£9,476-13s- 9d
1898	£8,075- 7s-11d
1899	£3,000- 0s- 0d
1900	£1,977- 9s- 9d
1901	£498- 4s- 6d
1902	£586- 2s- 4d
1903	£244- 8s- 6d
1904	£185- 6s- 3d
1905	£168-19s- 2d
1906	£158-16s- 7d
1907	£ 58- 8s- 0d
1908	£ 49- 9s- 4d
TOTAL	£24,876-17s- 6d

The cost of approximately £25,000 can be translated into some £1,250,000 at today's values, but there can be no doubt that the cost of the work, if done today, would have been considerably more.

The development of Warwick Park housing started in 1898, but it was a relatively slow and piecemeal development of a few houses or a single house at a time. Pelton's Directory for 1899 which calls the road Home Park Road, lists five houses which increased to ten by 1900 and sixteen by 1901 and the road was now called Warwick Park. By 1903, Kelly's Directory shows that there were 25 houses.

The 1901 Census confirms that there were sixteen occupied houses, but also that there were a further twelve houses not yet occupied, or at least not yet inhabited, and a further four under construction.

The sixteen houses recorded as occupied in the Census were lived in by five retired people – a hotel proprietor aged 47, a widow aged 65, a spinster aged 66, a retired gilder and shopkeeper aged 65, a retired Iron merchant aged 56 – and four 'living on their own means', the balance being a solicitor, a timber agent, a Head Master, an Organist, a Stockbroker, an insurance broker, a paper box manufacturer, and an insurance manager. Thirteen of the houses had servants – one had four, two had three, three had two, and seven had only one.

The south side of the road was the first to be developed and initially these houses were numbered sequentially 1, 2, 3, 4 and so on. But this had inherent problems, as did the initial naming of the spine road and its off-shoots as Warwick Park. (See Chapter 12 for a more detailed explanation.) However, by 1904, the issue of road-naming and numbering had been settled. As a result, Warwick Park was separated from its branch roads and the system of numbering in Warwick Park had been changed to the current even numbers on the south side and odd numbers on the north. It is interesting that in 1905, none of the north side had actually been numbered, possibly because only four houses had been built on the north side; and all of these were *above* what was subsequently called 'Blatchington Road'.

By 1904, the Burgess Rolls (of electors) showed that there were 30 residences in 'Warwick Park' with (according to the then electoral rules) a corresponding 30 electors. By 1910, the number of houses in Warwick Park had increased to 39. But the development was still essentially the south side and only five were on the north side, again all above Blatchington Road. Because development was relatively piecemeal, plots of land remained undeveloped for a long time, but allowance was made, not always accurately, for an appropriate house number. (For example, today the sites of Nos. 52 and 64 are separated only by the West Station railway cutting; there are only two houses between No. 41 and No. 53 and they are actually now in Blatchington Road; and Nos. 69 and 75 are next door to each other, with a somewhat idiosyncratic No. 69+ infilling between them.)

This study is essentially to do with the first major period of development up to 1914 – the first 20 years of the development of the Warwick Park Estate – when the First World War effectively halted development until the late 1920's/early 1930's.

But before this hiatus happened, it is now apparent in hindsight that the Warwick Park Estate, while not a failure, was not the success it was hoped to be. The reasons for this are several but what can now be seen fairly easily in hindsight, was not apparent at the time.

CHAPTER 10

THE BUILDERS OF WARWICK PARK

The Marquess and his Agent never had any intention of building the houses in the Warwick Park Estate. They had put in the infra-structure of the Estate – roads, a bridge, sewers, drains – according to a plan which they believed would optimise the land use in terms of numbers of plots, relative to the land area and the cost of installing that infra-structure, and the potential value. They now needed builders, whether speculative or commissioned, to put up the houses, and as soon as possible.

As they saw it, the Estate as defined by the January 1897 map and plan and still called the Home Farm Estate, was some 109 acres or 66 plots. Taking about 10% for roads and pavements meant an average of about $1^1/_2$ acres a plot, but they were not all of equal size. They were smaller towards the Pantiles and larger from Blatchington/Roedean Roads up to Forest Road. The Estate was essentially Portions I and II of Brackett's original survey of 1893 and consisted of all the Home Farm Estate

- from the Pantiles in the west up to Forest Road in the east;
- and from the Hastings railway cutting in the north, to the Frant Road in the south.

Their view of the proposed development in the 1890s was somewhat different from how current residents would view the Warwick Park Estate. We, living as we do *within* the Estate, are inclined to look from the centre outwards and would regard Forest Road, Birling Road and Frant Road as, at best, peripheral or even outside the Estate. But at the time of development, they looked at it from the outside in, and these roads were definitively part of the Estate – in fact, they constituted in linear terms about half of the boundaries of the Estate. So much so that eleven (one in six) of the 66 plots planned in January 1897 for the Estate would have *fronted* on to Forest, Birling or Frant Roads, and not on to Estate's other six planned roads.

It is relevant, even if not desperately interesting to the general reader, to record how many plots were originally planned in 1897 for each road and how many were actually developed before 1914 – in some cases more, because plots were sub-divided; in other cases, none – to show the difference.

	No. of plots (1897 plan)	No. of plots by 1914		
Current Road Name		Developed as planned	Sub-divided (No. of houses)	Not developed
Right-hand side				
Warwick Park				
to Rodmell Rd.	11	1	18	1
from Rodmell Rd. to Roedean Rd	7	1	10	3
from Roedean Rd. to Forest Rd.	6	0	3	5
Frant Road				
to Rodmell Rd.	4	4	–	–
Rodmell Road	1	1	–	–
Roedean Road	3	3	–	–
Sub-total	**26**	**10**	**28**	**9**
Left-hand side				
Warwick Park				
from Blatchington Rd. to Forest Rd.	13	2	2	10
Blatchington Rd.	14	8	13	1
Nevill Gate	6	1	0	5
Forest Road	2	2	2	0
Birling Road	5	5	5	0
Sub-total	**40**	**18**	**22**	**11**
Total	**66**	**28**	**50**	**20**

So by 1914, a total of 78 houses had been built on the 66 planned plots. But only 28 of them had been built on the plots as planned and 50 (essentially semi-detached) houses had been built on 18 plots which had been sub-divided into as many as four plots each, leaving 20 plots of the original plan still completely undeveloped.

This is a considerable change from what was envisaged only 17 years earlier in 1897. How and why did such a change occur?

We cannot be entirely sure since there is little documentary evidence, but we can make reasonable assumptions.

The Estate, at a notional 66 plots, was potentially up to that time the largest single development of its nature and character in the history of

Tunbridge Wells.[29] Previous developments of a similar nature had been smaller. The progenitor, Calverley Park, was originally only 24 houses; Calverley Park Crescent originally 17; Nevill Park only 11 and Hungershall Park the same; while Calverley Park Gardens, Lansdowne Road and Grove Hill Gardens were still only 20-30; and the somewhat later Broadwater Down was originally only about 30 houses.

There would seem to have been no question of the Estate being developed by one builder, since Tunbridge Wells did not have a builder capable of handling so many plots (or more importantly, of financing the development of so many on a speculative basis). It should be remembered that before the First World War, and even until after the Second, most houses were rented, not sold, and this was equally true of the better type of house. So a speculative builder renting his properties would not have the quick return on his investment which an immediate sale would provide, but rather would have limitations on further capital investment, as well as what we now call 'cash-flow' restrictions, spread over a much longer period.

There were also no national builders, as there are today, who could have handled the project in its entirety. Even the major London builders, such as Cubitt, John Johnson or Gibbs & Flew Ltd, would not have considered managing a development so far (35 miles) from London[30]. The development opportunities in London would have been still considerably more attractive than any Tunbridge Wells had to offer.

So the development of the Warwick Park Estate was to rest essentially with local builders.

At this point, it is relevant to make a distinction between the role of the developer and that of the builder. The developer took a risk. He chose the site; he bore the development cost; he selected *and paid* the builder; he marketed the property to renters or buyers, and if either of

---

[29] The only development in Tunbridge Wells which would have exceeded the size of Warwick Park was the Liptraps Park development of about 150 acres and 230 plots to the west of Pembury Road, which was planned by the financier, Francis Peek, and the architect, William Barnsley Hughes. It was to be a mixed housing development, ranging from small artisan houses near the new Southborough (High Brooms) railway station up to 7 acre plots, near to Sandhurst Park and Sandown Park. The development was proposed in 1893 and got under way mainly with the artisan houses, but the finance for it literally died when Francis Peek expired in 1899; and so it was never completed as planned.

[30] The 1864 Cheap Trains Act which created cheap travel for workers with the Workman's Ticket (for travel to work before 7am) was in any case designed to bring workers *into* London, and not take them *out*.

these were slow in coming forward, he could have a problem. Wise developers would plan early and seek to ensure that they had potential customers before the first sod of earth was turned. But this could not always be guaranteed, and there was always a risk.

Of course, some developers were also builders (or should one say that some builders were also developers), so the roles merged; and provided that both roles had sufficient capital to fund their part of the project, there was no problem. The Warwick Park Estate, as we shall see, was to have its share of both developers and developer-builders.

When the Warwick Park Estate was first offered for development, local developers/builders did not fall over themselves to acquire the sites. The map and plan was published in January 1897, but the first applications to the Borough Council for planning permission were not made until a year later – January 1898 – which hardly suggests that there was a rush. There had been a slight delay in completing the main (Warwick Park) road, but that should not have been a deterrent to *planning*.

When the planning applications started, the rate of applications was a diminishing flow, rather than an increasing cascade. There were a total of 18 houses in 1898 for which planning permission was sought; 15 in 1899; only 5 in 1900, 4 in 1901 and one in 1902; but the applications increased to 7 in 1903 but declined to one in 1904. So Warwick Park could not have been the success for which the Marquess had hoped and for which he had invested £25,000 for the infra-structure.

It must be admitted that there is some dissonance between different sets of records. Abergavenny records show some 78 houses 'on lease' in Warwick Park by 1914, while the Minutes of the Works Committee of the Borough Council (which officially approved all planning applications) show only 58 approvals. This may be due to some ambiguity in the Works Committee records – listing, for example, approval for four houses on 'the Home Farm Estate' without specifying the plot or partial-plot numbers which could lead to single-entry or multiple entry listing. But the diligent reader can judge for him/herself by studying Appendix 5.

It is also clear from what was built compared with what was intended, that the local developer/builders were determined men who were only willing to build what they thought would 'sell', or maybe more precisely what *they* thought that *they* could 'sell'. This is the only logical explanation for the sub-division of plots, with *semi*-detached houses being built on a sub-plot. They may well have been right. They may well have had a better feel for the market than the Marquess and his Agent. But equally, they may have had a better feel for *their* market, rather than the whole market. Whatever the explanation, and we shall never know, the local developer/builders carried the day and built what they wanted to offer.

It is difficult to judge why the Marquess was not more emphatic – after all, it was his land and his infrastructure, he was extremely powerful locally and right or wrong, he was used to having his own way. So why was he not more insistent in laying down what was expected?

The straight answer is that we do not know. We can only infer that there may not have been much enthusiasm among the local developer/builders for his concept and since he had invested quite a lot of money by any standard, he was keen to recover it; and therefore he gave way to what they felt were suitably 'commercial' pressures. There may well have been other factors, such as his age, the premature death of his Agent, George Macbean, and the ever-approaching prospect of vastly increased royalties from Welsh mining and iron-making when the loan had been repaid.

But the outcome is clear. Warwick Park was not a coherent or comprehensive development and this was primarily due to local developer/builders developing it piecemeal, to meet their own interests, their own timescale and their own priorities.

Who were these developer/builders? Leaving aside a number of individuals who had their houses designed by their own architect, there were eight developers who built more than one house on the Estate before 1914:

Estimated No. developed before 1914 by:

Henry Vaux Wild	18
L.S.Beale & Sons	18
W.S. Putland	9
S.E. Haward	3
H.Dear	3
Carlos Crisford	2
E.Drewitt	2
Thomas Bates*	2 *(but he built 9 & designed 7)
Total	57

The details of the specific houses built by the developers/builders, as well as the seven individuals, will be found in Appendix 6.

Despite the fact that Henry Vaux Wild actually built the same number of houses on the Warwick Park Estate as Louis Beale before 1914, there can be no question that Louis Beale was the more important developer.

Louis Beale (1853 – 1939) was responsible for the development of a number of estates in Tunbridge Wells – Linden Park Road, Mount Ephraim Mansions, Kingswood Road and Madeira Park. He would seem to have been a good salesman – his advertising for Madeira Park claimed somewhat optimistically that it was 'about three minutes from the Pantiles and the South Eastern Railway Station'. Obviously, the Victorians walked very much faster than we do today.

It may be that his involvement with, and commitment to Madeira Park which he started to develop in 1893, may have reduced his ability to take a full part in the development of the Warwick Park Estate.

Louis Beale with his eldest sons, Louis (left) and Bertram (right)

The difference between the proposed and the actual development of Madeira Park does suggest that Beale had a strong tendency to try to cram as many houses on as little space as possible. The original plan for Madeira Park (printed by Beale) showed 74 plots, helped by having a (never-built) connecting road between the east and west sides of the broadly-square development, and also by having a plot reserved, and actually used, for a connection with what was later Rodmell Road. But in the end, only 60 houses were ever built in Madeira Park which indicates that other events, or opinions, must have prevailed.

Planning permission for the development of Madeira Park was given on 14th April 1893. It would seem that this was a financial venture initiated by Louis Beale and probably funded by him as well. This puts his investment nearly on a par with that put up by the Marquess for the development of the Home Farm Estate. It is true that the development of the Home Farm Estate was for a larger acreage and that meant greater road building costs, but the returns should have been higher for the Marquess since more expensive houses would generate and justify higher Ground Rents. In the end, Madeira Park was developed with some 60 detached houses while the Home Farm Estate with ten times the acreage, achieved less than 80 developments before 1914.

The first house in Madeira Park (No.5) was given planning permission on 14th September 1894 and in the following fourteen years some 39 houses were built, of which Beale was responsible for the vast majority – some 35. This is not a particularly high building rate – an average of only about three a year – and this no doubt reflects the level of demand as well as capital investment considerations.

The house-building market in his day was essentially a rental rather than a purchase market, so cash-flow was much slower and it took much longer to get your capital investment back then, than is the case today. It raises the question of how did Louis Beale who left school at 14 to work for his father, a carpenter, manage to build so many houses? Who provided his capital (at least initially)? A friendly bank? (William Henry Delves [1829-1922], who was Mayor in 1900 and a leading light in Tunbridge Wells business, was among many things a banker. Was he a friend of Louis, or his mentor or benefactor?) Other friends? His father? His wife or her family? A silent business partner?

Louis Beale's descendants are not sure of the answer or answers, but they can supply certain clues. Louis was an excellent planner and organiser and clearly had enormous drive and self-confidence, characteristics which the family believe came more from his mother than his father. His father was nonetheless a competent and hard-working tradesman who developed, with Louis's help, a successful general building company and who left £5,638 when he died in 1888 at the age of 69. That was no doubt useful capital for the company, but what may have been more useful was Louis's lifelong and very active membership of no less than five Masonic Lodges. Certainly the Marquess of Abergavenny was a member of one of those lodges and this no doubt gave Louis a certain commercial advantage in Tunbridge Wells. According to his descendants, he was also Secretary of the Knights Templar Lodge, of which the Earl of Harewood, the husband of the Princess Royal, was Master.

Louis was also very shrewd and hard-headed and in those days of lower interest rates, borrowed money at 1% or even $1/2$%, against his existing developments in order to finance further developments. Since annual rents were conventionally set at 5-8% of original cost, an interest rate of 1% was not too punitive. Family legend has it that he built over 100 public houses for brewers in Kent and Sussex and this would have been an additional source of working capital since, while the brewers may have negotiated a keen price, Louis would have been paid in stages and on completion and so he did not have to wait for a return on his capital, as he would with rented residential property. He was also very demanding – family legend has it that he would not take on a bricklayer unless he could regularly lay 2000 bricks a day (i.e. 250 bricks an hour, or 4 a minute, spread over an eight hour working day). And on top of all that, he was a shrewd salesman. Again, family legend tells of him showing a Midlands manufacturer and his wife one of his new houses in Kingswood Road, for which he intended to ask £12,000. However, he overheard the wife whispering to her husband "I do like this. We must have it", so when the man asked the price, Louis immediately said £16,000 – and got it.

Madeira Park was not declared a Public Highway (i.e. responsibility for its upkeep being taken over by the Council) until March 1902. By comparison, Warwick Park which started 3-4 years later and was much less developed at the time with housing, had been declared a Public Highway in June 1899. This clearly reflects the very much greater ability of the Marquess to inject capital into a development.

Beale was to build 14 houses in Warwick Park in the seven years 1898-1904. With one exception, Plot 20 (now The Homestead) which is adjacent to Madeira Park, all the houses were on the southern side between Rodmell Road and Nevill Street and most (8) were semi-detached houses on sub-divided plots. Beale probably chose to build on these sites because of their proximity to Madeira Park and also because they were the most 'sellable' because of their proximity to the Pantiles.

Beale houses in Warwick Park

But there is clear evidence from the lease which Beale signed with the Marquess in September 1898 that he went along with the Marquess on the surface, but in reality he had other views. The lease was for eight plots – Nos. 3–10 – on the southern side between Rodmell Road and

Nevill Street. The lease was for 99 years starting 29th September 1898 and specified a nominal peppercorn ground rent for all eight plots for the first year, followed by an annual ground rent of £165 for the remainder. However, if four or more of the *plots* were undeveloped in any one of the initial five years, then the ground rent was halved to £82-10-0.

Beale shrewdly exploited this. It is clear from the fact that over time he actually developed the eight plots into 15 houses, that he had a different perception from the Marquess of what he wanted to develop, or thought would 'sell'; and it is surprising that the Marquess or his agent did not object. But Beale also chose to stretch out the development over time, without doubt to his own commercial advantage. In the first five years, only $2^1/_2$ plots were developed, although five houses were built, so he paid only half the ground rent. A further three houses were built on $1^1/_2$ plots in the marginal fifth year, so it is probable that he got away with half the ground rent for another year. (It hardly needs to be said that he was never out of pocket – the ground rents he charged to the tenants of his sub-divided plots, covered his liability to the Marquess, whether whole or half.)

After 1903, Beale seems to have stopped further development in Madeira Park and reduced it substantially in Warwick Park.

The reason for this is unknown – he may have had 'cash-flow' problems, but equally he may have been developing fresher pastures. It may also have been due to the growth of population in Tunbridge Wells slackening considerably at the turn of the century.

There were two further Beale developments in Warwick Park in 1904 and 1907, and then no less than four in 1909. It is of interest to note, although it is difficult to interpret the fact, that five of the fifteen sub-leases in Warwick Park were granted to Beale children – on plots 10a and 10b on 17th July 1903, to Bertram Saxon Beale (later Capt. Bertram Beale MC, Managing Director of Beale & Sons); on plot 8b on 17th July 1903 to Louis Bernhardt G. S. Beale (later Sir Louis Beale); on plot 6a to Miss Daisee (sic) Beatrice Beale and plot 9b to Miss Elsie Olive Beale, both on 24th December 1909 – surely a Christmas present from their father. The fact that Louis Beale was to retire in 1910 should also not be overlooked.

Beale & Sons Ltd remained in business until the Second World War and in particular were responsible for the construction of a further nine houses in Warwick Park (Nos. 94-112, but not No. 100) between 1927-1934. (See Chapter 14 for a more detailed explanation.)

Henry Vaux Wild (1838-1926) who was to build 16 houses in Warwick Park between 1898 and 1910, also concentrated his developments in a specific area of Warwick Park – essentially what came to be called Blatchington Road from 1904. He was also responsible for three houses which face onto Warwick Park – Park House (Plot 40F, originally 51 Warwick Park but now 2 Blatchington Road and in 1913, the home of the Mayor for that year, Cllr. James Silcock JP) and the adjacent Nos. 53 (Plot 40F and originally called 'St.Agnes') and 55 (Plot 41A and originally called 'Charlwood'), Warwick Park.

Wild was a developer and not a builder. He employed an architect to design and a builder to build. For example, in the case of No. 53 and No. 55, which were both built in 1900, his architect was W. Elliot of Folkestone and his builder was Thomas Bates of Nevill Terrace, Tunbridge Wells. These were substantial houses, originally built with eight bedrooms but only one bathroom, which was normal by the standards of those days, and one with a library and the other with a study, besides the usual living rooms. Both became residential-care homes after the Second World, although one (No. 53) has recently been converted into six flats.

Wild took the only extant photographs of the Home Farm and the New Road on 2nd. January 1899. Why he did so, when his prime interest was in what is now Blatchington Road, can be explained by the fact that in the coming year, he was to develop for his client, Mr. E.J.Carter, the site which became Cliff House or No. 67 Warwick Park. From the Abergavenny Archive, it would seem that Wild was seen as slightly sharp or pushy as a developer (which some may think is no different from the norm today). There are a number of references to him in the Archive which imply some dislike, if not distrust, as well as references to not paying Ground Rent on time, and not being allowed commissions.

No. 67 Warwick Park

Henry Wild had moved in 1897 from the modest 3 Norfolk Road to the much grander 'Kinnellar', 4 Eden Road, which virtually overlooked the sites he was subsequently to develop in Blatchington Road. His career as a developer is slightly puzzling and somewhat short-term. He first appears at the very beginning, just weeks after Haward and Beale, in April 1898 and was very active, particularly in what was to become Blatchington Road, until 1904. He then switched his attention much further north to Stephen's Road, where he was to develop 24 houses (Nos. 84-122, plus another 5) between 1904 and 1906. But he returned again to Blatchington Road, in 1906 and 1910; and after that, there is no record of his involvement in the Warwick Park Estate. He was to live another 16 years, dying at 21, Madeira Park on Boxing Day,1926 at the age of 88.

What is the explanation? The most obvious is simply old age – by 1910 he was aged 72. Even when he started to develop what was to become Blatchington Road, he was already 60. But it could also have been that having built so many houses, his capital was depleted or over-extended as far as further building development was concerned, or that 'sales' had not been sufficiently encouraging to justify further building development.

But there are certain puzzling considerations about Wild's business relationship with Thomas Bates, which suggest that Wild was almost certainly instrumental in helping Thomas Bates to set up on his own.

Thomas Bates (1864-1930).
There is some confusion about Bates's role as a developer and builder. Clearly he could have been no more than a builder at first, with his mentor Henry Wild providing him with the work. But this seems to have changed fairly rapidly. He appears to have developed only two sites before 1914, although he did design seven and build nine houses on the Estate in that time.

While he started as a builder, building what were generally the larger houses on the Estate for others, he subsequently became a developer as well as a builder. The fact that his name appears only twice before 1914 on the planning applications, does suggest that up till then, he was essentially a builder of other people's houses. He was certainly the builder for Henry Wild in the late 1890's and up to 1901. He built Cliff House (Plot 43) in 1901, and in 1903-4, he was responsible for building 'Standish House' in Roedean Road (Plot 26A) for Henry Dear; and in 1909 he built 'Tarquin' in Roedean Road (Plot 25) reputedly for his own

Standish House

use, but he never occupied it.

Interestingly, in view of the fact that he tended to build the larger houses, he does not seem to have used an outside architect for his designs. While he was building for other developers, the architect would have been chosen by the developer. But fairly early on, from about 1903 until at least 1913, Bates's plans carry the name L. Towner as architect, with the working address of 6 Nevill Terrace, which clearly suggests that Towner was Bates's in-house architect.

In fact Leonard Benjamin Towner, born in Hastings in 1882, was Thomas Bates's nephew, from his wife's side of the family. The fact that he was at the age of only about 21 ostensibly responsible for the architectural plans, might raise an eyebrow (or two) these days. The implications of this are discussed later in the next chapter on the architects of the Warwick Park Estate.

Thomas Bates retired through ill health in 1927 and died in 1930, leaving an estate of £10,969-8s-9d, a slightly higher amount than his mentor/partner/colleague Henry Vaux Wild did in 1926. In the 1920's, his business employed over 200 men and it passed to his three sons on his retirement. They continued the development of the company, with 1934 being a particularly successful year, in which they built the 'Courier' offices in Grove Hill Road (now demolished), the Ritz cinema (subsequently the ABC cinema, but closed in 2000) opposite the Town Hall, and were responsible for the widening of Forest Road. They continued the business until the retirement of the youngest of them in 1966.

W.S. Putland was the son of Alderman Putland who was a 'founding father' of the Borough of Tunbridge Wells. He lived initially at 34 High Street and subsequently at 42 Grove Hill Road. He used his neighbour at 34 High Street, James G.D. Armstrong, as his architect in 1899 for his first six houses – the semi-detached houses, Nos.64-70 and 76-78 Warwick Park and Strange & Sons as his builders. However by the time he had moved to Grove Hill Road, he had switched to Thomas Bates as both his architect and builder for the somewhat larger (detached) Nos. 80 and 82 Warwick Park, which were built in 1902 and the much larger Warwick Ridge (now 148 Forest Road) which was built in 1904.

S. Edwin Haward may well have intended to become a developer, and was indeed the first to put in a Planning Application for Warwick Park in January 1898. But his involvement did not go beyond 1898 and this may have been due to the pressures of his other business – S.E.Haward & Co.Ltd[31], the ironmongers, which was actually only incorporated in 1897, although founded some 32 years earlier. Or it could have been that he realised that property development was deep water and not suited to his temperament, since he may have been deterred by the law suit which involved him with Miss Sarah Prior and the Marquess of Abergavenny.

Nos. 68–70 Warwick Park

Haward was clearly an entrepreneur, rather than a property developer, and was responsible for building only three houses (one detached, two semi-detached) in Warwick Park. Building houses was intended to be a profitable business diversification, but he may well have rued the day that he did so.

One of the houses he built – The Pines, Plot 11b, or subsequently The Laurels, or No.40 – was to lead to the only known property law case in Warwick Park.

Nos. 38–40 Warwick Park (No. 40 on the left).

---

[31] The limited company S.E.Haward & Co.,Ltd was set up in 1897 with a capital of £17,000 which was increased in 1899 to £23,000. Balance Sheet assets in 1899 before the increase in capital were estimated at £23,743 and a profit of £2,148-4s-4d declared, with a dividend of 8%. Indicative of the small world which was Tunbridge Wells, was that the Chairman of the Company was Alderman W.H. Delves and the Company solicitors were Cripps, Son & Daish, at whose offices the AGM was held. Haward's shop survived until recently in Goods Station Road, and continues as part of Sandall Perkins.

Before the house was actually built, Haward entered into a lease on 17th September 1898 with Miss Sara Prior of Primrose Bank, Crowborough at a rent of £60 per year. It is not clear whether Sara Prior had made her intentions known, but she intended to sub-let to boarders and/or tenants and consequently "she exhibited (in her front window) placards containing the words 'Apartments To Let'."

This was quite unacceptable to the Marquess and to the intended nature and style of the Warwick Park Estate. The lease between the Marquess and Haward specifically forbade the carrying-on of any trade or business and consequently the Marquess issued a writ on 23rd March 1900 against Haward and Prior, restraining both or either 'from using the house or permitting to be used … for the business of a lodging-house keeper, or in any other manner than as a private house'.

It is likely that Haward was careless or ignorant of the niceties of sub-leasing; and he was swift to be co-operative. Miss Prior was much less so, and she seems to have had a genius for prevarication. Initially she 'had the 'flu'; then she had fallen over the balustrading; then she was considering taking a house at Southborough which would cost £70 a year 'which frightened her'; and finally she demanded £200 'on the advice of her nephew and his solicitor and Mr. Hughes QC, a friend of the family' in compensation.

This led to Haward issuing a summons on 11th June 1900 against Prior 'for failing to concur'. Prior's defence was that she 'did not accept that Warwick Park was laid out as a building scheme or that houses erected thereon could only be used as private residences'. It is amazing that in settling this 'storm in a teacup' no less than 81 documents were submitted to the Court. Needless to say, the Marquess won his case.

· Front · Elevation ·
Nos. 72–74 Warwick Park

Carlos Crisford was born in 1845 in Brede, Sussex, the eight child of a builder. His parents, James and Eliza, were undisputedly English and his Spanish Christian name is no doubt due to his parents' liking for slightly exotic names – his male siblings included Frederic *(sic)*, Amos and Caleb. By 1881, his elder brother, Amos, was living in Eastbourne and is listed as an Architect. Carlos was also living separately in Eastbourne, with his widowed mother and unmarried brother and sister, and is listed as an Architect's Assistant. But by 1891, he is an Architect and Surveyor. He only built two houses – the charming Nos. 72-74 – in Warwick Park. One can only surmise that the reasons why he did not build other houses there – maybe his capital was limited, maybe he considered the opportunities in Eastbourne better, or maybe the practical considerations in 1899 of organising a development from a distance of 30 miles were too daunting.

There is also evidence to suggest that the last two developers – Dear and Drewitt – were not builders/developers as such, but individuals who thought that owning more than one house was a good investment.

Henry Dear, who lived at Ventnor, Blatchington Road, only developed three houses – Standish House in Roedean Road and two adjoining sites, Nos. 84 and 86 Warwick Park. He used Thomas Bates as his builder and architect.

Edwin Drewitt also only developed three houses, all of them side-by-side in Blatchington Road. He was to be particularly upset when the spur in Warwick Park in which his three houses lay, was suddenly renamed Blatchington Road (for very good and practical reasons). He led the short-term and unsuccessful opposition to the change of name. (See Chapter 12 for more details.)

There were also at least nine individuals who had houses built for themselves. This brings the total to only 66. The explanation of the discrepancy between this and the Abergavenny record of 78 in 1914 has been given earlier in this chapter.

All these developers took their own 'patches' for development – for example, Beale at the lower reaches of Warwick Park, close to Madeira Park, but with houses which were one step down (in terms of size and price) from the houses he was offering in Madeira Park, an early example of astute market segmentation; Wild almost exclusively in what became Blatchington Road, offering a cross-section of semi- and detached houses; and Bates, as a comparative late developer, having to take sites where he found them in Warwick Park, Blatchington Road, Upper Cumberland Walk and subsequently Nevill Gate, but always concentrating on larger, more expensive properties. The table below provides the geographical division of the Estate by its principal developers:

Geographical Division of the Estate by principal Developers

	Beale	Wild	Putland	Bates	Other	Total
Warwick Park	27	1	9	4	16	54
Blatchington Rd.	–	17	–	4	3	21
U.Cumberland Walk	–	–	–	5	–	5
Rodmell Road	–	–	–	–	–	–
Roedean Road –	–	–	2	–	2	
Nevill Gate	2	–	–	2	2	6
Birling Road	2	–	–	–	3	5
TOTAL	31	18	9	17	24	99
Madeira Park	37	–	–	–	3	40

It is also relevant to record the changing level of involvement over time. All the original developers had dropped out by 1940. Beale was the principal developer and survived up till 1940. Bates was a late starter but came through strongly between 1915-1940. Wild was a strong player until 1910, but vanished totally thereafter. And the same was true for Putland. The following table illustrates the involvement by the major developers over time:

Warwick Park Estate – No. of houses by Developer

Developer	Pre-1915	1915-1939	Post 1939	Total
Beale	18	13	–	31
Wild	18	–	–	18
Bates	6	9	–	15
Putland	9	–	–	9
TOTAL	51	22	–	73

CHAPTER 11

THE ARCHITECTS OF WARWICK PARK

The developers and builders of Warwick Park have been discussed in some detail, but it is of course the 'architects' who created the style of Warwick Park as we know it, although they would have been under some constraint by the developers as to size of plot, size and type of house, and cost.

It is therefore sad that Warwick Park did not have, as did Calverley Park, a Decimus Burton as its architect, or even a single *dominant* architect.

The Warwick Park Estate, reflecting not only the fragmented nature of its development but also the extended period of development over 80 or more years, has had no less than 46 identifiable architects, of whom over half (24) designed only one house.

Some of those 46 architects were not qualified architects as we would know them today. At the turn of the 20th century, the professional status and qualifications of the architect had not yet been fully established. Indeed it was not until the Architectural Registration Act of 1938 that the use of the title 'Architect' was restricted by law to those who had qualified by examination.

Before then, the Royal Institute of British Architects (RIBA) had succeeded in restricting its *new* membership from 1929 to those who had qualified by examination, but it had had to allow those who were practising before 1929 to be Licentiate members (LRIBA) and until the 1938 Act, it was open to anybody to call him/herself an 'Architect' if they so wished.

The late 19th and early 20th centuries were a period of flux in architecture. A major issue which raged was whether architecture was an art or a science; and the definitions or requirements as to knowledge, expertise, experience and/or qualifications were not as strict or as clearly defined as they are today. At that time, it would seem that the surveyor who today is not an *integral* member of an architectural practice, although his expertise is a fundamental and original input, was in a stronger position than he is today, since he appears to have been responsible for all the technical detail of a building (including technical specifications and drawings), while the architect was responsible for the more strategic and aesthetic considerations such as siting, layout, architectural style and appearance, and was less involved in technical detail than he is today.

The architect today has now taken over many of the technical aspects as well, and the surveyor has relatively lost out. There is no doubt that the Royal Institute of British Architects (founded as the Institute of British Architects in 1834 and allowed to call itself Royal in 1866) is in a stronger position today than it was then.

The 'architects' of the Warwick Park Estate are, it must be confessed, 'a mixed bag'. Some had formal qualifications; others had none. Some were qualified architects; others were qualified surveyors (even for individual houses built in the 1960's and 1970's); others were neither.

The 24 'architects' who designed more than one house on the Estate, were:

WARWICK PARK ESTATE – ARCHITECTS

ARCHITECT	NO. OF HOUSES	SPECIFIC HOUSES
Pre-1915		
William Elliot	12	Nos.1-9, 2-4 & 21-23 Blatchington Rd Nos. 53, 55, 67 Warwick Park
Leonard Towner	16	Nos.11-15, 6-8 & 16-18 Blatchington Rd. 'The Homestead', 'Ardmore' & 'Melrose', Upper Cumberland Walk; Nos. 84-88 Warwick Park; 'Standish House '& 'Tarquin', Roedean Road; 'Warwick Ridge' nka 148 Forest Rd
Beale & Sons	15	Nos.8-36, 48, Warwick Park
James G.D.Armstrong	6	Nos.64-70, 76-78 Warwick Park
Thos. Bates	4	Nos. 80, 82 Warwick Park; Nos. 17, 19 Blatchington Rd.
G.H.Strange	3	Nos.38-40, Warwick Park + Nevill Ground Cricket Pavilion
Carlos Crisford	2	Nos. 72-74 Warwick Park
W. Harold Hillyer	1	'Court Lees' No.69, Warwick Park
Stanley Philpot,LRIBA	1	King Charles Church Hall
W. Barnsley Hughes	1	No.1 Warwick Park – Offices/Warehouse
Other 'single architect' houses	10	
Sub-Total	**69**	

1920-1939

Thos. Bates	12	Nos. 10-14 Blatchington Rd.; Nos. 4, 57, 59, 67a Warwick Park; 'Byways','Chimneys' & 'Birchmead', Nevill Gate; 'Tidebrook' nka 'Willow Bank', 'Cumberland Cottage', Upper Cumberland Walk.
Beale & Sons	13	Nos.83-85, 90-98 ,102-112 Warwick Park; No.2 & 'Nevill House', Nevill Gate.
Stanley Philpot, LRIBA	1	Brookside' (No.35) and part No.69, Warwick Park
Other 'single architect' houses	3	
Sub-Total	**29**	

Post-1945

Countryside Properties	23	All in Richmond Place
Henry Osborne Associates	13	Nos.13-29 Warwick Park & Nos.1-4 Oak Tree Close
Philip Beauchamp ARIBA	5	'Russets',RandomTiles 'nka , 'Highview', 'Hillbrow', 'Pinewood', Roedean Rd; No. 100 Warwick Park
Trevor L. Banks	4	'Five Oaks', 'Willow Lodge', 'Springbank', 'South Riding', Rodmell Road and Upper Cumberland Walk
T.C.Gibbons,LRIBA	3	'Southwinds' and Nos. 2 & 3, The Drive
R.& A.Bates, RIBA	2	Nos.2 & 6 Warwick Park
Cecil Burns & Guthrie	2	No.116, Warwick Park and 'Blaven', Roedean Road
John J. Cardwell	2	Nos. 61 & 63, Warwick Park
Basil Fountain, AIAS	2	No.65, Warwick Park & Bhadreswar, Rodmell Road
Mayall, Webb & Hart	2	'Hillside' & 'Phoenix', Roedean Road
Otford Design	2	Nos.44 & 44a Warwick Park
R.A.Buckingham	2	'Fulbeck' & 'Woodentops' nka Greenways, Upper Cumberland Walk
RB Consultants	2	'Edgewater' & 'Tumblewood', Rodmell Road
D.P.Winter, AIAS	2	Nos.85a &85b Warwick Park
Other'single architect' houses	9	
Sub-Total	**70**	

TOTAL ARCHITECTS	**46**
TOTAL HOUSES/BUILDINGS	**167**

Numerically, the most prolific 'architect' in Warwick Park was Thomas Bates's architect, **Leonard Benjamin Towner** (1882-1963), who was also his nephew. Towner submitted his first designs under his own name for approval by the Council in 1903 when he was barely 21. However we should not be misled into thinking that we have a genius in our midst. Certainly the controls and the required qualifications at that time were such that a 21 year-old could have submitted designs, but the designs submitted by Towner throughout his known career in Tunbridge Wells (1901 – 1913) were not original – they were variants of designs submitted by his predecessor, **William Elliot**, who was Henry Wild's architect between 1898 and 1901.

William Elliot and Leonard Towner run a very close race as to who designed the most houses. Technically, Leonard Towner wins with 16 applications against only 12 for Elliot. But since he was copying and varying Elliot's original designs, we have no choice but to give the laureateship to Elliot as the man who created the style of the Warwick Park Estate.

No. 86 Warwick Park

What do we know about Elliot? The short answer is virtually nothing. We do know that when he submitted his first designs in 1898, he lived at 57 Ovington St, London SW, but by January 1899 he had moved to 33, St. John's Street, Folkestone and that by 1900 he had moved again to 63, Brockman Road, Folkestone. Neither of these two addresses are where you would expect an architect to live and there is no record of him at either in the 1901 Census. We also know that he is not listed with the R.I.B.A. But we do not know his qualifications (although they were less relevant then as now); we do not know any of his other work; we know nothing about him as an individual. What we can infer is that he was a perfectly competent architect (whether he was qualified or not); he may have chosen after a while not to continue working on developments in Tunbridge Wells because of the problems of travel; or he may have died, but there is no matching record of his death in 1900 or 1901. It is more probable that he may have been caught out in the classic individual architect's dilemma – that when you have produced sufficient designs and variants of those designs, so that they can be duplicated with minor variations by a less expensive 'architect', your services are no longer needed.

Certainly Elliot was employed by Wild as the developer and with Bates as the builder, and he worked for them from 1898-1901 on some 12 houses, by which time he had established the style for what would become Blatchington Road, and also had had a major influence on the upper part of Warwick Park with the designs for 53, 55, and 67 Warwick Park and with designs which could also be transferred into Roedean Road.

1 Blatchington Road

It is pertinent to note that there was a hiatus in the named architect around 1901-3. The last time Elliot was named in a planning application was in January 1901; then followed an interval when the architect was declared as 'Thomas Bates & Co.', and Towner first appeared (at least officially) in July 1903 when he was all of 21.

However the style which Elliot created and which Towner continued, was not unique – it was derivative of many other middle-class houses of the period and this is a not unreasonable judgement to make, since middle class housing cannot usually afford to be original or unique. In broad terms, it can be called part 'Jacobethan'/part Arts and Crafts style, and this style, which was common at the time, was also the inspiration of most of the Beale houses in the pre-1915 period. Elliot's work can be recognised in Warwick Park by its square turrets (e.g. No.1 Blatchington Road, No.86 Warwick Park) and by its consistent style, whether detached or semi-detached.

51 & 53 Warwick Park
(51, now 2 Blatchington Road).

The second leading 'architect' after Elliot/Towner has regrettably to be **'Beale & Sons'**. This is *not* a comment on the quality of the architecture, but rather regret that we cannot identify an *individual* contribution in the design of Beale houses, either pre-1915 or from 1920-1939. It is possible that Louis Beale himself may have had something to do with the designs before 1900 since, according to family legend, when Louis left school at the age of 14, he attended Technical School at night and gained a teacher's certificate for drawing, plans and perspective, but we do not know for sure.

It is not surprising when the role and status of the architect was still in the process of definition, that those people involved in making things happen i.e. the builders, should offer design services as well. The name(s) of the Beale architects for some 28 houses built over a period of some 40 years are unknown. Only once did a Beale planning application go forward with the name of the architect identified – a certain L.S. Hatchard. It was for what became No.112 which was the first of the Beale developments in Warwick Park after the First World War. The plans were approved by the Council on 18th November 1927, but they were never built. Beale & Sons quickly submitted a *virtually identical* design with Beale & Sons listed as the architect; and this alternative was also approved by the Council and was built instead.

The third architect in terms of numbers of houses is very recent and is also corporate, namely **Countryside Residential**, which built 28 dwellings in what is now Richmond Place in 1998-2000. Most of these are in pastiche Regency or Kent/Sussex Weald styles and most are detached.

The fourth architect in numerical terms was **Henry Osborne Associates** of London who designed for the builders, Brickland Houses Ltd (also of London), in the mid-1960's. Their first development was in 1964 for the four bungalows in Oak Tree Close which was carved out of the garden of Oak Cottage – No. 41 Warwick Park. Their second development (and their last in the Warwick Park Estate) was in 1966-68 when they designed nine chalet houses, Nos. 13-29 Warwick Park, on the land which had been originally designated for the Ornamental Garden, with two lakes, waterfalls and a Band Stand, and which had been subsequently used for animal grazing and allotments. (See Chapter 14 for more detail.)

There were a number of other architects who are of interest:

Carlos Crisford was both a developer and his own architect, and may well have used his own brother who is described in Census returns as a builder. Since he came from Eastbourne, he may have believed the initial intention of Warwick Park to emulate the social success of Eastbourne, but after building two charming semi-detached houses (Nos. 72-74), he did not carry on. His background has already been described in Chapter 10.

James Armstrong was the original architect for the developer W.S. Putland. He designed six identical but very pleasant semi-detached houses (Nos. 64-70 and 76-78 Warwick Park). However it seems likely that despite his talent, he lost out to financial or other considerations since Putland who had used Bates to build Armstrong's designs, subsequently changed to Bates to *design* and build the next-door houses (Nos. 80 and 82 Warwick Park).

No. 42 Warwick Park

C.H. Strange, ARIBA was an architect whose family business was Strange & Sons Ltd., the Tunbridge Wells builders. He designed and they built two semi-detached 'villas', Nos. 38-40 Warwick Park, for the ironmonger S.Edwin Haward, but interestingly Haward did not use him for the larger detached house, No. 42, which was built subsequently next door. G. H. Strange became a Borough Councillor. The only other building attributed to him on the Warwick Park Estate is the Cricket Pavilion in the Nevill Ground, designed and built in record time (some 12 weeks) to replace the one burnt down in 1913, ostensibly by 'Suffragettes'.

C. H. Strange, ARIBA

Harold Hillyer only designed one house in Warwick Park – No.69, Court Lees – which is the only Neo-Georgian house in Warwick Park and is a close but smaller copy of Edwin Lutyens' Middlefield in Great Shelford, Cambridgeshire. Before designing Court Lees, which is believed to have been his first independent commission, Hillyer worked with Sir Astin Webb, the leading Edwardian architect, on the design of the façade of Buckingham Palace in 1908, the Admiralty Arch in 1908, and the Victoria & Albert Museum in 1906. He was killed in 1916 during the First World War, having been the Royal Engineer officer in charge of the mining of Hill 60 at Ypres in April 1915, which was the first 'mine' to be exploded in the First World War, and for which he received the Military Cross.

Capt. Harold Hillyer, RE, MC

69 Warwick Park – in the mid-1920s

King Charles the Martyr Church Hall

Stanley Philpot, LRIBA, was an architect with offices in the High Street, who lived at No.12 Warwick Park from 1913-26 and subsequently at No.69. Just before the First World War, he was responsible for the design of the King Charles the Martyr Church Hall at the bottom of Warwick Park, which is solid, practical but stylish in a discreet and muted way. In 1922, he designed 'Brookside' (No. 35 Warwick Park) a large detached and handsome house in the Kentish Weald style, whose large garden was subsequently sold off in the 1980's for development. No other work by him is known in Warwick Park, apart from some fairly substantial alterations which he made to 'Court Lees' (No. 69) in 1928-9.

No. 1 Warwick Park

Head of Bacchus

W. Barnsley Hughes was a prolific architect in Tunbridge Wells, being responsible for the Molyneux Park Estate c.1890, the Friendly Societies' Hall in Camden Road with its splendid Camden Elephants entablature, and the magnificent stable-block built for Sir David Salomons at Broomhill. In the early 1890's, he also designed the Liptraps Park Estate and his 'busyness' with this, potentially Tunbridge Well's largest development, is no doubt why he was responsible for only one building in Warwick Park, the offices and warehouse at No.1 for the wine merchants, E. Robins & Sons Ltd. It is a handsome building with an amusingly appropriate keystone of Bacchus over the main window.

Philip Beauchamp, ARIBA, was an architect who practised in a number of partnerships – Branson & Beauchamp in the 1950's, Beauchamp & Addey in the 1960's – and was particularly responsible for some four detached houses (Russets, and Random Tiles in 1950, Hillbrow and Pinewood in 1964) in Roedean Road and also for 100 Warwick Park in 1955.

An architect who deserves particular mention is **Michael Winter, RIBA**. He has built only one house on the Warwick Park Estate – for his wife and himself – in 1995, but The Boundary House in Upper Cumberland Walk has a mould-breaking, award-winning design which has been widely praised. It is without doubt the most original house, not only in Warwick Park, but also probably in Tunbridge Wells as well.

Only 12 of the 45 architects of Warwick Park have been described in any detail in this Chapter. Lack of any mention should not necessarily be taken as criticism. It is simply that not enough is known – who they were, what were their qualifications, was the design early or late work, what other buildings have they done – to make any meaningful comment.

The Boundary House

If only Warwick Park had had a Decimus Burton, or at least one dominant architect, or had just been developed over a much shorter time-span.

If only... Then what is today a very pleasant estate, could have been so much more.

CHAPTER 12

THE NAMES OF THE ESTATE AND THE ROADS

The first name for the Estate, or more specifically its spine road, was **not** Warwick Park.

Because the land for development was part of the Eridge Estate and was specifically the Home Farm Estate, the development was initially called the Eridge Estate Development, but more familiarly the Home Farm Building Scheme. There seems to have been a fair degree of confusion about the name and Home Farm and Home Park seem to have been inter-changeable. The Minutes of the Borough Works Committee seem to favour Home Farm Estate in 1895, Home Park Estate in 1896, reverting to Home Farm estate in 1897 and 1898, but it was possible to have the site referred to by both names in the same set of minutes.

The 'Plots for Sale' Prospectus which was produced in January 1897 did not have any names for the roads – they were just listed as 'New Road'.

The first proposed name for what was to become Warwick Park, was King Charles's Road, no doubt reflecting the proximity of the Church of King Charles the Martyr at the western end of the site. The first reference to King Charles's Road is to be found on the outline map prepared by William Roper FSI and submitted for outline approval to the Council on 14th November 1895[32]. It also featured in H.Michell Whitley's proposal and map of the Ornamental Gardens in April 1897, and it is also to be found on some planning applications as late as April 1903. But it clearly did not achieve either popular or official approval, and the more commonly used names in the records for the period 1897-1900 were Home Park Road or the Home Farm Estate.

But the road was renamed or should one say, officially named Warwick Park in 1900, without doubt by, and in recognition of, the Abergavenny family and their connection with the Earls of Warwick. Initially there was some confusion between Warwick Park as the name for the whole area – the Estate – and for the principal or spine road. On a number of maps and references, the road is called Warwick Park *Road* to

---

[32] On this plan, the only other named road was Home Park Road to describe what was subsequently Roedean Road.

distinguish between the two, but *Road* was subsequently and fairly quickly dropped when the concept of the Estate did not catch on. The confusion even extended to the Ordnance Survey which as late as its 1909 edition was calling the road Warwick Park 'Warwick Road'.

It would seem that the cause of all this confusion was that initially the whole estate and *all its roads* were intended to be called Warwick Park and if this were to be the case, there was no need to distinguish between the estate and the roads. There was a good *and local* precedent for this. Camden Park, less than a mile away, was built between 1860 and 1890 and consisted of one main road with a number of branches, all of which were called Camden Park. It is clear that Warwick Park started off in the same manner, but there must have been some confusion about exactly where to find a house since virtually all the houses had names only and very few had numbers (and the numbering in any case was not logical). Warwick Park was much bigger than Camden Park, so the problem of finding a 'name-only' house on the principal road or one of its branches, was compounded.[33]

But it would seem that the problem in Warwick Park was appreciated early. On 15th January 1904, the Works Committee referred a letter from Mr. Gaisford, the Marquess's Agent, about the naming of the side roads to the Watch Committee, who were responsible for road naming and numbering. The Watch Committee considered it at their next meeting which was a month later. The letter proposed that the side roads should be named Rodmell Road, Blatchington Road and Roedean Road.

Rodmell, Blatchington and Roedean are Abergavenny estates in Sussex. Rodmell is a small manor and village just south of Lewes, which has The Abergavenny Arms as its pub. The village is probably best known for being the weekend home of Leonard and Virginia Woolf from 1919 until her tragic death there in 1941. Roedean (which is part of Rottingdean) is best known for its girls' school and is a few miles west of Rodmell; and West Blatchington is now part of Brighton and Hove[34].

The Watch Committee accepted this proposal without discussion on

---

[33] For the record, the Camden Park system has never been changed, although some of the new infill roads in Camden Park have names of their own.

[34] Birling Road was not included in this application although it was a boundary road to the Estate. Birling Place is another Abergavenny property. The 4th Earl was Rector of Birling for many years.

18th February 1904. (It is interesting to note that there is no record between 1895-1908 of the Watch Committee ever officially approving the name Warwick Park.)

Their decision produced a swift and antagonistic response from local residents, who seem to have accepted that the side roads should be renamed, but in particular did not like the name 'Blatchington'. Ten days later, the Watch Committee were considering a letter from Mr. E. Drewitt (who lived at Lyndale, Warwick Park – now No.4 Blatchington Road) forwarding a petition signed by the owners and residents of 'Blatchington Road', petitioning that the name should be altered and also enclosing a letter from Mr. Gaisford (on behalf of the Marquess) on the matter. The inference of the Minute is that the Marquess was sympathetic to their request but the Watch Committee was adamant, and resolved: "That the Memorialists be informed that the Committee are not prepared to alter the name of the road." And so Blatchington Road remains Blatchington to this day.

Following this, it was a matter of weeks before the Watch Committee resolved on 26th May 1904 that all residents be given two months' notice of the proposed numbering of the houses on the Warwick Park Estate. There were of course a large number of undeveloped plots, some of which got divided up subsequently, others of which have never been developed. This is the probable explanation for Warwick Park's somewhat peculiar numbering system and particularly the gaps between numbers.

House names[35] have now largely gone out of fashion since they are felt today to be a little pretentious; and sequential numbering is simpler and more logical, particularly for visitors and strangers. But initially virtually every house in Warwick Park had a name. It is surprising how many house names were (and still are) largely meaningless. The name is often a hybrid, such as Beechcote or Micheldene, whose origin was

---

[35] The need for house names arose because of the development of postal services and particularly with the introduction of the Penny Post in 1840. But it was soon clear, with the increasing volume of mail in major towns and cities, that a more practical form of addressing individual residential property was required. So the system of numbering streets in towns which had arisen in the 18th century, was applied to residential roads, and particularly to the new suburbs from about the 1860's. However the system took time to take hold - in the case of roads with few houses, it was thought to be unnecessary, and in any case many people preferred to have a name, which was thought to have more cachet with its overtones of a larger house or even a country residence. It was only at the beginning of the 20th century that the numbering system became (almost) universal, at the insistence of the GPO. But even now (2007), there are many houses in the Warwick Park Estate with names and no numbers. (See Appendices 5 and 6 for examples.)

known only to its originator; or is obscure, such as Tresco, Glenesk, Ashington or Airlie, reflecting a geographical or sentimental association now probably long forgotten; or are practical or descriptive, if a little uninspiring, such as Park House, Brookside, Woodside, The Laurels, The Pines, or Rosebank. The original house names in the Warwick Park Estate will be found listed in Appendices 5 and 6.

The last (or maybe it is only the latest) act in the naming of the Warwick Park Estate occurred at the end of 1999 when the site which would have been serviced by Road No.4 in 1898, was at last developed by Countryside Residential. They wanted to call it Nevill Grange and it was marketed as such by them, but the Royal Mail, based 25 miles away in Redhill, Surrey, objected not unreasonably on the grounds that there were already six thoroughfares in Tunbridge Wells with the name Nevill, and that in any case, Grange meant house or barn, and not thoroughfare. The Council then proposed Beau Nash Drive which was universally disliked by local residents, who suggested that the name should have a local association, such as Home Farm or Gro[o]m Brook (for the streams which run under the site and down to the Pantiles and onto Groombridge.)

The Council, when faced with universal dislike of their proposal, showed a [then] typical response of having no further interest in choosing a relevant local name.

At a Highways Committee meeting, the Council accepted by votes of 3-2 with three abstentions, the proposal of three new residents of the development who had not even taken up residence at the time. They first of all wanted Regency Drive, which they thought properly reflected the quality and style of the development into which they were buying. However the Royal Mail refused this proposal on purely practical grounds, so they then changed their minds to Richmond Place, a name designed like Nevill Grange to sound upmarket and justify the prices they were paying.

It need hardly be said that Place is inaccurate as a description of a winding 300-yard cul-de-sac; and Richmond has no relevance to Warwick Park.

CHAPTER 13

ASSESSMENT OF THE WARWICK PARK DEVELOPMENT UP TO 1914

Warwick Park was a development which went wrong – not disastrously so, but it never achieved its initial promise. It was not a failure as such. It was just not the success *as an estate* that it was hoped to be, or could have been.

There was no single reason for this, but several, and it is difficult to allocate degrees of responsibility between them.

Some were beyond the control of the Marquess:

- **Unrealised at the time, Tunbridge Wells was past its development peak.** By the time the Warwick Park development got under way, the population growth of Tunbridge Wells was beginning to plateau, but the Marquess was not to know this. Tunbridge Wells had grown remarkably from just under 6,000 in 1831 to just over 10,000 in 1851, to just under 20,000 in 1871 and just over 29,000 in 1891, a rate of increase of about 5,000 every ten years. But that growth rate was to halve in the next twenty years and virtually not grow at all in the next forty. It only grew 6,000 to just over 35,000 between 1891-1911 and was not to reach 40,000 until 1961, some 50 years later. So it is clear in retrospect, but not so at the time, that Tunbridge Wells had passed its peak in growth by the 1890's; and this must have affected the demand for housing.

Population of Tunbridge Wells

Year	No.	Increase/Decrease
1801	1,000 (est)	-
1831	5,929	4,929
1841	8,302	2,373
1851	10,587	2,285
1861	13,807	3,220
1871	19,410	5,603
1881	24,309	4,899
1891	29,296	4,987
1901	33,373	4,097
1911	35,697	2,324
1921	35,568	–129
1931	35,367	–201
1941	No Census	
1951	38,397	3,030
1961	40,340	1,943

Source: OPCS National Census

- **Competition from other developments in Tunbridge Wells.** There were obviously other property developments being carried out in Tunbridge Wells at broadly the same time and depending on what they were and how well they were marketed, they represented competition for Warwick Park. Without knowing in any detail how well these other developments were marketed (and one must recognise that marketing then was not the high-powered technique it is today), one must say that from what we know of Warwick Park marketing, it does not seem to have offered too much competition. It was fortunate for Warwick Park starting effectively in 1897, that most of the reasonably large developments in Tunbridge Wells were in the past – although the recent past – such as Linden Park in 1886, Molyneux Park in 1891, and Boyne Park, Madeira Park and Liptraps Park in 1893. Clearly there was a building boom in the early 1890s in Tunbridge Wells, based on the euphoria generated by achieving Borough status in 1889, the enthusiasm and drive of its citizens and the optimism which this generated. But these earlier developments may have skimmed off much of the latent demand of the period and this, coupled with the overall diminishing demand indicated above, must have had some effect on the response to Warwick Park.

- **Warwick Park was too large a development for local builders.** Local developers were relatively small builders who built a few houses at a time, sold or rented them and then used the sale income or rental collateral to develop the next few. As a result, there was no local developer who could have built the whole estate of 66 plots simultaneously and in a comprehensive style. It was therefore inevitable that the Warwick Park Estate would be developed by a number of builders who had different ideas about the best type and size of house to build, the easiest customers to sell to, and the pace of development they were prepared to follow. It was the pressure of local developers (who may have understood local housing needs better than the Marquess and his Agent) which led to the splitting of the original 66 plots into many smaller plots – some plots being divided into four, others into two or three, while only about a third remained as single undivided plots. All of this led to a fragmented and incohesive development spread over too long a period.

- **The First World War** created a hiatus for all development in Britain. Warwick Park had distinctly faltered well before the First World War, but the War made sure that this continued until the late 1920's. This situation would have been compounded by the Abergavenny Estates being run between 1915-1927 by Trustees, who would have had many things on their minds, other than Warwick Park.

Other reasons were within the control of the Marquess:

- **Size of the development.** If the Marquess had realised the limitations of local builders, he might have been able to approach a larger developer from possibly London, such as Cubitts, who might have been able to handle the whole estate comprehensively. He could have talked at least to the developer whom Bracketts said was interested in developing the whole estate.

- **Nature of the development.** If what was built is any guide, the Marquess does not seem to have imposed any conditions about the nature of the development. He was to allow plot-splitting, detached and semi-detached houses on variable plot sizes; and there is no coherent style or nature to the Estate, as can be found at Nevill Park or Broadwater Down. It could be that he was so determined to have a return on his investment that he bowed to the pressures of local builders.

- **Random development.** He allowed builders in effect to choose their own sites which led to the Estate being developed very patchily. He had been specifically advised by Henry Michell Whitley not to allow random development.

- **Extent and pace of development.** He allowed developers to build single houses. This might have been acceptable for individuals building their own houses, but he should have insisted on larger, more comprehensive development – the most that was ever being developed by one builder at the same time was four houses.

Some of the reasons can be put down to the results of circumstance:

- **Determination to develop the Estate.** The Marquess's determination to develop the Estate seems to have declined over time. This may have been due to his increasing age – he was 74 in 1900 – and also the sudden death in 1902 of George Macbean, his Agent, who must have been a driving force behind the development. But possibly the biggest factor was the renegotiated royalty agreement with the Blaenavon Iron & Steel Co. and the Nantyglo & Blaina Ironworks Co. in 1906, which suddenly turned an annual income from them of about £3,000 into about £30,000. If the motivation for developing Warwick Park was financial, then the need was removed.

- **Discouraging problems** during development such as the Settled Land issue, the sewerage dispute with the Corporation, negotiations with the railways and the road-builders, and the unevenness of the terrain. There can be no doubt that the problems discovered in levelling the Nevill Ground must have been a deterrent to developing the land in the upper reaches of Warwick Park and some of the plots are still undeveloped.

- **Increased costs.** Although the Marquess seems to have accepted at first a development cost of £50,000+, it is clear that this was cut back to about £20,000 as a result of more limited plans which eliminated a bridge and a couple of roads, and firm negotiation which lowered costs. Nonetheless, the final cost at about £25,000 was about 25% higher than the pro-rata original estimate. This must have irritated the Marquess whose aim was to make money, not to lose it.

- **The failure to establish an Ornamental Garden in Warwick Park**, which would have done much to give both style and a certain cohesion to the Estate, was essentially due to the vacillation of the Borough Council on the issue of Summer/Winter Gardens, which was not resolved until the creation of Calverley Grounds in 1919/21. It would have been a relatively small garden, but it could have been a significant factor.

However, whatever the factors involved and whether or not they were post hoc or propter hoc, it has to be recognised that Warwick Park never achieved the *style* of the earlier 'Park' developments. Whatever its aspirations or pretensions, Warwick Park could never match Calverley Park, Nevill Park, Hungershall Park or Camden Park, which although developed over a number of years, nonetheless have a more coherent and consistent style.

An unwitting but clear indication that the drive had gone out of the development of Warwick Park is to be found in the Marquess's reply to a letter dated 25th May 1906 from the Pantyles Rifle Club. He agreed with their request for a 100 yard and 50 yard 'Morris Tube' rifle range at the top of Warwick Park (effectively Plots 50 and 53) and told them that no rent would be charged, but that he reserved the right to reclaim the site whenever he wished. That site has remained a rifle range to this day. The only apparent change over the past 100 years is that of the name of the Club – to St. Peter's Rifle Club.

CHAPTER 14

SUBSEQUENT DEVELOPMENT AFTER THE FIRST WORLD WAR

The development of the Warwick Park Estate after the First World War was similar to that pre-War. It was random, largely unplanned and generally piecemeal. The drive had gone out of the development long before the 1st. Marquess's death in 1915 at the age of 89; and subsequently the Trustees would have been pre-occupied in running the whole estate for the 2nd Marquess who had been certified as incapable of doing so, without being too concerned about picking up the development of a languishing Warwick Park Estate.

A comparison (using Kelly's Directory[36]) for 1914 and 20, 40 and 60 years later, shows how later development progressed with the greatest development being between 1954 and 1974, an unusual situation for an Estate which was started in the late 1890's:

No. of residential houses*

	1914	1934	1954	1974
WARWICK PARK	38	54	58	77
No. on south side	*33*	*43*	*44*	*52*
No. on north side	*5*	*11*	*14*	*25*
BLATCHINGTON ROAD	14	19	19	20
RODMELL ROAD	–	1	1	6
ROEDEAN ROAD	3	3	6	11
NEVILL GATE	–	6	6	6
TOTAL	55	83	90	120

*Houses, not residences or households, or plots.

There was an hiatus in development in the 1920's as the British economy recovered from the War, but after 1927 (coincidentally or maybe relevantly, the year the 2nd.Marquess died) there were signs of development beginning again, particularly in Warwick Park above Nevill Gate. The development was the activity principally of one company – Beale & Sons Ltd., now under the control of Louis Beale's son, Captain Bertram Beale, MC. They built eleven detached houses

---

[36] 1974 was fortuitously, but fortunately for this comparison at 20-year intervals, the last year in which Kelly's Directory for Tunbridge Wells was published.

(nos. 92 -112 Warwick Park, with the exception of no.100, and 4, Nevill Gate) between 1928-34.

Ten houses in seven years is not a particularly fast rate of development, but it does reflect the same development policy exercised by the company before the War – build several houses on what was originally just one plot on the 1897 plan; if possible sell the house before you build it (rather than let it, as was the case before the War); if not, do not overstretch yourself by building too many too soon; which is why it took seven years to build ten houses. (But it should be also recognised that Beale was not just concerned with developments in Warwick Park, but did have other building sites, such as in Forest Road, at the same time.)

No. 106 Warwick Park

No. 108 Warwick Park

Beale's started their development up the hill and then moved down. The earliest development started on Plot 49 on which seven houses were built – nos.108-112 in 1928, nos. 102-106 in 1930 and no.98 in 1933, which was also the year in which 4 Nevill Gate was built. Then Plot no.48 was developed in 1934 as two houses, nos. 94 and 96. Two of the houses were sold in advance – nos. 108 and 96 – and at no time were more than three houses under development. Beale's were clearly cautious, reflecting the relative lack of capital of a local builder and the desire to put as many houses on a plot as would be reasonably acceptable.

The other major builder after the War was Thomas Bates, although most of the work done can be attributed to his three sons. Thomas Bates actually retired in 1927 and died in 1930, but his three sons carried on the company and designed and built two attractive and unique semi-detached houses on Plot 41b (now Nos. 57 and 59), which had a pleasant verandah across the front of each house and a loggia at the back.

They were also in other major developments in Tunbridge Wells such as the building of the Courier offices in Grove Hill Road, the cinema site (Essoldo/ABC/Ritz) at the Mount Pleasant/ Church Road crossroads in 1934 (now under re-development) and the widening of Forest Road.

No. 57 Warwick Park

No. 59 Warwick Park

The period 1934-50 was one of virtual hiatus in the growth in the number of houses, which is not surprising in view of the economic recession in the Thirties, the total stoppage of new residential building during the Second World War and the austerity imposed in the period of recovery after the War.

Of all the roads, Blatchington Road and Nevill Gate are the most consistent in terms of type of house and architectural style, since most of the building plots in these roads were developed in a relatively short period of time – Blatchington pre-1910 and Nevill Gate in the mid-1930s.

Rodmell Road and Roedean Road were the 'late developers' of the Estate, most of Rodmell being post-1954 and about half of Roedean also being post-1954. Nonetheless Roedean Road still retains its pre-1914 character, while Rodmell (which as Nevill Lane, or Cut-Throat

Lane, had served an essentially practical rather than residential purpose) lacks the style and character of the rest of the Estate.

Warwick Park shows the most varied style of all:
- partly because it is the longest road with the largest number of plots;
- partly because a large number of its plots were not developed in the initial pre-1914 phase;
- and partly because it has had the largest number of different builders who have each imposed their own development criteria on both the type of house built and its architectural style.

The south side (even numbers) of Warwick Park has twice as many houses as the north side and developed much faster, the majority (33 out of 38) being completed by 1914. In contrast, the majority of the north side houses (14 out of 25) were completed after 1934. The reason for more houses on the southern side has been that the northern plots had been much less likely to be sub-divided and a large plot had been earmarked for the Ornamental Gardens.

The development of the Ornamental Gardens site was belated but somewhat surprising, since it had never been zoned for residential use and a Town Planning Agreement dated 18th January 1939 specified that the land should be maintained as an open space 'in perpetuity'. By the 1960's, perpetuity seems to have come to mean 25 years.

In early 1965, an outline planning application for nine houses on the site was submitted by Henry Osborne Associates of London N.1, who were the architects, on behalf of Brickland Houses of London W.1, who were the prospective purchasers of the land, provided that they received planning permission.

The land was some 1.976 acres and it (or at least the leasehold of the land) would seem to belong to the Trustees of A. Corlett (who presumably had died recently). The sale was being handled by Geering & Colyer of 22-26, High Street. Whether the freehold still remained with the Marquess is not known, but probably not, since the Marquess sold many freeholds in Warwick Park to sitting leaseholders in the late 1940's and in the 1950's.

It was quickly realised that the site was not shown on the Town Planning Map as 'for residential use' but as a *private* open space and the Agreement of 1939 was resurrected. The signatories to the Agreement had been the Marquess, Lord Nevill, the Tunbridge Wells

Borough Council and somewhat surprisingly, the Marquess Camden and the *Uckfield Rural District Council* (inexplicably, unless it had to do with rights over the water of the Grom Brook which flowed through the site).

It is sad these days that so much information and so many files from the recent past are 'weeded' before just a few are put on microfiche, while older files are never 'weeded' and are classed as 'historic'. So in the case of the development of the Ornamental Gardens site, we cannot be absolutely sure what happened only 40 years ago, although the 'bare bones' are reasonably clear.

It would seem that the Borough Council, or more precisely the Borough Surveyor, was in favour of the proposal because the agreement of the signatories to waive the Agreement of 1939 seems to have been obtained very quickly, and initial outline planning permission was given in a matter of only about three months. A factor which may have influenced permission being granted, was that the developers proposed with great acuity (if not even public-spiritedness), that one of the plots (what would have been No.11, Warwick Park) should be developed with 14 garages, of which the freehold should be given to the owners of nos. 10-36 opposite, who had no garages or space to park their cars. Today the garage area is somewhat run-down and not all the garages are still owned by the residents opposite.

Garage area today.

Once outline planning consent had been given, it was only a matter of time (about nine months) before detailed plans were approved in 1966. The development went in three phases of planning and construction – nos. 13 to 23, then 25 and 27 and finally 29, but all were complete by the end of 1968.

In retrospect, it was probably inevitable, once the Borough Council had rejected the site (as long ago as 1910) as a public Winter (or Summer) Garden, that it would eventually be developed as housing, although the relative steepness of both sides of the site (Warwick Park and Cumberland Walk) coupled with the water-course in the middle, may well have been the reason why it took so long. Certainly within living memory (the 1950s and early 1960s), there were allotments and sheep grazing on the site – in other words, within about 200 yards of the Pantiles.

The architect of what was eventually built on this site wrote in his proposal to the Council of his desire to try and preserve "the character of this rather unique (sic) wooded valley". Whether he is to be believed or not, is debatable. Most people today would feel that if he did try, he certainly did not succeed.

No. 17 Warwick Park

No. 21 Warwick Park

Most of the development after the Second World War, with the exception of the nine houses on the Ornamental Gardens site in the 1960's and the Countryside development of 23 houses and five 'social housing units' in 1999, was of individual houses, largely 'infilling' on larger plots. Examples of these are:

• Nos. 61 and 63 built in 1949 as so-called 'cottages' on what was part of plot 42, at a time when government regulations limited the building cost of a house to £1,500;
• No.65 built in 1950 on part of the garden of No.67 (Plot 43) when the same regulations applied;
• No. 100 built in 1955 on Plot 49a;

No. 65 Warwick Park

150

- No. 114 built in 1958 and No.116 in 1964, built on the north corner plot of 'Ferrylands', on the corner of Forest Road and Warwick Park. No.114, which had little architectural merit as well as major foundation problems, has subsequently been demolished and been replaced in 2005 by a much handsomer and larger 'Arts & Crafts' pastiche design which is nonetheless somewhat too large for its site, in relation to its neighbours;

No. 114 Warwick Park

- No.69+ built in 1973 on part of the garden of No.69. The somewhat idiosyncratic and confusing No.69+ is so numbered because it was built by the owner of No.69 for his own use and he did not like the idea of living in 69a or 69b. Since there is no No.71 nor No.73, it is to be hoped that common sense will eventually prevail and it will be renumbered;
- No.75 built in 1983 on Plot 45 after no less than nine previous applications had been rejected by the Council between 1975 and 1982. No less than 10 conditions were attached to the final approval when it was given;
- Nos. 85a and 85b built in 1974 as two detached houses on part of the garden of No.85 (which was built on part of Plot 53, which in its turn was built as 4 Nevill Gate, by Beale in 1933);
- and there were also developments such as The Drive (of five houses), built between and behind Nos. 86 and 88.

The Countryside development of 1999 is of some note since its spine road is essentially the same as the one (no.4) which should have been built in 1898, but never was. There have been many attempts over the years to develop this hilly site which is approximately $6^1/_2$ acres. It is the land which was to the rear and left-hand side of No.92. In the eight years between 1974 and 1982, there were eight applications, ranging from 3 to 28 houses, and all of them were refused by the Council.

Countryside seem to have been involved since the 1982 application, although the land was not actually sold to a developer until December 1994, when Bryant Homes paid a reputed £3.5 million for it. By this time, the site was designated in the TWBC Local Plan for private housing development including social housing. Bryant attempted to get planning consent over the next two years without success, and their proposals were rejected by councillors unanimously, or nearly so. Bryant appealed against the Council's decision and even took the issue to a Public Inquiry, at which the Inspector upheld the Council's decision.

Bryant's frustration at making a large investment in land for which they could not get planning permission can be easily imagined; and so they agreed to allow Countryside Properties nine months in which to get permission for an alternative scheme. Countryside had one major advantage. They had been responsible for developing Highgrove, a residential road at the higher, southern end of the site, leading into Birling Road; and whether by accident or design, they had retained a small piece of land which would provide access to the south, as well as from Warwick Park on the north, of the site. Two points of access could be important for a development, even thought TWBC was opposed to any road being a through road. Even so, while TWBC Planning officers recommended that Countryside's application in November 1997 should be allowed, it was defeated narrowly in Committee by 7-8 at the beginning of December.

Richmond Place

Bryant Homes allowed Countryside extra time and with suitable 'tweaking', the Countryside application was approved on 29th April, 1998 for some 23 'executive' homes then priced at between £300,000 and £750,000 and accessed from Warwick Park; and five 'social housing units' i.e. 'affordable housing', accessed from Highgrove.

Richmond Place

The other main development since the Second World War has been the conversion of what were considered to be houses which were too large, into smaller flats. Some eleven houses in Warwick Park were converted – mostly into two or three flats per house, but there was one of seven and another of nine flats, so it can be seen that the houses were large. There were also five conversions into nursing or retirement homes, although the economic returns and increased legislation concerning these, has lead to one reverting to a single-occupancy house, another two being converted to six flats and a fourth being demolished to make way for 24 flats. There are other signs of a move towards divided houses being restored to single occupancy, largely as a result of City salaries and bonuses.

What Warwick Park has avoided is any demolition of an original house, followed by the construction of a row of town houses, which can be found on the Frant Road and elsewhere. This may be because the sites were thought too small for wholesale redevelopment, which may be ultimately a small benefit deriving from the original builders' determination to build several houses on the plots which Abergavenny had intended for only one house. But it could also be that there are still plots which have never been built on, largely because they are difficult or unsuitable.

What we have in Warwick Park today is an area which, while it may not be the best address in town, is nonetheless highly regarded and desirable. Its position can be gauged by the fact that every year at the pantomime at the Assembly Hall, jokes are made about the 'nobs' of Warwick Park and yet there are much richer areas in Tunbridge Wells. Perhaps it is chosen for this 'accolade', because Warwick Park is bigger and better known; and therefore makes an easier target for a wider audience.

What can be said is that Warwick Park is leafy; it is hilly; it is spacious; it is fairly quiet and peaceful; and it is reasonably central. Its overall style is 1890-1910, but it now has many variations from this. To some, it may be a curate's egg – good in parts – but for most residents, there are few grounds for complaint. And yet, in relation to the original intent behind it, it can only be called a qualified success.

It is not a failure, but it could have been so much more – the verdict which applies for all of us, to so much in life.

APPENDIX 1:

ACTS OF PARLIAMENT RELATING TO THE ABERGAVENNY ESTATES

1540	31	Henry VIII c.2	
1543	34&35	Henry VIII c.4	
1555	2 & 3	Phillip and Mary c.22	
1610	7	James I c.41	
1627	3	Charles I c.11	
1673	13	Charles II c.17	
1678	18&19	Charles II c.20	
1864	27&28	Victoria c.ix:	Earl of Abergavenny's Estate Act 1864
1871	34&35	Victoria c.4:	Earl of Abergavenny's Estate Act 1871
1880	43&44	Victoria c.4:	Marquess of Abergavenny's Estate Act 1880
1946	9&10	George VI c.1:	Marquess of Abergavenny's Estate Act 1946

Settled Land Acts

19&20	Victoria c.120:	Settled Estates Act 1856
21&22	Victoria c.77 :	Settled Estates Act 1858
27&28	Victoria c.45 :	Settled Estates Act 1864
39&40	Victoria c.30 :	Settled Estates Act 1876
40&41	Victoria c.18 :	Settled Estates Act 1877
45&46	Victoria c.38 :	Settled Land Act 1882
52&53	Victoria : c.36:	Settled Land Act 1889
53&54	Victoria : c.69:	Settled Land Act 1890
15	George V:c.18:	Settled Land Act 1925
6&7	George VI: c.25:	Settled Land and Trustee Act 1943

APPENDIX 2:
ABERGAVENNY RENT ACCOUNT 1895–1909

ESTATE	1895	1896	1897	1898	1899	1900	1901	1902	1903	1904	1905	1906	1907	1908	1909
Eridge/TW/Rotherfield	20,720	20,778	19,895	18,135	18,014	18,455	18,962	20,219	20,039	20,247	20,081	19,972	20,630	21,016	21,020
South Down	6,548	5,539	5,304	5,446	5,390	5,409	5,294	5,442	5,151	5,105	5,379	5,674	5,165	5,159	5,178
W.Sussex	682	611	733	754	664	695	728	674	702	757	747	769	790	814	817
Kent	611	711	262	261	269	251	351	350	253	252	252	252	252	252	252
Sub-total	28,561	27,639	26,194	24,596	24,337	24,810	25,335	26,685	26,145	26,361	26,459	26,667	26,837	27,241	27,267
Monmouthshire & Herefordshire**	14,401	14,363	14,531	13,644	13,524	13,490	13,486	13,689	13,567	13,334	13,580	14,439	5,894	5985	6,160
Worcestershire	2,436	2,211	2,245	2,548	2,147	2,036	2,226	2,089	2,187	2,166	2,268	2,363	2,227	2,270	2,435
Sub-total	16,837	16,574	16,776	16,192	15,671	15,526	15,712	15,778	15,754	15,500	15,848	16,757	8,121	8,255	8,595
Mineral Rights total												2,773	29,513	22,057	22,128
TOTAL	45,399	44,214	43,033	40,791	40,008	40,339	41,049	42,465	41,899	41,910	42,308	*48,970	*64,197	*64,471	*57990

* Includes Mineral Rights of £2,773 in 1906, £29,513 in 1907, £22,057 in 1908 and £22,128 in 1909
** The drop in income between 1906 and 1907 is due entirely to Mineral Rights being listed separately for the first time

Source: ABER 2/40

APPENDIX 3:

ABERGAVENNY HOUSEHOLD RUNNING COSTS 1890–1903

HOUSEHOLD	1890	1891	1892	1893	1894	1895	1896	1897	1898	1899	1900	1901	1902	1903
Eridge Castle	£6,236	£6,892	£6,253	£3,241	£2,595	£2,645	£2,186	£1,950	£1,529	859	£2,483	2,158	£1,754	£1,352
Eridge Garden	£268	£281	£262	£256	£130	£351	£239	£251	£459	76	£382	5	£446	517
Eridge Park	£146	£183	£199	£221	£86	£101	£131	£129	£123	30	£186	62	£167	166
Eridge Stables	£949	£1,178	£981	£1,055	£748	£719	£379	£230	£92	71	£179	317	£534	442
Game	£127	£207	£175	£119	£188	£403	£455	£419	£327	384	£376	50	£704	510
Sub-Total	**£7,726**	**£8,741**	**£7,870**	**£4,892**	**£3,747**	**£4,219**	**£3,390**	**£2,979**	**£2,530**	**£3,020**	**£3,606**	**£3,692**	**£3,605**	**£2,987**
London House	£445	£620	£565	£512	£574	£544	£538	£483	£485	510	£512	520	£566	537
Nevill Court	-	-	£777	£879	£1,890	£2,023	£867	£982	£324	?	£152	?	?	?
TOTAL	**£8,171**	**£9,361**	**£9,212**	**£6,283**	**£6,211**	**£6,786**	**£4,795**	**£4,444**	**£3,339**	**£3,530**	**£4,270**	**£4,212**	**£4,171**	**£3,524**

The figures clearly reflect where the family were principally living - at Eridge in 1890-1892, then at Nevill Court in 1894-95.

They also reflect certain economies from 1893, but certain costs, such as Garden and Park, are relatively fixed.

Source: ABER 2/40

APPENDIX 4:
ABERGAVENNY GROUND RENTS IN TUNBRIDGE WELLS 1899

Abergavenny Annual Ground Rents (GR) in Borough of Tunbridge Wells, 1899

Folio	Road/Site	Earliest Lease Date	Duration	GR (range)	Acreage	Total GR	Av. GR per acre
No.							
120/121	Broadwater Down	29.9.1860	99 years	(£20-£47)	121.99	£1347-10-6	£11- 1- 0
122/123	Frant Rd.(east side)	29.9.1865	94 years		15.22	£ 437- 1- 6	£28-14- 3
124	Frant Rd.(west side)	1856	75 years	£20	11.451	£ 318-10- 0	£27-16- 3
124	Birling Road	29.9.1869	60 years	£18-10-0 (8 cottages)	2.408	£ 71-15- 0	£29-16- 0
125	Coach & Horses			£38	0.05	£ 38- 0- 0	£760
125	Corn Exchange			£80	0.28	£ 80- 0- 0	£285-14- 3
125	Nevill Street			£234	1.125	£ 234- 0- 0	£208
125	Market Terrace			£66	0.15	£ 66- 0- 0	£440
126	Montacute Gardens	29.9.1882	77 years	£8	2	£ 64- 0- 0	£32
126	Linden Park	29.9.1885	99 years	(£5-£25)	9.842	£ 150- 0- 0	£15- 5- 0
127	Linden Gardens	29.9.1888	58 years	£10	2.037	£ 55- 0- 0	£27
127/128	Eridge Road	29.9.1871	75 years	£5-10-0	3.542	£ 158- 0- 0	£44-12- 0
129	Nevill Park	29.9.1831	75 years	£40	100.25	£ 684-17- 6	£6-16- 8
129	Nevill Terrace			£40	0.25	£ 40- 0- 0	£160
130/130A	Warwick Park	29.6.1898	99 years	(£10-£25)	93.915	£881-10- 0	£9- 7- 9
TOTALS					390.924	£4929-19- 0	£12-12- 0

Source: ABE

APPENDIX 5:

WARWICK PARK ESTATE: PLOT DETAILS: PRE-1914

WARWICK PARK ESTATE: PLOT DETAILS
According to the Brackett report of February 1897 and related map.
(Brackett's suggestions in italics)

Block No.	ROAD & Current House No.	Original House Name	Orig. Plot No.	Rev. Plot No.	Acreage A-R-P	Frontage Feet	Return Frontage* Feet	Depth Feet	Annual Ground Rent (£)
1	Warwick Park								
	4		1		0-0-23	50		150	18
			2		0-0-20	50		150	18
	6			2a		25		150	
	8			2b		25		150	
			3		0-0-33	50		150	18
	10	Beechcote		3a		25		150	
	12	Widford Villa		3b		25		150	
			4		0-0-36	50		150	18
	14	Wyvern		4a		25		150	
	16	Glenesk		4b		25		150	
			5		0-1-01	50		150	18
	18	Almvik		5a		25		150	
	20	Kimberley		5b		25		150	
	22		6	6a	0-1-03	50		150	18
	24	Wynfeld	7		0-0-36	50		150	18
			8		0-2-07	70		150	25
	26	St.Benet's		8a		35		150	
	28			8b		35		150	
			9		0-2-24	50		150	25
	30	Highlea		9a		25		150	
	32	Warwick House		9b		25		150	
			10		1-0-22	50		150	25
	34	Ashington		10a		25		150	
	36	Milford		10b		25		150	
		Each plot available for the erection of one pair of villas							
			11			175	175		50
	38	Glentworth		11a		50		150	
	40	The Laurels		11b		50		150	
	42	Warwick Towers		11c		75	175		
	Frant Road								
	9	Reidhaven	12			75	230	205	50
	7	King Charles' Vicarage	13			80		190	50
	5		14			80		173	50
	3		15			80		155	50
2	Warwick Park								
			16		1.1.07	180		120(max)	36
	44			16A		150		120(max)	30
	48			16B		80		120(max)	22
	52		17		1.01.20	165		120(min)	36
		Suggested cutting these 2 plots into 6 of about 60ft. frontage, for each of which a Ground Rent of of £18 could be asked.							
3	Warwick Park								
	41	Oak Cottage	18			188		260	60
			19			150		280(min)	48
		Sub-dividing recommended							
4	Rodmell Rd.	The Homestead	20			425		Irregular shape	60
		Splitting suggested							

158

APPENDIX 5 *(continued)*

Block No.	ROAD & Current House No.	Original House Name	Orig. Plot No.	Rev. Plot No.	Acreage A-R-P	Frontage Feet	Return Frontage* Feet	Depth Feet	Annual Ground Rent (£)
5	Warwick Park								
	·		21			128		140(min)	30
	64	Micheldene		21a		32		140	
	66	Bridgeside		21b		32		140	
	68	Ravensdene		21c		32		140	
	70	Rosebank		21d		32		140	
			22			120		120(min)	30
	72	St.Malo		22a		30		120	
	74	Trefri		22b		30		120	
	76	Morven		22c		30		120	
	78	Airlie		22d		30		120	
			23			130	120		30
	80	Newlands		23a		65		120	
	82	Uplands		23b		65	120		
6	Roedean Rd.								
			24			340		380(max)	50
		Warwick Lodge	24A						
		Tarquin	25			168		380(max)	50
			26			160	210		50
		Ventnor	26a						
7	Blatchington Rd.								
	1	Rolandseck	27			50	150		15-15-0
			28			50		100-137	15-15-0
		Montrose		28a		25		100-137	
		St. Fillans		28b		25		100-137	
			29			50		100-137	15-15-0
	7	Hazeldene		29a		25		100-137	
	9	Ellerslie		29b		25		100-137	
	11	Mountain Ash	30			50		100-137	15-15-0
	13	Aldbro	31			50		100-137	15-15-0
	15	Inge Va	32			50		100-137	15-15-0
	17	Kingmere	33			50		100-137	15-15-0
	19	Berry Croft	34			50		100-137	15-15-0
	21	Knavesmire	35			50		100-137	15-15-0
	23	Warwick Park Cottage	36			50		100-137	15-15-0
		Plot combined with 36	37			150		100-137	18.10.0
		* Applies only to corner sites							
8	Blatchington Rd.								
			38			308		266(max)	38
	18			38A					Peppercorn
	16	Ambleside		38B					8
			39			185		395	46
	14			39A			46		14
	12			39B			46		
	10	Trevone		39C			46		14
	8	Hartland		39D			46		
			40			160	320		50
	6	The Rowans		40A		80		320	
	4	Lyndale		40B		80		320	
	2	Park House		40C		80	240		

APPENDIX 5 *(continued)*

Block No.	ROAD & Current House No.	Original House Name	Orig. Plot No.	Rev. Plot No.	Acreage A-R-P	Frontage Feet	Return Frontage* Feet	Depth Feet	Annual Ground Rent (£)
8	Warwick Park								
			41			150		355	46-10-0
	53	St. Agnes		41A		70		240	
	55	Charlwood House		41B		80			
			42			150		375	46-10-0
	57			42A					
	59			42B					
	63			42C					
	65			42D					
	67 & 67a	Cliff House & Cliff Cottage	43			150		385	45
	69 & 69+	Courtleas	44			150		450	45
	75		45			150		410(min)	46-10-0
	Nevill Gate (LH)		46			160	350		50
	Nevill Gate (RH)		47			155	340		45
	Warwick Park								
			48			150		260	45
	83			48A					
	85			48B					
			49			240		230	50
	85a			49A					
	85b			49B					
	2nd Cricket pitch	Plot not developed	50			390	140		44
			Sub-division of plots 49 & 50 suggested						
	2nd Cricket pitch	Plot not developed	51			140		318 (min)	35
	2nd Cricket pitch	Plot not developed	52			130	320		35
9	Warwick Park								
	Rifle range	Plot not developed	53			150	420		40
	Jnct. Forest Rd.								
	148 Forest Rd	Warwick Ridge	54			550		285(max)	45
10	160 Forest Rd.		55			380	460		50
	Warwick Park		56			465		308(max)	50
	114			56A					
	112			56B					
	110			56C					
	108			56D					
			57			200		335	50
	106			57A		100			
	104			57B		100			
			58			200		345	50
	102			58A		100			
	100			58B		100			
	98		59			200		363	50
			60			200	400		57
	96			60A		100			
	94			60B		100			
	Birling Rd.								
			61			460	700		60
			62			200		520	62
			63			200		520	63
			64			200		520	60
		Heatherlands	65			440		500	56-15-0

* Return Frontage applies only to corner sites.

APPENDIX 6: WARWICK PARK ESTATE, HOUSE RECORDS FROM TWBC ARCHIVES

WARWICK PARK ESTATE

Location	Application No.	Description	Approval Date	Owner	Builder	Surveyor	Other information
Home Farm Estate	1731	New roads/sewers	31.01.1896	Marquess of Abergavenny	Walter Arnold	William Roper	
Home Farm Estate	1900	Bridge over LBSC Rail	11.12.1896	Marquess of Abergavenny	Pauling & Co.		
Home Farm Estate	2004	Entrance to Madeira Park	15.10.1897	Marquess of Abergavenny	Walter Arnold	William Roper	
Home Farm Estate	2097	18 Cottages	Refused	Marquess of Abergavenny			Permission refused
Home Farm Estate	2394	Diversion of sewer	Refused	Marquess of Abergavenny			Permission refused

House No.	Original House Name	Plot No.*	Application No.	Type of House**	Approval Date	Original Developer/Owner	Architect	Builder	No. of bedrooms***	Other information
SOUTHERN (or LH) SIDE										
2		1a	SW/1/66/173	Single-storey house	31.05.1966	R.D. Bates	R&A Bates		2 bed	Part of No.6 site-
4		2a	5653	Detached house	18.02.1921	Thos. Bates	Thos Bates & Son	Thos. Bates & Son	3 bed	Listed as a 'Subsidy House' & originally No.6
6	Holly House	2a	SW/1/68/107	House/Studio	01.05.1968	Harold A. Bates	R&A Bates	R.D. Bates		Part of No.6 site- garage for 3 cars
8		2b	4426/4436	Detached house	14.10.1910	B. Saxon Beale	B. Saxon Beale	Beale & Sons	6 bed	2 bedrooms in attic
10	Beechcote	3a	2065	Semi-det. Villa	28.01.1898	L.S. Beale	Beale & Sons	Beale & Sons	5 bed	1 bedroom in attic
12	Widford Villa	3b	2065	Semi-det. Villa	28.01.1898	L.S. Beale	Beale & Sons	Beale & Sons	5 bed	1 bedroom in attic
14	Wyvern	4a	2120	Semi-det. Villa	01.04.1898	L.S. Beale	Beale & Sons	Beale & Sons	4 bed	
16	Glenesk	4b	2120	Semi-det. Villa	01.04.1898	L.S. Beale	Beale & Sons	Beale & Sons	4 bed	
18	Alnvik	5a	2163	Detached house	27.05.1898	J.H. Chapman	Beale & Sons	Beale & Sons	5 bed	1 bedroom in attic
20	Kimberley	5b	2258	Detached house	02.12.1898	L.S. Beale	Beale & Sons	Beale & Sons	6 bed	1 bedroom in attic
22		6	2511	Detached house	16.03.1900	L.S. Beale	Beale & Sons	Beale & Sons	6 bed	2 bedrooms in attic
24	Wynfeld	7	3231	Detached house	29.08.1903	L.S. Beale	Beale & Sons	Beale & Sons	6 bed	1 bedroom in attic
26	St. Benet's		3304	Detached house	15.01.1904	L.S. Beale	Beale & Sons	Beale & Sons	6 bed	1 bedroom in attic
28		8b	3189	Detached house	15.05.1903	L.S. Beale	Beale & Sons	Beale & Sons	5 bed	
30	Highlea	9a	2857	Detached house	11.10.1901	L.S. Beale	Beale & Sons	Beale & Sons	5 bed	
32	Warwick House	9b	2857	Detached house	11.10.1901	L.S. Beale	Beale & Sons	Beale & Sons	5 bed	
34	Ashington	10a	2858	Semi-det. Villa	11.10.1901	L.S. Beale	Beale & Sons	Beale & Sons	4 bed	
36	Milford	10b	2858	Semi-det. Villa	11.10.1901	L.S. Beale	Beale & Sons	Beale & Sons	4 bed	
38	Glentworth	11a	2078/2060	Semi-det. Villa	29.01.1898	S.E.Haward	Strange & Sons	Strange & Sons	5 bed	
40	The Laurels	11b	2078/2060	Semi-det. Villa	29.01.1898	S.E.Haward	Strange & Sons	Strange & Sons	5 bed	Subject to litigation by the Marquess - see text
42	Warwick Towers	11c	2180/2092	Detached house	29.06.1898	S.E.Haward	Charles Norton	?	7 bed	Smoking Room on 2nd floor
Rodmell Road Junction										
RODMELL ROAD										
	Reidhaven nka Rodmell House	12	2007/2067	House	14.01.1898	Mr. H. C. Lander	H. C. Lander		10 bed	Basement& attic/Servants' Hall
44	Craig-Side	17	18700	Bungalow	24.05.1965	Mrs .M. E. C. Smith	Huntley & Lawson ARIBA	J.E. Skinner	3 bed	Infill of Nevill Villa garden. Outline app SW/55/233
44a	Nevill Rise Cottage	17	7324	Stable conversion	20.09.1929	Mr. H.J. Bennett	John Jarvis & Co.	John Jarvis & Co.	2 bed	Conversion of stables of Nevill Villa,No.7 Frant Rd.
46	Derreen	17	11681	Bungalow	19.02.1954	Mr. Sydney R. Miles	Mr. S. R. Miles	Simmons Bros.	2 bed	Est. cost £2,500
	Bhadreswar			Bungalow	21.04.1953	Mr. Alonzo Allen	Basil H. Fountain AIAS	Richard Thorpe Bros.	3 bed	1bed in attic. Small dispute over drive/crossover
WARWICK PARK										
44	Farthings	17	TW/82/0858	Semi-detached house	22.07.1982	Simmonds Trust	Otford Design		3 bed	Conversion of garages into 1 house/1 flat+ garages
44a		17	TW/82/0858	Semi-detached flat	22.07.1982	Simmonds Trust	Otford Design		1 bed	Conversion of garages into 1 house/1 flat+ garages
46	The Mount Stables	17		Stables						
48		17a	4594	Detached house	08.09.1911	B. Saxon Beale	Beale & Sons	Beale & Sons	5 bed	Integral 'Motor House'
52		17b	4517	Detached house	28.04.1911	Mr. W. W. Starmer	Ernest Willard	Soper & Jones	7 bed	Music Room & 2 bed in attic
	Railway Bridge									

161

APPENDIX 6 (continued)

House No.	Original House Name	Plot No.*	Application No.	Approval Date	Type of House**	Original Developer/ Owner	Architect	Builder	No. of bedrooms***	Other information
	WARWICK PARK									next Railway Bridge
64	Micheldene	21a	2266	16.12.1898	Semi-det. Villa	W.S.Putland	James G.D. Armstrong	Strange & Sons	6 bed	
66	Bridgeside	21b	2266	16.12.1898	Semi-det. Villa	W.S.Putland	James G.D. Armstrong	Strange & Sons	6 bed	
68	Ravenside	21c	2266	16.12.1898	Semi-det. Villa	W.S.Putland	James G.D. Armstrong	Strange & Sons	6 bed	
70	Rosebank	21d	2266	16.12.1898	Semi-det. Villa	W.S.Putland	James G.D. Armstrong	Strange & Sons	6 bed	
72	St. Malo	22a	2336	28.04.1899	Semi-det. Villa	Carlos Crisford	Carlos Crisford	Miller Holmes	6 bed	3520 sq. ft
74	Trefri	22b	2336	28.04.1899	Semi-det. Villa	Carlos Crisford	Carlos Crisford	Miller Holmes	6 bed	3520 sq. ft
76	Morven	22c	2425	19.08.1899	Semi-det. Villa	W.S.Putland	James G.D. Armstrong	Strange & Sons	6 bed	3520 sq. ft
78	Airlie	22d	2425	19.08.1899	Semi-det. Villa	W.S.Putland	James G.D. Armstrong	Strange & Sons	6 bed	3520 sq. ft
80	Newlands	23a	2905	24.01.1902	Detached house	W.S.Putland	Thomas Bates	Thomas Bates	6 bed	Plan signed by Henry Wild
82	Uplands	23b	2905	24.01.1902	Detached house	W.S.Putland	Thomas Bates	Thomas Bates	6 bed	Plan signed by Henry Wild
	Roedean Road Junction									
	ROEDEAN ROAD									
	Hillbrow	pt.24	16993	07.10.1964	Detached house	Mr. Vincent Byrne	Beauchamp & Addey ARIBA	P. M. Clifford	3 bed	
	Pinewood	pt.24	18105	1964	Detached house	Mr. Vincent Byrne	Beauchamp & Addey ARIBA	P. M. Clifford	3 bed	App with 7 conditions. 0.085 hectare
	Blaven	pt.24	TW/78/0210	03.11.1978	Chalet bungalow	Mrs. W. B. Lake	Burns, Guthrie & Part.		3 bed	
	Warwick Lodge nka Roedean Manor	24	2450	13.10.1899	Detached house	Edwin W. Wix	W. Campbell Jones	Strange & Sons	8 bed	Cellar, attic, garage, conservatory
	Tarquin	25	3854	13.09.1907	Detached house	Mr. Thomas Bates	Leonard Towner	Thomas Bates	8 bed	Cellar, attic
	Standish House	26a	3175	24.03.1903	Detached house	Henry Dear	Thomas Bates/Towner	Thomas Bates	7 bed	Est. cost £2400. Pursuant to Sec.64 of 1936 Act.
	Russets		10584	22.09.1950	Detached house	Mr. C. P. Beauchamp	Branson & Beauchamp ARIBA	?	4 bed	Est. cost £2,400
	Random Tiles nka Highview		10622	20.10.1950	Detached house	Mr. Arthur R. Chapman	Branson & Beauchamp ARIBA	?	4 bed	Est. cost £1,800
	Goodrington nka Springfield		10638	24.11.1950	Bungalow	Mr. Arthur F. Stewart	Mr. A.F. Stewart	Mr. A. F. Stewart	4 bed	Est. cost £3,500
	Hillside		SW/1/57/205A	02.10.1957	Bungalow	Mr. Harold A. Bowman	Mayal, Webb & Hart	Direct labour	3 bed	Est. cost £3,500
	Phoenix		SW/1/57/205A	02.10.1957	Detached house	Mr. Harold A. Bowman	Mayal, Webb & Hart	Direct labour	3 bed	
	WARWICK PARK									
84	Esperance	26b	3217	10.07.1903	Detached house	Henry Dear	Leonard Towner	Thomas Bates	7 bed	20,000 sq. ft.
86		26c	3175	23.04.1903	Detached house	Henry Dear	Leonard Towner	Thomas Bates	7 bed	Cellar / not less than 23,000 sq. ft.
	THE DRIVE									
	Emmes	pt.26c			House-conversion					Conversion from No.88 outbuildings
2	Southwinds	pt.26c	SW/1/63/300	26.08.1963	Detached house	M. F. Martin	T. C. Gibbons, LRIBA	M. F. Martin	3 bed	Est. cost £6,000
		pt.26c	SW/1/63/251	26.08.1963	Detached house	M. F. Martin	T. C. Gibbons, LRIBA	M.F. Martin	3 bed	Est. cost £5,500
3		pt.26c	SW/1/63/299	26.08.1963	Detached house	M. F. Martin	T. C. Gibbons, LRIBA	M. F. Martin	3 bed	Est. cost £5,500
	WARWICK PARK									
88	Rydal Court	26c	4129/24646	26.03.1909	Detached house	Thomas Bates	Leonard Towner	Thomas Bates	6 bed	Separate Coal/Wood/WC now converted to house
90	The Cedars	48	8637/9082	20.09.1935	Detached house	Beale & Sons	Beale & Sons	Beale & Sons	6 bed	4 acres. House now converted into flats.
92	Blinkbonnie	47b	7640/8604	21.11.1930	Detached house	Beale & Sons	Beale & Sons			7640 missing from archives
	RICHMOND PLACE									
		None	SW/1/57/291	06.11.1957	Outline for 10 houses	Mrs. Mather Hume/ Bracketts			Various	Outline consent for 10 houses expired 25.02.1970
		None	TW/98/268	13.05.1998	23 houses/ 5 social units	Countryside Properties	Countryside Properties	Countryside Properties	Various	At least 16 applications to develop 1974-1998
		None	TW/98/269	13.05.1998	22 houses/ 5 social units	Countryside Properties	Countryside Properties			Although approved, not built as such
	WARWICK PARK									
94		48a	8280/8315	18.05.1934	Detached house	Beale & Sons	Beale & Sons	Beale & Sons	5 bed	1 acre. 8280 never built
96		48b	8450	29.11.1934	Detached house	Mrs. M. Johns	Beale & Sons	Beale & Sons	4 bed	1 1/4 acres
98		49	8218	24.11.1933	Detached house	Beale & Sons	Beale & Sons	Beale & Sons	6 bed	1 1/2 acres
100		pt.49	12157/13426	06.04.1955	Detached house	H. Sandford	Philip Beauchamp	J. Crates & Son	3 bed	Est. cost 3,200

House No.	Original House Name	Plot No.*	Application No.	Approval Date	Type of House**	Original Developer/ Owner	Architect	Builder	No. of bedrooms***	Other information
	WARWICK PARK									
102	Glenwood	49b	7559/7617	18.07.1930	Detached house	Beale & Sons	Beale & Sons	Beale & Sons	5 bed	25,000 sq. ft.
104		49c	7496	23.05.1930	Detached house	Beale & Sons	Beale & Sons	Beale & Sons	5 bed	2,500 sq. yds
106		49d	7334/7467	14.03.1930	Detached house	Mr. H. Hargreaves	Beale & Sons	Beale & Sons	4 bed	4,000 sq. yds
108	Presteign	49e	6950	16.12.1927	Detached house	Mr. E. Godfrey Browne	Beale & Sons	Beale & Sons	5 bed	20,000 sq. ft.
110		49f	7030/7363	20.04.1928	Detached house	Beale & Sons	Beale & Sons	Beale & Sons	4 bed	9,600 sq. ft.
112		49g	6946	18.11.1927	Detached house	Beale & Sons	L.S. Hatchard	Never built	4 bed	Why never built?
			7009	23.03.1928	Detached house	Beale & Sons	Beale & Sons	Beale & Sons	3 bed	Virtually identical to 6946
114	Sellwood	pt.55	SW/1/55/171	27.08.1955	Detached house	S.C. Jager	T.G. Gibbons		3 bed	Never built. Est. cost £3,000
			SW/1/58/64	05.03.1958	Detached house	Frederick Holland	Frederick Holland	Direct labour		
116		pt.55	SW/1/64/114	01.04.1964	Detached house	Mrs. V.E. Taylor	Cecil Burns & Guthrie	P. Bishop/ Constel	4 bed	Est.Cost £11,000
	Corner The Hermitage nka Littlehurst	55	3209	10.07.1903	Detached house	Miss Berry	A. William West	J. Levey & Sons	6 bed	Morning Room, Servants' Hall, basement: 6 rooms
	Forest Rd. & WP Forest Road junction									
	BIRLING ROAD									
	Heatherlands	65	2691	29.03.1901	Lodge & Stables	Mr. E. Davison	Spurrell & Murray	Mark Martin	3 bed	Lodge- no bathroom or dining room. Now demolished
	Heatherlands	65	3057	14.11.1902	House	Mr. E. Davison	Spurrell & Murray	Strange & Sons	6 bed	Billiard room in cellar. House now demolished
31/32			3630/3655	11.05.1906	2 semi-det. Houses	Mr. L Bernhardt Beale	Beale & Sons	Beale & Sons	5 bed	3630|6 bedlapproved, but superceded by 3655
33			3661	25.06.1906	House	Mr. C.F. Clapham	Beale & Sons	Beale & Sons	5 bed	Photographic Dark Room
34			4371	15.07.1910	House	Mrs. Malden	Allen Foxley	Beale & Sons	6 bed	Mrs. Malden's sitting room on 1st Floor
	NORTHERN (or RH) SIDE									
1		0a	2496	02.02.1900	Offices /Warehouse	E. Robins & Sons Ltd.	W. Barnsley Hughes	J. Laney & Son		Living room/bedroom in attic
3	King Charles C.H.		4972	05.09.1913	Church Hall	Mr F.L. Berridge	Stanley Philpot LRIBA	NK		Date of completion 29.02.1920. Flat above.
5			5801	19.05.1922	Detached house	Messrs. Beale & Sons	Messrs. Beale & Sons	Messrs. Beale & Sons	5 bed	Attic, garage
7	Redshaws		TW/96/1601	14.03.1997	Detached house	QCB & D.L. Hitch	J.P. Hitch & Associates	Chinplex Ltd.	5 bed	Proposed Georgian style changed to Edwardian
	The land between here and Rodmell Road was originally intended to be an Ornamental Garden				It was eventually developed as Nos.13-29 in 1965-69				65-68	1.976 acres in area
	Car Park. 17 garages and forecourt		SW/1/65/90	03.09.1965	8 houses/14 garages	Brickland Houses	Henry Osborne Assoc.			Outline permission. One plot used for 14 garages and given to residents on opposite side of road
13		Land	SW/1/66/24	05.01.1966	17 garages & forecourt	Brickland Houses	Henry Osborne Assoc.	J.Bath	4 bed	Type C: - 4 bed house
15		never	SW/1/66/286	31.08.1966	Chalet house	Brickland Houses	Henry Osborne Assoc.	Brickland Builders(Kent)	4 bed	Type C: - 4 bed house
17	Copper Beech	given	SW/1/66/286	31.08.1966	Chalet house	Brickland Houses	Henry Osborne Assoc.	Brickland Builders(Kent)	3 bed	Type A:- 3 bed house
19		a plot	SW/1/66/276	31.08.1966	Chalet house	Brickland Houses	Henry Osborne Assoc.	Brickland Builders(Kent)	3 bed	Type A:- 3 bed house
21		number	SW/1/66/276	31.08.1966	Chalet house	Brickland Houses	Henry Osborne Assoc.	Brickland Builders(Kent)	3 bed	Type A:- 3 bed house
23			SW/1/66/276	31.08.1966	Chalet bungalow	Brickland Houses	Henry Osborne Assoc.	Brickland Builders(Kent)	3 bed	Type B:- 3 bed bungalow
25			SW/1/66/276	31.08.1966	Chalet house	Brickland Houses	Henry Osborne Assoc.	Brickland Builders(Kent)	4 bed	Type C: - 4 bed house
27			SW/1/66/402	07.12.1966	Chalet bungalow	Brickland Houses	Henry Osborne Assoc.	Brickland Builders(Kent)	3 bed	Type B: bungalow but with 4 bed
29			SW/1/68/43	06.03.1968	Chalet house.	Mr. J.Clark	Henry Osborne Assoc.	Brickland Builders(Kent)	4 bed	
35	Brookside	None	5780	24.03.1922	Dwelling house/garage		Stanley Philpot	T.Bates & Son	4 bed	Cellar
	RODMELL ROAD									
	Edgewater	None	TW/82/636	03.06.1982	Detached house	Mrs. J Corlett	RB Consultants	Eldovet Ltd	4 bed	App. Subject to 12 conditions
	Tumblewood	None	TW/82/636	03.06.1982	Detached house	Mrs. J Corlett	RB Consultants	Eldovet Ltd	4 bed	Previous App TW/82/167 for 3 houses refused
	Patty Moon nka Willows	None	SW/1/56/139	27.06.1956	Detached house	Mr. Raymond W. Whittaker	Philip Beauchamp ARIBA	Ambrose H. Allcorn Ltd	3 bed	Outline permission:SW/1/55/195;est. cost£3,500
	Five Oaks	pt.20	TW/78/463	05.09.1978	Bungalow	Lingbury Property Co.Ltd	Trevor L. Banks	W. C. Manners Ltd	4 bed	Area for 4 plots : 1.8 acres
	Willow Lodge	pt.20	TW/78/463	05.09.1978	Detached house	Lingbury Property Co.Ltd	Trevor L. Banks	W. C. Manners Ltd	4 bed	Built on garden of The Homestead
	Springbank	pt.20	TW/78/463	05.09.1978	Detached house	Lingbury Property Co.Ltd	Trevor L. Banks	W. C. Manners Ltd	4 bed	following death of Sir Clifford Wakely

APPENDIX 6 (continued)

House No.	Original House Name	Plot No.*	Application No.	Approval Date	Type of House**	Original Developer/Owner	Architect	Builder	No. of bedrooms***	Other information
	OAK TREE CLOSE									
1		pt.18	SW/1/64/464	13.11.1964	Single-storey dwelling	Brickland Houses Ltd	Henry Osborne Assoc.	J.H.Bath of Tonbridge	3 bed	Oak Tree Close - 2 acres
2		pt.18	SW/1/64/464	13.11.1964	Single-storey dwelling	Brickland Houses Ltd	Henry Osborne Assoc.	J.H.Bath of Tonbridge	3 bed	Originally named Cottage Close, but following protests, changed to Oak Tree Close
3		pt.18	SW/1/64/464	13.11.1964	Single-storey dwelling	Brickland Houses Ltd	Henry Osborne Assoc.	J.H.Bath of Tonbridge	3 bed	No.2 - negligence claim :October 1982
4		pt.18	SW/1/64/464	13.11.1964	Single-storey dwelling	Brickland Houses Ltd	Henry Osborne Assoc.	J.H.Bath of Tonbridge	3 bed	
	UPPER CUMBERLAND WALK									
	Tidebrook nka Willow Bank	19a	5620	19.11.1920	Bungalow	Mr. T. Bates	T. Bates & Sons	T. Bates & Sons Ltd	3 bed	Listed as a 'Subsidy House'
	The Homestead	19b	4744	24.05.1912	Detached house	Mr. T. Bates	Leonard Towner	T. Bates & Sons Ltd	5 bed	1 bed in attic
	South Riding	20	4669	12.01.1912	Detached house	Mr. T. Bates	Leonard Towner	T. Bates & Sons Ltd	6 bed	
	Brook Cottage	pt.20	TW/78/463	05.04.1978	Detached house	Lingbury Property Co.Ltd	Trevor L. Banks	W. C. Manners Ltd	4 bed	Cellar, artist's studio
	Beverley Stables nka The Coach House	4.S	4320/4395	15.04.1910	Dwelling Hse & Art Studio	Mr. Alexander H. Kirk	H. Bukeley Creswell FRIBA	T Bates & Sons Ltd	4 bed	Motor House, Coach House, 4 stables, 3 bedrooms
	Ardmore	5.S	3477	10.03.1905	Stables and Cottage	Mr. T. Clive Davies	Geo. Mansfield & Son		3 bed	
6	Knocklofty	6.S	4847/4880	21.02.1913	Detached house	Mr. . T. Bates	Leonard Towner	T .Bates & Sons Ltd	4 bed	Reconstruction of Aspenden Cottage/stables
7	Melrose		5850	12.09.1922	House	S. S. Weeks	Cecil Burns		6 bed	Opp. Tennis Club entrance
	Fulbeck		4938	16.05.1913	Detached house	Mr. T. Bates	Leonard Towner	T. Bates & Sons Ltd	5 bed	
	Woodentops nka Greenways		SW/1/67/13	01.02.1967	Detached house	Richard Alfred Buckingham	R. A. Buckingham	R. A. Buckingham	4 bed	
	Boundary House site		TW/87/1666	31.03.1967	Detached house	Mrs. Buckingham	R. A. Buckingham	not built		Outline application refused, appeal rejected
	The Boundary House		TW/94/1025	12.10.1994	Detached house	Kent County Estates	Barton Willmore Partners	not built	5 bed	Permission with 11 conditions
			TW/94/1292	20.02.1995	Detached house	Kent County Estates	J. M. Leeson RIBA		4 bed	11 conditions; cost:site £65k; construction £235k
						Mr. Michael Winter	Michael Winter, RIBA			Bedrooms on ground floor; living quarters 1st.floor
	WARWICK PARK									
41	Oak Cottage Railway Bridge	18	5639	17.12.1920	Cottage	Major P.H.Bird	Connor Bros (Builders)	Connor Bros.	4 bed	Listed as 'Subsidy House'-2 acres
	BLATCHINGTON ROAD (LH Side)									
1	Rolandseck	27	2141	13.05.1898	Detached house	Henry Wild	W.Elliot	T.Bates & Sons Ltd	7 bed	Turret
3	Montrose	28a	2140/2379	13.05.1898	Semi-det. Villa	Henry Wild	W.Elliot	T.Bates & Sons Ltd	5 bed	
5	St.Fillans	28b	2140/2379	13.05.1898	Semi-det. Villa	Henry Wild	W.Elliot	T.Bates & Sons Ltd	5 bed	
7	Hazeldene nka Scotscraig	29a	2339	14.04.1899	Semi-det. Villa	Henry Wild	W.Elliot	T.Bates & Sons Ltd	5 bed	
9	Ellersile	29b	2339	14.04.1899	Detached house	Henry Wild	W.Elliot	T.Bates & Sons Ltd	5 bed	
11	Mountain Ash	30	3293	18.12.1903	Detached house	Henry Wild	Leonard Towner	T.Bates & Sons Ltd	8 bed	4 bed in attic
13	Aldro	31	3293	18.12.1903	Detached house	Henry Wild	Leonard Towner	T.Bates & Sons Ltd	8 bed	4 bed in attic
15	Inge Va	32	3232	11.09.1903	Detached house	Henry Wild	Leonard Towner	T.Bates & Sons Ltd	8 bed	
17	Kingsmere	33	2832	13.09.1901	Detached house	Henry Wild	Leonard Towner	T.Bates & Sons Ltd	6 bed	Alterations signed by Towner. Cellar.
19	Berrycroft	34	2832	13.09.1901	Detached house	Henry Wild	T.Bates & Sons	T.Bates & Sons Ltd	6 bed	Alterations signed by Towner. Cellar.
21	Knavesmire	35	2654	11.01.1901	Detached house	Henry Wild	W.Elliot	T.Bates & Sons Ltd	6 bed	3 bed in attic; rellar
23	Warwick Park Cottage	36/37	2654	11.01.1901	Detached house	Henry Wild	W.Elliot	T.Bates & Sons Ltd	6 bed	3 bed in attic; cellar
25	Oakholt	37		1960's						
	BLATCHINGTON ROAD (RH Side)									
2	Park House	40d	2401	27.06.1899	Detached house	Henry Wild	W.Elliot	T.Bates & Sons Ltd.	8 bed	4 bed on top floor. Area: 7,000 sq. ft.
4	Lyndale	40c	2555	15.06.1900	Detached house	Edwin Drewett	W.Elliot	T.Bates & Sons Ltd	7 bed	Lived in by Edwin Drewett
6	The Rowans	40a	3378	29.07.1904	Detached house	Edwin Drewett	Leonard Towner	T.Bates & Sons Ltd	8 bed	4 bed in attics. Cellar. 12,700 sq.ft.
8	Hartland	39c	3425	25.11.1904	Detached house	Edwin Drewett	Leonard Towner	T.Bates & Sons Ltd	8 bed	Cellar & Attics
10	Trevone	39b	6452	10.09.1925	Detached house	T.Bates	T.Bates & Sons	T.Bates & Sons Ltd	5 bed	
12			6000/6026	20.07.1923	Detached house	T.Bates	T.Bates & Sons	T.Bates & Sons Ltd	8 bed	App.under Sect.25 of 1919 Act
14		39a	5968/5976	25.05.1923	Detached house	Henry Wild	T.Bates & Sons	T.Bates & Sons Ltd	6 bed	2 bed in attic
16	Ambleside	38e	4344	10.06.1910	Detached house		Leonard Towner	T.Bates & Sons Ltd	4 bed	Cellar

APPENDIX 6 (continued)

House No.	Original House Name	Plot No.*	Application No.	Approval Date	Type of House**	Original Developer/Owner	Architect	Builder	No. of bedrooms***	Other information
	WARWICK PARK									
53	St.Agnes	40f	2456	27.10.19	Detached house	Henry Wild	W.Elliot	Thomas Bates	8 bed	Area 5,500 sq.ft.
55	Charlwood	41a	2611	28.09.1900	Detached house	Henry Wild	W.Elliot	Thomas Bates	8 bed	Area 7,500 sq.ft.
57		41b	7407	24.01.1930	Semi-det.	Thomas Bates	Thomas Bates	Thomas Bates	4 bed	Garage
59		41b	7407	24.01.1930	Semi-det.	Thomas Bates	Thomas Bates	Thomas Bates	4 bed	Garage
61		42a	10082	21.12.1948	Cottage	Jack Hart	John J.Cardwell	G.Paddock	3 bed	4 bed changed to 3 bed+boxroom.Est.cost £1,850
63		42b	10081	21.12.1948	Cottage	Alex Barker	John J.Cardwell	G.Paddock	3 bed	Est.Cost £1,700
65		pt.43	10544	14.07.1950	Detached house	E.M.Collingwood	Basil Fountain AIAS	B.Scrage & Hill	3 bed	Est.Cost £2,600
67	Cliff House	43	2478/3482	22.12.1899	Stables/Dwelling over	E.J.Carter	W.Elliot	Thomas Bates	8 bed	Cellar(wine,larder,coal,boots,cycles)
67a	Cliff Cottage	pt.43	2822	02.08.1901	Detached house	E.J.Carter	Thomas Bates	Thomas Bates	1 bed	Coachhouse/2stalls/loose box/harness room
69	Court Lees	44	4497/4532/	07.04.1911		Keith Fenton Crawford	W.Harold Hillyer	John Jarvis	6 bed	Extended in 1928&1933; converted to flats 1961
			4564/7137/8055/8530/15360			Richard Millard	Geering & Collyer	G.F.Penn (?)	3 flats	Est. cost of conversion £2,000
69+		pt.44	25229	28.03.1973	Chalet bungalow	Richard Millard	Geering & Collyer	W.D.Edwards	3 bed	Infilling of No.69 site - built on croquet lawn
75	Woodlands		TW82/1333	28.03.1983	Detached house	Lingbury Property Co.		Mr. Manners	4 bed	Permission granted subject to ten conditions
			9 previous applications	1975-1982 refused	House in front of No.75					Site 0.32 hectares
			TW93/0268	18.06.1993						
	Nevill Gate junction									
	NEVILL GATE									
	Byways	pt.46	6200	23.05.1924	House	Mr.R.W.Wallace	T.Bates & Sons	T.Bates & Sons Ltd	5 bed	
	Nevill Cottage	pt.46	4208	10.09.1909	Detached House	Marquess of Abergavenny	J.Richardson		4 bed	External wc; no bathroom
	Chimneys	45a	6402	22.05.1925	House	Messrs.T.Bates& Sons	T.Bates & Sons	T.Bates & Sons Ltd	3 bed	
	Birchmead	45a	6402	22.05.1925	House	Messrs.T.Bates& Sons	T.Bates & Sons	T.Bates & Sons Ltd	3 bed	
		pt.47	7711	20.03.1931	House	Messrs.Beale & Sons	Beale & Sons	Messrs. Beale & Sons	5 bed	Garage
2	Nevill House	pt.47	7705	20.03.1931	House	Messrs.Beale & Sons	Beale & Sons	Messrs. Beale & Sons	5 bed	Garage
	NEVILL GROUND									
			2121	01.04.1898	Cricket Pavilion	TW Athletic Club Ltd.				
			2223	14.10.1898	Pavilion	TW Athletic Club Ltd.				
			2265	02.12.1898	Covered Stands	Cricket,Football & Athletic Club				
			?	17.02.1899	Pavilion	Cricket Week Committee				
			2695	30.05.1902	Grandstand	Major Spens				
			3208	12.06.1903	Cricket Stand	Messrs.E & A.Wilson				
Tennis			4166	Allowed	Temp.Grandstand	Cricket,Football & Athletic Club	G.H.Strange ARIBA	Strange & Sons Ltd.		
			4930	24.04.1913 Allowed	Cricket Pavilion					
	WARWICK PARK									
83		pt.47	8016	25.11.1932	House	Messrs. Beale & Sons	Messrs. Beale & Sons	Messrs. Beale & Sons	5 bed	
85		48	7985/8012/8184	25.11.1932	House	Messrs. Beale & Sons	Messrs. Beale & Sons	Messrs. Beale & Sons	4 bed	Changed from 4 to 5 to 4 bed with 2 bath
85a		pt.49	TW/74/0559	16.09.1975	House	Nevill Developments	D.P.Winter, AIAS		4 bed	
85b		pt.49	TW/74/0559	16.09.1975	House	Nevill Developments	D.P.Winter, AIAS		4 bed	
	CRICKET FIELD									
	St.Peter's Rifle Club	Plots 50, 51, 52								
99		53	SW/1/63/69	03.04.1963	Outline permission	Miss S.J.Brunt	Ibbett, Mosely Card&Co. Ellis, Clark & Gallannaugh	J.H.Bath of Tonbridge	4 bed	property sold to J.P.Cook in 1965
99		pt.54	SW/1/65/371	05.01.1966	Detached house	J.P.Cook	Ernest Vinall	Never built	4 bed	3bed&living room 1st.flr; 1 bed grnd flr.
Jnct.	Warwick Ridge	54	3346	13.05.1904	Detached house	W.S.Putland	Leonard Towner	T.Bates & Sons Ltd	7 bed	Superceded previously approved plan
WP & Forest Road rka 148 Forest Road		54	3361	24.06.1904	Detached house	W.S.Putland				

Key: *as defined in 1897 Roper map **as stated in Application *** provided as indicator of house size

165

SOURCES, BIBLIOGRAPHY, MAPS and PLANS

1. General Background to Tunbridge Wells (Chapter 1 et passim)

Sources:
Abergavenny Archive: East Sussex County Records Office, Lewes, Sussex
Tunbridge Wells and the Calverley Estate: John Britton, London, 1832
Borough of Tunbridge Wells: Archives & Council Minutes, passim 1893-1915
Census Returns 1841-1901
Companies House
Kelly's Directory of Tunbridge Wells, 1892-1974
Centre for Kentish Studies, Maidstone, Kent
Kent & Sussex (Tunbridge Wells) Courier, passim
Pelton's Illustrated Guide to Tunbridge Wells, 1881
Beechings' Homeland Handbooks: Tunbridge Wells of Today: c.1895
Royal Tunbridge Wells Official Guide: at least 15 editions

Bibliography:
Frederick Alderson: The Inland Resorts and Spas of Britain: David & Charles, 1973
Brian Austen: Tunbridge Ware: Foulsham, 2001 3rd.edition
Margaret Barton: Tunbridge Wells : Faber & Faber, 1937
The Buildings of England: West Kent and the Weald: ed. By Nikolaus Pevsner, Penguin: Second Edition 1976
Butler & Hetherington: Around Royal Tunbridge Wells: Frith Book Co. 2002
Frank Chapman: Tales of Old Tunbridge Wells: Froglet Publications, 1999
Terence Davis: Tunbridge Wells. The Gentle Aspect: Phillimore, 1976
Roger Farthing: Royal Tunbridge Wells. A Pictorial History.: Phillimore, 1990
Farthing, Myles & Robinson: Centenary History of the Tunbridge Wells Lawn Tennis Club, 1999
John Fuller: The Church of King Charles the Martyr: Friends of the Church of King Charles, 2000
Margaret A. V. Gill: Tunbridge Ware: Shire Publications, 1997
Royal Tunbridge Wells in old picture postcards: European Library, 1983 & 1999
Willard Connely: Beau Nash: Werner Laurie, 1955
History of the Tunbridge Wells Cricket Club: Bi-Centenary 1782-1982: 1982
Jean Maulsdon: Tunbridge Wells As It Was: Hendon Publishing 1977
Lewis Melville: Society at Tunbridge Wells in the Eighteenth Century – and After : Eveleigh Nash, London, 1912
The Nevill Cricket Ground Centenary 1898-1998: Tunbridge Wells Cricket Club, 1998
M.L.J.Rowlands & I.C.Beavis: Tunbridge Wells in Old Photographs. Alan Sutton, 1991
Tunbridge Wells. A Second Selection. Alan Sutton, 1994
Royal Tunbridge Wells: Past and Present: ed. by J.C.M.Given: Courier Publishing, 1947

Royal Tunbridge Wells Civic Society: The Residential Parks of Tunbridge Wells: Local History Monograph No. 4: 2004
Royal Tunbridge Wells Civic Society: 400 Years of the Wells: Local History Monograph No. 5: 2005
Alan Savidge: Royal Tunbridge Wells: A History of a Spa Town: Midas Books 1975 and (revised and updated) Oast Books 1995
Tunbridge Wells and Rusthall Common: A History and Natural History: Tunbridge Wells Museum and Art Gallery, 2001
Edgar Yoxall Jones: A Prospect of Tunbridge Wells: Lambarde Press, 1964
H.P.White: Forgotten Railways (of) South East England: David & Charles, 1976

2. The Abergavenny Family and 1st Marquess; and the development of Warwick Park (Chapter 2 et passim).

Sources:
The Abergavenny Archive in the East Sussex County Records Office, Lewes: passim
Borough of Tunbridge Wells: Archives & Council Minutes, passim 1893-1915
Burke's Peerage and Baronetage
Kent County Records Office, Maidstone: passim
The Kent & Sussex (Tunbridge Wells) Courier, passim
Probate Office: passim

Bibliography:
The Iron Industry of the Weald: Henry Cleere & David Crossley: Leicester University Press, 1985
Lady Dorothy Nevill: Memoirs: n.d.
The Peerage of Great Britain, Burke 1910
Andrew Roberts: Salisbury, Victorian Titan: Weidenfeld & Nicholson, 1999
Richard Shannon: The Age of Disraeli, 1868-1881: the Rise of Tory Democracy: Longmans, 1992
Richard Shannon: The Age of Salisbury, 1881-1902: Longmans, 1996
Robert Stewart: The Foundation of the Conservative Party 1830-1867: Longmans 1990

3. Maps and Plans

Maps
Jan Kip – A vista of Tunbridge Wells, 1719 (printed) - various editions/versions
John Bowra – Tunbridge Wells: 1738 (printed)
T. Stidolph – Tunbridge Wells: 1838 (printed)
J. Colbran – Tunbridge Wells: 1853 (printed)
Ordnance Survey – Tunbridge Wells: Kent and Sussex: 1897, 1909 (printed)
Parishes of Tunbridge & Frant – Kent/Sussex Boundary map: 1894 (hand-drawn, Kent County Records Q GAZ 23)

Plans (mainly hand-drawn, and from the Abergavenny Archive at the East Sussex County Records Office in Lewes)

The Eridge Estate: 1878 (overdrawn with possible road layouts) ESCRO/ACC/363/Box 3

Brackett & Sons: Plan of Home Farm Estate, Tunbridge Wells: November 1893: ESCRO/ACC/363/Box 3

Henry & Percivall Currey: Alternative Plans A, B, & C: July 1894 ESCRO: ACC/363/64/Box 3

Borough Surveyor's Plan of Proposed Highways: September 1896: ESCRO/ACC363/Box 3

The Home Farm Estate, Tunbridge Wells: January 1897 (printed): drawn by W. Roper: ESCRO: ACC/363/76.

Plan for Ornamental Gardens on 'King Charles' Road', April 1897: ESCRO: ABE Box 3g

Abergavenny Estate Office Plan of Warwick Park plots (several versions) 1900-1904 ESCRO: ACC/363/63; ACC/363/15

Terrier of Frant Parish c.1800/1846 by T.Budgen: ESCRO: ABE27E; ABE59; ABE 105

Tunbridge Wells Loop-line Deposited Map: KAO Q/RUm 314 B

ACKNOWLEDGEMENTS

The publishers have sought to establish the copyright holders of all illustrations in this monograph. If they have failed unwittingly, they offer their apologies and will rectify their mistake in any reprint.

Many old prints, maps and postcards prior to the 20th century are generally, by their very age, out of copyright; and since each can be found in a number of public and private collections, it is not realistic to attribute any one collection as a source or copyright holder.

We would however like to make the following specific acknowledgements:

To the 5th and 6th Marquesses of Abergavenny, without whose Archive, now at the East Sussex County Records office in Lewes, this history could not have been written. The 5th Marquess encouraged the writer and read the original manuscript, saying that it had told him much about his family which he did not know, and he looked forward to seeing it in print. Sadly, this was not to be. The 6th Marquess deserves our gratitude for permission to reproduce seven maps relating to the development of Warwick Park, which clearly show far better than any words can, how the plans for development kept changing.

To the Tunbridge Wells Borough Council for providing access to planning records and Council Minutes, which proved invaluable for both writing and illustrating this history.

To John, Peter and Ivor Beale for providing photos of, and information about Louis Stephen Beale and his family.

To Ann Bates, for providing a photo of, and information about her grandfather, Thomas Bates.

The print of Tunbridge Wells Station c.1850 in Chapter 2 is the copyright of the Ironbridge Gorge Museum, whose permission to reproduce is gratefully acknowledged.

INDEX

A

Abergavenny 14, 16, 20, 25, 29, 30, 69, 72, 75, 76, 81, 93, 94, 96, 114, 125
Abergavennys, The 16, 17, 18
   1st Earl 15
   2nd Earl 15, 16, 19, 29
   3rd Earl 16, 29
   4th Earl 16, 17, 19, 29
   5th Earl 15, 17, 28, 30, 31
   1st Marquess (see also 5th Earl) 13, 15, 17, 24, 28, 29, 31, 32, 37, 145
   2nd Marquess (*see also* Earl of Lewes) 12, 19, 24, 47, 55, 145
   3rd Marquess 24, 37
   4th Marquess 24
   5th Marquess 1, 3, 24, 25, 28, 169
   6th Marquess 25, 169
Abergavenny Archive 2, 120, 166, 167, 169
Abergavenny Estates 14, 19, 46, 93, 142
Abergavenny family 2, 11, 13, 14, 16, 17, 142
Abergavenny Household Expenditure 21, App. 3
Abergavenny, Marquess of 9, 11, 13, 14, 18, 20, 22, 23, 24, 31, 33, 34, 36, 47, 48, 49, 51, 57, 61, 63, 72, 77. 80, 89, 97, 98, 99, 104, 105, 106, 108, 111, 114, 115, 116, 117,118, 119, 123, 124, 139, 141, 144, 148
Abergavenny Mineral Rights in Wales 23-24, 143, App. 2
Abergavenny, 'the Peer-Maker ' 27, 33
Abergavenny Rents 20, App. 2
Abergavenny, 'the Tory Bloodhound' 33, 34
Abergavenny Trustees 26, 38, 145
Architectural Registration Act, 1938 127
Armstrong, James G.D. 122, 128, 133
Arnold & Sons, Walter 104

B

Bates, Thomas 3, 27, 44, 45, 47, 115, 120, 121, 122, 125, 126, 128, 146
Bath 7, 8
Beale 44, 119, 120, 126, 128, 145
Beale, Louis Stephen 3, 27, 42, 43, 45, 46, 48, 115, 116, 118
Beale & Sons 115,132
Beauchamp, ARIBA, Philip 129, 135
Beau Nash 7, 8, 140
Bergavenny (see also Abergavenny) 5, 14, 28
Birling Road 43, 53, 65, 67, 69, 95, 96, 97, 101, 102, 111, 112, 126
Birling Park Avenue 53, 54, 98
Blaenavon Iron & Steel Co. 23, 25, 26, 143
Blatchington Road 45, 47, 102, 105, 106, 108, 110, 112, 120, 121, 125, 126, 138, 139, 145, 147
Bluemantles CC 84, 88

Borough Improvement Association	75
Brackett, William	
27, 37, 38, 39, 48, 57, 60, 63, 65, 72, 73, 75, 102, 103, 111, 143	
Brickland Houses Ltd	148
Broadwater Down	1, 17, 55, 60, 65, 113, 143
Bryant Homes	151-152
Burton, Decimus	1, 39, 127, 136

C

Calverley Park	1, 39, 65, 113
Calverley Park Crescent	113
Camden, Marquess	36, 48, 75, 76, 80, 149
Camden Park	1, 75, 138
Censuses, 1841-1961	9, 49, 52, 109, 141
Central Station (see also West Station/ Loop-line)	10, 116
Charlton, John (Arthur)	79, 82, 83
Child's Bank/Child, Messrs	20, 23
Claremont Road	46
Cliff House (*see also* No. 67, Warwick Park)	120, 121
Colbran, John	40, 50
Companies House	89
Conan Doyle, Sir Arthur	91
Cottages proposed	65, 67, 94, 108
Countryside Residential Properties	129, 132, 140, 150, 151
Courier, The (Kent & Sussex/Tunbridge Wells)	
11, 19, 30, 32, 35, 42, 48, 55, 80, 81, 83, 84, 86, 92, 97, 104	
Cranbrook, Earl of	19, 93
Cricket in Tunbridge Wells	74-92
Cripps, William Charles	27, 37, 40, 41, 48, 76, 80, 93, 96, 97, 98, 99
Crisford, Carlos	115, 124-125, 128, 133
Cumberland Walk	16, 37, 44, 67, 69, 95, 97
Currey, Henry	27, 39, 61, 63, 65, 72, 102, 108
Cut-Throat Lane	53, 101, 147

D

Dear, Henry	115, 125
Delves family	50, 57
Delves Farm	49, 50
Delves, William (1807-1886)	12, 20, 36, 37, 50, 51, 52, 54
Delves, William Henry (1829-1922)	20, 41, 47, 48, 53, 117
Devonshire, Duke of (*see also* Gilbert & Eastbourne)	39, 63, 95
Disraeli, Benjamin	29, 34
Drake, Augustus	27, 37, 38, 39, 61, 63, 72, 93, 94, 95, 96
Drake & Lee	22, 37, 38, 40
Drewitt, Edwin	115, 125, 139
Drive, The	151

E

Eastbourne (see also Devonshire & Gilbert)	1, 39, 63, 68, 102, 103, 124, 125, 133
Elliot, William	120, 128, 130, 131
Eridge Castle/Eridge Park	15, 16, 31, 34, 49
Eridge/Eridge Estate	1, 4, 15, 16, 17, 18, 20, 21,31, 34, 38, 40, 49, 53, 56, 57, 61, 72, 73, 100, 137
Eridge Gardens	20
Eridge Hunt	31, 35
Eridge overdraft	22
Eridge Road	47

F

Farmcombe Road	60
Farthing, Roger	3
First World War	110, 134, 142
Fletcher Lutwidge, Major C. R.	13, 47, 48, 76
Forest Brickworks	103
Forest Farm	49
Forest of Varieties, A	5, 6
Forest Road	33, 35, 37, 40, 42, 52, 56, 57, 60, 61, 67, 68, 74, 90, 91, 93
Frant/Frant Road	6, 14, 49, 53, 57, 60, 65, 101, 111, 112

G

Gaisford, Ernest Charles	35, 37, 106, 138, 139
Gilbert, John Davis (see also Devonshire and Eastbourne)	39, 40, 63, 95
Grom Brook	16, 49, 140, 149

H

Hackness Hall	30
Hastings railway line	51, 57, 60, 65, 77, 97, 102, 111
Haward, Samuel Edwin	27, 47, 48, 115, 120, 123, 133
Highgrove	152
Hillyer, Harold	3, 128, 133
Hillyer, OBE, John	3
Hollamby, Henry, Tunbridge Ware Factory	101
Home Farm	23, 27, 38, 49, 50, 51, 52, 53, 94, 95, 107, 120
Home Farm Estate	1, 13, 16, 17, 18, 35, 37, 39, 40, 49, 50, 57, 65, 69, 75, 76, 79, 93, 97, 103, 108, 109, 111, 114, 116, 117, 137
Hughes, W. Barnsley	103, 113, 128, 134, 163
Hungershall Park	1, 16, 17, 53, 113

I

Improvement Commissioners	9, 11, 12
Industrial Revolution	26, 32
Iron industry in the Weald	15
Incorporation of Tunbridge Wells	12

J
Jarvis, John — 79

K
Kavanagh, Mr. — 79
Kelly's Directory — 45, 109, 145
King Charles the Martyr, Church of — 5, 33, 35, 41, 82, 84
King Charles the Martyr Church Hall — 134
King Charles's Road — 137
Kingswood Road — 43, 116, 118
Kip, Jan — vi, 7

L
Lewes, Earl of (*see also* 2nd. Marquess) — 19, 55
Liptraps Park — 113, 142
London, Brighton & South Coast Railway (LB&SCR) — 10, 11, 106
Loop line (*see also* Central & West Stations) — 51, 57, 110
Lower Cricket Ground — 74
Lutyens, Sir Edwin — 134

M
Macbean, George Evan — 27, 35, 37, 38, 40, 41, 47, 48, 57, 63, 67, 68, 69, 72, 76, 93, 94, 95, 96, 97, 98, 99, 104, 105, 108, 115, 143
Madeira Park — 43, 44, 46, 101, 116, 117, 118, 119, 121, 125, 142
Mellor, T. E. W. — 27, 41, 42, 48
Molyneux, Whitfield & Co. — 55, 77
Montgomery, Lt. General Bernard — 88
Mottram, Trevor — 82-83

N
Nantyglo & Blaina Ironworks Co. — 23, 25, 143
National Union of Conservative Associations — 29, 33
Nevill — 1, 15, 19, 24, 25, 28, 29, 30, 36, 48, 53, 55
Nevill Arms — 98
Nevill Court — 20, 21, 108
Nevill family — 15, 24, 25, 29
Nevill Gate — 54, 77, 83, 98, 105, 112, 126, 145, 147
Nevill Gate, No. 4 — 146, 151
Nevill Ground — 38, 65, 67, 69, 74-92, 94
Nevill, Hon. Ralph Pelham — 19
Nevill Lane — 55, 96, 101, 147
Nevill, Lord George — 31, 48, 55
Nevill, Lord Henry (*see also* 3rd. Marquess) — 24, 30, 48, 55, 76, 80
Nevill Park — 1, 16, 17, 65, 113, 143
Nevill Pavilion — 80, 81, 83-85, 133
Nevill Street — 49, 53, 57, 60, 98, 101, 106, 118
Nevill Terrace — 47, 122

North, Lord Dudley	5, 14
Norfolk Road	44, 45, 47, 120

O

Ornamental Garden(s)	67-69, 132, 137, 144, 148, 149, 150
Osborne Associates, Henry	129, 132, 148

P

Pankhurst, Mrs.	84
Pantiles, The	7, 16, 50, 65, 75, 106, 111, 150
Pantyles Rifle Club	41, 144
Paxton, Joseph	39
'Peer-Maker', The	33
Pelton's Directory	109
Philpot, LRIBA, Stanley	128, 134
Plan A	65, 69, 72, 73, 76, 100
Plan B	65, 67, 69, 72, 73, 76, 100
Plan C	65, 67, 69, 72, 73, 76, 100
Population of Tunbridge Wells	8, 9, 11, 141
Portion I	60, 61, 65, 69, 73, 111
Portion II	60, 61, 65, 69, 73, 100, 111
Portion III	60, 61, 65, 69, 73, 100, 102
Prior, Miss Sarah	123-4
Putland, W.S.	115, 122, 126, 133

Q

Queen Elizabeth	15
Queen Henrietta Maria	6
Queen Victoria	9
Queen Catherine of Braganza	6

R

Ratepayers' Association	75
Reform Acts of 1832, 1867 and 1884	31, 32
Richmond Place	101, 140, 151, 152
Rodmell Road	53, 67, 101, 102, 105, 108, 112, 116, 118, 126, 138, 145, 147
Roedean Road	47, 53, 67, 101, 105, 108, 112, 126, 138, 145, 147
Roper, William	37, 38, 72, 75, 77, 79, 80, 83, 95, 137
Royal Institute of British Architects (RIBA)	127
Rusthall	6

S

Salisbury, 3rd. Marquess of	29
Salomons, Bt, Sir David	13, 76, 135
Settled Land Acts	19, 25, 93, 94, 96
Smithfield Market	51
South Eastern Railway (SER)	10, 11, 49

South Frith	6
Spa	5
Spa Hotel	48, 52
Speldhurst	6, 14
Spens, Major Lionel	76, 87
Standish House, Roedean Road	122, 125, 128
Stidolph, Thomas	49
Stone-Wigg, J.	77
Strange, ARIBA, C.H.	85, 133
Strange & Sons	83, 122, 128, 133
Suffragettes	84, 91, 92, 133
Sussex Weekly Advertiser	74
Swan Hotel	97

T

'Tarquin', Roedean Road	122, 128
Tonbridge	6, 8, 9, 14
Tory Bloodhound, The	33, 34
Towner, Leonard Benjamin	122, 128, 130, 131
Tunbridge Wells Borough Council (*see also* Watch & Works Committee)	
	2, 67, 68, 69, 95, 96, 97, 105, 114, 118, 132, 140, 144, 148, 149, 152
Tunbridge Wells Cricket Club	84, 85, 86, 87
Tunbridge Wells Cricket, Football and Athletic Club Ltd	
	76, 78, 85, 87, 88, 89, 105
Tunbridge Wells Football Club	85-88
Tunbridge Wells Hockey Club	85
Tunbridge Wells Improvement Act, 1835	9, 11
Tunbridge Wells Incorporation, 1889	12, 68
Tunbridge Wells Lawn Tennis Club	85, 86, 88
Tunbridge Wells Tradesmen's Association	12, 37, 44, 75, 76, 79
Twitten, The	54, 98

U

Upper or Higher Ground	74, 75
Upper Cumberland Walk	125, 126, 135

W

Warwick Park	1, 5, 10, 11, 13, 17, 18, 23, 38, 42, 43, 49, 67, 69, 73, 75, 77, 98, 101, 103, 108, 110, 112, 114, 115, 118, 125, 126, 127, 136, 137, 138, 141, 142, 143, 145, 148, 151, 152, 153
Warwick Park Estate	1, 2, 11, 24, 38, 49, 63, 65, 93, 95, 103, 110, 111, 113, 116, 127, 128, 130, 133, 142, 145, 148

Warwick Park - Individual Houses

No. 1	128, 134-5
Nos. 2 and 6	129
No. 11	149
No. 12	134

Nos. 13-29	129, 148-150
No. 35 (Brookside)	129, 134
Nos. 38-40	82
No. 41 (Oak Cottage)	81
No. 42	82
Nos. 44 and 44a	129
Nos. 61 and 63	150
Nos. 64-70	74, 79
No. 65	150
No. 67 (*see also* Cliff House)	120, 121, 150
No. 69 (Court Lees)	1, 128, 133, 134
No. 69+	151
No. 75	151
Nos. 76-78	74, 82
Nos. 80 and 82	74, 82
Nos. 83-85	129
Nos. 84-86	125
Nos. 85a and 85b	129, 151
Nos. 86 and 88	128, 151
Nos. 90-98	129
No. 92	69, 93
Nos. 94-96	146
Nos. 94 -112	119, 146
No. 100	119, 135, 146, 150
No. 114	151
No. 116	151
Warwick Ridge (nka 148 Forest Road)	123
Warwick the Kingmaker	15, 33
Watch Committee (Tunbridge Wells Borough Council)	138, 139
Webb, Sir Astin	134
West (or Brighton) Station (*see also* Central Station & Loop-line)	11, 47, 57, 60
Whitley, Henry Michell	27, 39, 40, 63, 65, 67, 68, 102, 137, 143
Wild, Henry Vaux	27, 44, 45, 46, 47, 106, 115, 116, 119, 120, 121, 122, 126
Williamson, Andrew	37, 107
Winter, RIBA, Michael	129, 135
Works Committee (Tunbridge Wells Borough Council)	95, 97, 105, 106, 114, 137, 138
Wyborne Grange	52

Y

Yorkshire Times	32